Praise for *Occult America*

"Teases out fascinating stories of the 'dreamers and planners who flourished along the Psychic Highway.' "
—DANIEL STASHOWER, *The Washington Post Book World*

"A treasure trove . . . What Mr. Horowitz has done is link the mystical history of the United States into a coherent, fascinating narrative. . . . His section on fascism and the occult is the clearest I've ever read."
—SUSAN CORSO, The Huffington Post

"A brilliant job of tracking down how positive thinker Norman Vincent Peale borrowed his core self-help philosophy from a religious movement called New Thought."
—JULIA DUIN, *The Washington Times*

"Employing extensive research while writing with an authoritative tone, Horowitz succeeds in showing how a 'new spiritual culture' developed in America."
—*Publishers Weekly*

"Treats esoteric ideas and movements with an even-handed intellectual studiousness that is too often lost in today's raised-voice discussions about religion and belief systems."
—CHRISTOPHER PORTER, *Washington Post Express*

"Patriots and paranoids alike have tramped through this field, and it badly needed sorting out. Mitch Horowitz does it with scholarship, style, and tales that evoke wide-eyed amazement."
—JOSCELYN GODWIN, professor of music, Colgate University

"This enthralling read tells the surprising story of how occult spirituality in America informed the ris rights, and the belief in the universality

OCCULT AMERICA

WHITE HOUSE SÉANCES, OUIJA CIRCLES,
MASONS, AND THE SECRET
MYSTIC HISTORY OF OUR NATION

MITCH HOROWITZ

BANTAM BOOKS TRADE PAPERBACKS
NEW YORK

A 2010 Bantam Books Trade Paperback Edition

Copyright © 2009 by Mitch Horowitz

Published in the United States by Bantam Books, an imprint of The Random
House Publishing Group, a division of Random House, Inc., New York.

BANTAM BOOKS and the rooster colophon are registered
trademarks of Random House, Inc.

Originally published in hardcover in the United States by Bantam Books,
an imprint of The Random House Publishing Group,
a division of Random House, Inc., in 2009.

Library of Congress Cataloging-in-Publication Data

Horowitz, Mitch.
Occult America : white house séances, ouija circles, masons, and
the secret mystic history of our nation / Mitch Horowitz.
p. cm.
Includes bibliographical references and index.
ISBN 978-0-553-38515-1
1. Occultism—United States—History.   2. Parapsychology—
United States—History.   I. Title.
BF1434.U6H67 2009
130—dc21
2009009864

Printed in the United States of America

www.bantamdell.com

Text design by Diane Hobbing

To Allison,
who makes everything possible

"*O Egypt, Egypt, there will remain
of thy religion only fables . . .*"

—HERMETICA

Contents

+ + +

Occult
America

• • •

WHAT IS THE OCCULT?

(And What Is It Doing in America?)

✦ ✦ ✦

Religious history, like literary or any cultural history,
is made by genius, by the mystery of rare human
personalities.

—HAROLD BLOOM, *THE AMERICAN RELIGION*

In the summer of 1693, the philosopher Johannes Kelpius and a small band of followers fled their Rhine Valley homeland. The region had once been a sanctuary of political independence and esoteric spirituality. It was now a charred land of devastation, crushed by the papal Habsburg Empire during the Thirty Years' War.

The twenty-one-year-old Kelpius, a protégé of mystical scholars who survived in the Rhine corridor, led his German pilgrims to the New World. Fewer than forty in number, they first traveled over land and later endured a five-month sea voyage, which proved less dangerous for the weather than for warring French and British ships crisscrossing Atlantic routes. By late June of 1694, the group reached Philadelphia, then a cluster of about five hundred houses. They settled along the wooded banks of the Wissahickon Creek outside town. There they lived a monastic existence, occupying caves and constructing a forty-foot-square log tabernacle topped with a telescope, from which they scanned the stars for holy signs. By sunlight and hearth fire, they studied astrology, alchemy, number symbolism, esoteric Christianity, Kabala, and other philosophies that had once flowered back home. Newcomers journeyed to America to join their Tabernacle in the Forest, and in the years following Kelpius's death from tuberculosis in 1708, they created a larger commune at Ephrata, Pennsylvania.

News drifted back to the Old World: A land existed where mystical thinkers and mystery religions—remnants of esoteric movements that had thrived during the Renaissance and were later harassed—could find safe harbor. And so began a revolution in religious life that was eventually felt around the earth. America hosted a remarkable assortment of breakaway faiths, from Mormonism to Seventh-day Adventism to Christian Science. But one movement that grew within its borders came to wield radical influence over nineteenth- and twentieth-century spirituality. It encompassed a wide array of mystical philosophies and mythical lore, particularly the belief in an "unseen world" whose forces act upon us and through us. It is called the occult.

The teachers and purveyors of the American occult—colorful, audacious, and often deeply self-educated men and women—shattered every stereotype, real and imagined, of the power-mad dabbler in dark arts. Rather than seeing mystical or magical ideas as a means to narcissistic power or moral freedom, they emphasized an unlikely ethic of social progress and individual betterment. These religious radicals, acting outside the folds of traditional churches and mostly overlooked or ignored in the pages of history, transformed a young nation into the launching pad for the revolutions in therapeutic and alternative spirituality that swept the earth in the nineteenth and twentieth centuries, even reigniting mystical traditions in the East.

Sons of Frankenstein

In her 1818 novel *Frankenstein*, Mary Shelley offered a stirring portrait—not sympathetic, but not as unsympathetic as many suppose—of the European occult in the Age of Enlightenment in the 1700s. Her budding scientist Victor Frankenstein was torn between the occult visions that drew him to science as a child and the materialist philosophy of his peers: "It was very different when the masters of science sought immortality and power; such views, although futile, were grand; but now the scene was changed. . . . I was required to exchange chimeras of boundless grandeur for realities of little worth." In the public mind, the occultist craved immortality, deific power, and limitless knowledge. It was an image that popular occultists often fed. The nineteenth-century French magician Éliphas Lévi fancied the occult arts "a science which confers on man powers apparently superhuman." England's "Great Beast" Aleister Crowley extolled self-gratification in his best-known maxim: "Do what thou wilt shall be the whole of the law."

The standard-bearers of the American occult took a different path. They sought to remake mystical ideas as tools of public good and self-help. The most influential trance medium of the nineteenth century, Andrew Jackson Davis—called the "Poughkeepsie Seer" after his Hudson Valley, New York, home—enthralled thousands with visions of heaven as a place that included all the world's people: black, white, Indian, and followers of every religion. In early America, the occult and liberalism were closely joined, especially in the movement of Spiritualism—or contacting the dead—whose newspapers and practitioners were ardently abolitionist and suffragist. For women, Spiritualist practices, from séances to spirit channeling, became vehicles for the earliest forms of religious and political leadership. The first American-born woman to become a recognized public preacher was Jemima Wilkinson. In 1776, at age twenty-four, she claimed to have died and returned to life as a medium of the Divine spirit, calling herself the "Publick Universal Friend."

The Friend, like the Rhine Valley mystics and Andrew Jackson Davis, remained a Christian. While her claims of supernatural rebirth and spirit channeling fell squarely within the occult framework, her religious perspective was unmistakably Scriptural. For a time, this was the nature of most American occultists (and it would never fully disappear). Few of them expressed any feelings of contradiction between Christian devotion and arcane methods of practice. Eventually, the occult and its acolytes came to branch ever more clearly into a separate and distinct spiritual culture, though not necessarily shedding a Christian moral outlook.

In the years between the Civil War and World War II, Americans took a do-it-yourself approach to many aspects of life, including the occult. Their enthusiasms resulted in strange inventions like the Ouija board, a boom in pop astrology, and a revolution in metaphysical mail-order courses and "how-to" guides. Breaking with the habits of the Old World, American occultists often proved wary of secret lodges and brotherhoods; they wanted to evangelize occult teachings as tools that ordinary men and women could use to contend with the problems of daily life. In their hands, methods that had once seemed forbidden or even sinister in the Old World—such as Mesmerism, soothsaying, and necromancy—morphed into a bevy of friendlier-sounding philosophies, some involving mind–body healing, positive visualization, and talking to angelic spirits.

The early-twentieth-century progressive minister Wallace D. Wattles, whose writing later inspired the book and movie *The Secret,* conceived of a psychical "science of getting rich," which he saw more as a program of wealth redistribution than a means of personal enrichment. Similarly, the black-nationalist leader Marcus Garvey attempted to harness the "mind power," or positive-thinking, principles so popular within American mysticism as a path to black liberation. Even at the highest rung of American politics, the Iowan farmer–seeker Henry A. Wallace, who served as Franklin Roosevelt's second vice president, drew ethical ideas from his lifelong passion for the occult and envisioned the dawn of a spiritually enlightened "New Deal of the Ages."

Since the mid-nineteenth century, denizens of the American occult had foretold a "New Age" in education, cooperation, and inner awakening. In the depth and reach of their careers, in their marriage of arcane methods with self-improvement philosophy, and in their determination to bring mysticism to the masses, they remade occultism into the harbinger of a new era in self-empowering and healing spirituality. Its arcane roots, however, became overgrown and forgotten.

The Silver Moon

Mysteries can be found wherever you look—especially when you're not sure what you're looking for. My brush with the occult began on a quiet Sunday morning in the mid-1970s at a diner in the Queens neighborhood where I grew up, a place of bungalow-size houses and cracked sidewalks that straddles the invisible boundary between the farthest reaches of New York City and the suburbs of Long Island. As a restless nine-year-old, I fidgeted at a table crowded with parents, aunts, and older cousins. Bored with the grown-up conversation, I wandered toward the front of the restaurant—the place where the real wonders were: cigarette machines, rows of exotic-looking liquor bottles above the cashier counter, brochure racks with dating-service question-naires, a boxy machine that could print out your "biorhythm." It was a carnival of the slightly forbidden.

One vending machine especially caught my eye: a dime horoscope dispenser. Drop in a coin, pull a lever, and out would slide a little pink scroll wound in a clear plastic sleeve. Unroll it and there appeared a brief analysis for each day of the month. I was a ripe customer. I had just borrowed a book of American folklore from our local library. It contained an eerie pentagramlike chart over which, eyes closed, you could hover a pin and bring it down on a prophecy: *A NEW LOVE; LOSS; GOOD HEALTH;* and so on. My prophecy read: *A LETTER.* At nine, letters rarely found me. But the very next day, one arrived—from the library. My hands shook when I opened it, only to remove a carbon-copied overdue slip. But still.

In the 1970s, the supernatural was in the air: I overheard my big sister on the phone considering whether ex-Beatle Ringo Starr had shaved his head in solidarity with the youth culture's Prince of Darkness Charles Manson. Books on ESP, Bigfoot, and "true" hauntings appeared in the Arrow Book Club catalogs at my elementary school. Friends huddled in basements for séances and Ouija sessions. *The Exorcist* was the movie that no one on the block was allowed to see. On TV, Merv Griffin and Mike Douglas chatted with clairvoyants, astrologers, and robed gurus. Everything seemed to hint at a strange otherworld not so far away from our own.

Or so it seemed that Sunday morning as I bounded back to the table to show off my star scroll. "Look what it says!" I announced, reading out predictions that were always just reasonable enough to come true. "Does it also say you're a sucker?" asked my grandfather, the perpetually exhausted manager of a flower shop. His lack of even the slightest curiosity about the mysteries of the world was as impossible for me to understand as my boyish enthusiasm was for him. While I didn't yet know the lines from *Hamlet—There are more things in heaven and earth, Horatio, than are dreamt of in your philosophy*—I felt their meaning in my guts. Peering down at my star scroll, I wondered: Where did this stuff come from? The zodiac signs, their symbols, the meanings—all this came from somewhere, *somewhere old*. But where—and how did it reach Queens?

Although I wouldn't know it until many years later, my dime-scroll philosophy contained a surprising likeness to the ideas of Claudius Ptolemy, the Greco–Egyptian astrologer–astronomer of the second century A.D. who had codified the basic principles of heavenly lore in his *Tetrabiblos*. In Ptolemy's pages stood concepts that had already stretched across millennia and followed a jagged path—sometimes broken by adaptations and bastardizations. They ranged from the philosophy of primeval Babylon to classical Egypt to Ptolemy's late Hellenic era to the Renaissance courts of Europe to popularizations of the nineteenth and twentieth centuries and, finally, to the star scroll bought by a nine-year-old one morning in a local diner (a place aptly named the Silver Moon).

In Ptolemy's day, astrology remained a mainstay of royal

courts and academies, but by the fourth century A.D. it would fall into disfavor under the influence of early Church fathers, who warned that divinatory practices were an easy portal for demonic powers. In the Church's zeal to erase the old practices—practices that had endured throughout the late ancient world (even Rome's first Christian emperor, Constantine, personally combined Christianity with sun worship)—bishops branded pantheists and nature worshippers, astrologers and cosmologists, cultists and soothsayers in ways that such believers had never conceived of themselves: as practitioners of Satanism and black magic. It was a new classification of villainy, entirely of the Church's invention. Once so characterized, the religious minority could be outlawed and persecuted, just as early Christians had been by pagan powers.

The fall of Rome meant the almost total collapse of esoteric and pre-Christian belief systems in Europe, as ancient books and ideas were scattered to the chaos of the Dark Ages. Only fortresslike monasteries, where old libraries could be hidden, protected the mystery traditions from complete destruction. By the time Greco–Egyptian texts and philosophies started to reemerge in the medieval and Renaissance ages, astrology and other divinatory methods began to be referred to under the name "occultism."

Occultism describes a tradition—religious, literary, and intellectual—that has existed throughout Western history. The term comes from the Latin *occultus,* meaning "hidden" or "secret." The word *occult* entered modern use through the work of Renaissance scholar Heinrich Cornelius Agrippa, who used it to describe magical practices and veiled spiritual philosophies in his three-volume study, *De occulta philosophia,* in 1533. The Oxford English Dictionary cites the first instance of the word *occult* twelve years later.

Traditionally, occultism deals with the inner aspect of religions: the mystical doorways of realization and secret ways of knowing. Classical occultism regards itself as an initiatory spiritual tradition. Seen from that perspective, the occultist is not necessarily born with unusual abilities, like soothsaying or mind reading, but trains for them. Such parameters, however, are loose: Spiritualism is impossible to separate from occultism. Whether believers consider channeling the dead a learned skill or a passive gift, its crypto-religious nature draws it into the occult framework. Indeed, occultism, at its heart, *is* religious: Renaissance occultists were particularly enamored of Jewish Kabala, Christian Gnosticism, Egypto–Hellenic astrology, Egyptian–Arab alchemy, and prophetic or divinatory rituals found deep within all the historic faiths, especially within the mystery religions of the Hellenic and Egyptian civilizations. They venerated the ideas of the *Hermetica,* a collection of late-ancient writings attributed to the mythical Greco–Egyptian sage Hermes Trismegistus. The name Hermes Trismegistus meant "Thrice-Greatest Hermes," a Greek term of veneration for Thoth, Egypt's god of writing, whom the Greeks conflated with their own Hermes (and later with the Roman Mercury). The *Hermetica* reflected the final stages of the magico-religious thought of Alexandria and formed a critical link between ancient Egypt and the modern occult.

The sturdiest definition of classical occult philosophy that I have personally found appears not in a Western or Egyptian context but in Sino scholar Richard Wilhelm's 1950 introduction to the Chinese oracle book *The I Ching or Book of Changes:*

> . . . *every event in the visible world is the effect of an "image," that is, of an idea in the unseen world. Accordingly, everything that happens on earth is only a reproduction, as it were, of an event in a world beyond our sense perception; as regards its occurrence in time, it is later than the suprasensible event. The holy men and sages, who are in contact with those higher spheres, have access to these ideas through direct intuition and are therefore able to intervene decisively in events in the world. Thus man is linked with heaven, the suprasensible world of ideas, and with earth, the material world of visible things, to form with these a trinity of primal powers.*

Of Dime Horoscopes

Back, for a moment, to the Silver Moon diner. What of the coin machine where I bought my horoscope that morning? It had its own story, one perhaps less august than that of ancient scholars or Renaissance courts but, to a young boy, no less fascinating. It was invented in 1934 by a clothing and securities salesman named Bruce King—or, as he was better known by his *nom de mystique,* Zolar. ("It comes from 'zodiac' and 'solar system,'" he explained. "Registered U.S. trademark.") His initiation was not in the temples of Egypt but on the boardwalks of Atlantic City, New Jersey. There he witnessed a goateed Professor A. F. Seward thrusting a pointer at a huge zodiac chart while lecturing beach-goers on the destiny of the stars. Professor Seward sold one-dollar horoscopes to countless vacationers—so many, rumor went, that he retired to Florida a millionaire. (The rumor, as will be seen, was true.)

Bursting forth from the boardwalks, Bruce King knew he had what it took to sell mysticism to the masses. "I felt the competition wasn't great," he told John Updike in *The New Yorker* in 1959, "and I could become the biggest man in the field." Zolar immersed himself in astrology, Tarot, palmistry, and all the "magical arts," on which he could expound with surprising erudition. "Everything I've ever known I've taught myself," he said. "I've studied psychiatry, sociology, and every field of human relations as well as the occult." For all his *have-I-got-a-deal-for-you* pitch, Zolar knew his material. His biggest breakout came in 1935, when the dime-store empire Woolworth's agreed to sell his pocket-sized daily horoscopes, the first generation of the mass-marketed horoscope booklets that now adorn the racks at supermarket checkout lines.

The secret to Zolar's success was that he spoke in a language everyone could understand. "I'm like the old two-dollar country doctor—a general practitioner," he once said. "If you want a specialist, you go somewhere else." Zolar could even sound like my grandfather when giving a reporter the lowdown on the resurgence of astrology in 1970: "It sounds kind of crazy—but you know that screwy play *Hair* that has that Aquarian thing?" Zolar was speaking, of course, of the rock musical's rousing opener, "Aquarius." "I think that's sold five million horoscopes."

So it had—and in America the old mysteries were on the move.

CHAPTER ONE

THE PSYCHIC HIGHWAY

+ + +

Yet who knows but the institution of a new order of labourers in the great Spiritual vineyard, is to prove the signal for the outpouring of such blessings as have been hitherto unparalleled in the history of our American Israel.

—WESTERN RECORDER, 1825

The Age of Reason could seem anything but reasonable for people with unusual religious beliefs—or those accused of them. In 1782, Switzerland sanctioned one of the Western world's last witch trials, which ended in the torture and beheading of a rural housemaid. In 1791, the Vatican sentenced the legendary Italian occultist called Cagliostro to death on charges of heresy and Freemasonry. Although his execution was stayed, the self-styled "High Priest of the Egyptian Mysteries" died of disease four years later in the dungeons of the Inquisition.

In eighteenth-century England, a young woman with the simple name of Ann Lee, living in the industrial town of Manchester on Toad Lane (where she was born in a leap year), told of magical visions and spoke of prophecies. The girl—who belonged to a radical Christian sect that would become known as the Shaking Quakers, or the Shakers—was hounded, beaten, and jailed on charges of sorcery and public disruption. Local authorities were aghast at the otherworldly possession that seemed to grip her and the other Shakers when they gyrated and shook in spirit trances. But she was not destined to become another casualty. Ann Lee escaped.

In 1774, the woman now called Mother Ann sailed from Liverpool to New York with eight followers and hangers-on. They included an unfaithful husband with whom she had already suffered through the birth and death of four infants. As the legend goes, the ship almost capsized in a storm. But Ann, in a state of eerie calm as waves crashed over the bow, told the captain that no harm would befall them. She reported seeing "two bright angels of God" on the mast. The ship survived.

After toiling at menial labor in New York City, the pilgrims—now twelve, minus Ann's husband—scraped together enough resources in 1776 to form a tiny colony in the knotty, marshy fields of Niskayuna, near Albany in New York's Hudson Valley. The twelve apostles, as they saw themselves, anointed the place Wisdom's Valley. It was a punishing, swampy stretch of two hundred acres swept barren by icy winds in the winter and transformed into muddy, mosquito-infested fields in the summer. Their neighbors were no friendlier than the landscape. Angry rumors painted Mother Ann and the Shakers—all sworn pacifists—as British sympathizers or spies. Revolutionary authorities briefly jailed the religious leader in Albany on charges of sedition. During a Shaker missionary trip to Petersham, Massachusetts, a band of thirty townsmen seized Mother Ann and subjected the celibate woman to the humiliation of disrobing, ostensibly to determine whether she was an English agent in drag. Some accused her of witchcraft or heresy. ("There is no witchcraft but sin," Mother Ann evenly countered.) But, oddly, the little sect—celibate, poor, steeped in a life of hard labor and little rest—began to grow.

Following a brutal upstate New York winter in 1780, two men from across the Hudson River in the farming community of New Lebanon took advantage of an early spring thaw to visit the Shaker settlement. The men were disappointed followers of one of the many Baptist revivals that had been sweeping the region, and they longed to see the woman whom followers called

Christ returned in female form. When they located Mother Ann and her colony in the wilderness, they were astonished at the small group's survival. They began asking Mother Ann about her mystical teachings and rumors of the sect's practices, in which members spoke in prophecies, saw visions of the dead, and danced, jumped, and shouted in the thrall of the Holy Spirit. "We are the people who turn the world upside down," Mother Ann enigmatically told them.

The men returned to New Lebanon to spread word of the people in the woods—and more curiosity seekers trekked to Niskayuna. Strange natural events drove newcomers into Mother Ann's little world. On May 19, 1780, many parts of New England experienced "The Dark Day"—a period when the daytime skies mysteriously blackened and the sun's rays were blotted out. The cause may have been a rash of local fires to clear fields, but the effect was panic over the coming of Armageddon. Mother Ann's warnings about the debased nature of the world suddenly seemed prophetic—and new converts came to her. To the Shakers, it was all expected. The previous year, Mother Ann had told her followers to store up extra provisions: "We shall have company enough, before another year comes about, to consume it all." Soon New Lebanon itself sprouted a much bigger colony, eventually sporting the immaculate whitewashed buildings, tidy yards, and brick meetinghouses for which the Shakers became famous.

Though Mother Ann died in 1784, her influence extended further in death than in life. The late 1830s saw the dawn of a feverish and profoundly influential period of Shaker activity called "Mother Ann's Work." The departed leader appeared as an otherworldly spirit guide directing a vast range of supernatural activity and instruction. Shaker villages—now spread as far south as Kentucky—recorded visits from spirits of historical figures and vanquished Indian tribes. The devout reported receiving ghostly visions and songs, which they turned into strangely beautiful paintings and haunting hymns (many of which still survive). Villagers spoke in foreign tongues, writhing and rolling on the floors in meetings that lasted all night—some even getting drunk on "spirit gifts" of unseen wine or Indian tobacco. In an

America that had not yet experienced the Spiritualist wave of séances, table tilting, or conversing with the dead, the Shakers foretold that beings from the afterlife would soon "visit every city and hamlet, every palace and cottage in the land." And events unfolding outside the manicured grounds of Shaker villages were already bringing that prophecy to life.

The Burned-Over District

The Shakers had laid down their roots in an area that would prove pivotal in American culture, its influence vastly surpassing its size. The region's role is as central to the development of mystical religions in America as the sands of the Sinai are to Judaism, and no account of American religion is possible without taking stock of it. The twentieth-century historian Carl Carmer called this area "a broad psychic highway, a thoroughfare of the occult." A snaking stretch of land in central New York State, it was a place of pristine lakes and rolling green hills, about twenty-five miles wide and three hundred miles long, extending from Albany in the east to Buffalo in the west. It became one of the main passages through which Americans flowed west. It remains so today as U.S. Route 20, an east–west highway that begins in New England, gently traversing the bends and slopes of Central New York's farmland before heading across the expanse of the nation to the Pacific Northwest. It is the longest continuous road in the United States. As fate and geography would have it, this great corridor cuts directly across a part of Central New York that in the nineteenth century became so caught up in the fires of religious revival movements—the fires of the spirit—that it became known as the Burned-Over District.

Before the Revolutionary War, the Burned-Over District was home to the Iroquois nation, whose remnants the new American government pushed out, partly in retaliation for the tribe's alliance with the British and partly to satisfy the land hunger of early settlers and speculators. And when settlers did arrive after the war, most of them unaware of the Indian lives that had been extinguished or hounded from the rich soil, the place seemed like an Eden of bountiful open land and vast lakes.

Throughout the first decades of the nineteenth century, itinerant ministers continually traveled the newly settled region, crisscrossing its hills and valleys with news of the Holy Spirit. The circuit-riding preachers and their tent revival meetings often left the area in a torrent of religious passion. For days afterward, without the prompting of ministers or revivalists, men and women would speak in tongues and writhe in religious ecstasy. Many would report visitations from angels or spirits.

Folklore told of the area once being home to a mysterious tribe—older than the oldest of Indian tribes, maybe even a lost tribe of Israel. These ancient beings, so the story went, had been wiped out in a confrontation with the Native Americans. Some believed their ghosts and messengers still walked, composing a world within a world amid the daily goings-on of Burned-Over District life.

The Burned-Over District's early religious communities thrived on a steady pool of migrants drawn to the region's abundant land. This new breed of Yankee, streaming westward from New England, was spiritually curious, ready to listen and believe. In the starlit nights of pioneer life, many minds and hearts turned to the whispers of the cosmos and the mysteries of what-might-be.

Apocalypse Postponed

If the Burned-Over District became a staging ground for a young nation's foray into unconventional and alternative religious ideas, it was in the mood and mind-set of its residents that the journey took flight. The mental habits of the Burned-Over District can best be understood by looking at one of the great schisms of American religious history. It concerns an early-nineteenth-century sect called the Millerites, later known as the Seventh-day Adventists. This group of believers, which numbered in the thousands by the 1840s, followed the utopian-millenarian ideas of a Freemason and Baptist clergyman named

William Miller. Born in Pittsfield, Massachusetts, Miller grew up estranged from his strict Baptist upbringing, more or less indifferent to religion. But after fighting in the War of 1812, he took up a common view among returning soldiers that his survival had somehow been divinely ordained. The former secularist came home with a deep interest in questions of immortality.

Convinced that the Bible was a record of literal truths, Miller undertook a comprehensive study to determine the time of Christ's return—and the millennium of peace he believed it would bring. Though only moderately educated, Miller spent fourteen years poring over Scripture, organizing and cross-referencing all that he found, and endeavoring—in true Yankee fashion—to find an orderly blueprint to God's plan. Miller's data pointed to the end as falling somewhere between March 21, 1843, and March 21, 1844. He later recast the final call to October 22, 1844. By the early 1830s, he had begun to gain a serious audience, first as one of the Burned-Over District's legion of itinerant religious speakers and later as a Baptist minister.

As Miller's portentous dates neared, hundreds and then thousands of followers gathered at tent revival meetings throughout Central New York. They filled—and sometimes overflowed—the biggest tent the nation had ever seen, one that could seat three thousand people. Once, near Rochester, a wind squall snapped fifteen of its chains and several inch-thick ropes, violently ripping the tent from its moorings like the opening of a gigantic clamshell. Amazingly, no one was hurt—which deepened local belief that Miller's movement was charmed. When an economic depression swept the Burned-Over District in the late 1830s and early 1840s, it served only to heighten the yearning for deliverance and the feeling that familiar institutions were slipping away.

A widely promulgated myth tells that as 1843 approached, the man the press called "Mad Miller" and his followers shed their last possessions, donned white "ascension robes," and waited on hilltops for the new advent. Stories abound in popular histories and local tales that some ran amok, engaging in "free love" and throwing money to the wind in anticipation of a world without wants or demands. Not only is this portrait historically inaccurate—without any viable source material in newspapers of the day—but it misunderstands the unusual blend of magical beliefs and practical habits that marked so many lives in the Burned-Over District.

In fact, Miller's followers never sold their belongings en masse, retreated to hilltops, or—except for rare cases—threw responsibility to the winds as they awaited their Savior. What few such episodes did occur were seized upon and exaggerated by those neighbors who mocked, and in some cases even physically attacked, the Millerites as they congregated in meeting halls and homes. Most evidence shows that these Yankee acolytes toiled right up to the point of Miller's end-times, working at their jobs, maintaining their farms, and attending school. Barns were swept, haylofts loaded, and fireplaces stoked before the arrival of the "last days." While followers believed in—and were passionate for—progress and perfection, they never abandoned the worldly. And this was the distinct habit of thought in the Burned-Over District: the ability to believe so deeply in the otherworld that it could be felt as a palpable presence but also to possess the soundness of mind and instinct to, in the Shaker formulation, keep hands to work even as hearts soared to God. It was a key facet of the occult and metaphysical mind-set being born in America.

The Universal Friend

The dreamers and planners who flourished along the Psychic Highway seemed to relish splitting apart orthodoxies, remaking Christianity as a new source of mystery and magic. One woman, in particular, today long forgotten, created in the mind of her followers a dramatically new idea of what a divine messenger could be. A New Englander by birth, she became the first American-born woman to found a spiritual order. Unlike Ann Lee, she wasn't seen as a female return of Christ but rather as a medium or channel possessed of the Divine Spirit. Her name was Jemima Wilkinson.

Wilkinson was born in 1752 to a moderately prosperous farming household of Quakers in Cumberland, Rhode Island. She lost her mother at age twelve and grew up under the care of older sisters, riding horses, gardening, and reading the basics of Quaker theology. The girl grew into a young woman of "personal beauty" who "took pleasure in adding to her good appearance the graceful drapery of elegant apparel," historian Stafford C. Cleveland wrote in his 1873 *History and Directory of Yates County,* which became the earliest biographical narrative of any repute of Wilkinson. Later in Wilkinson's life, onlookers commented on her fresh complexion and gently tanned skin, the ringlets of chestnut-brown hair that draped her neck, and her flashing black eyes. The attractive young woman presented a strikingly different figure than Mother Ann Lee—that is, if testimony from the spirit world can be relied upon.

Although no images survive of Mother Ann, some of her nineteenth-century followers doted on a "psychometric portrait" of their founder. The portrait was created by a New York artist who, when handed an object, claimed to clairvoyantly summon the vision of its owner. Whatever his abilities, the "psychometrist" was not attempting flattery. The supernatural image of Ann Lee revealed a dark, straight-haired woman with an unusually large forehead, dull eyes, and thick masculine lips. To her followers, it accurately captured a degree of world-weariness in Ann Lee far different from anything that would have been known by Jemima Wilkinson, raised amid the relative comforts of a successful New England farm.

By about sixteen, Wilkinson had been educated in the subjects expected of a girl from a modest estate—poetry, current news, and light literature. But in a short time she became wrapped up in a Rhode Island religious revival, and her life took a dramatically different turn. It was the last phase of the "Great Awakening" brought to New England by charismatic British preacher George Whitefield, who in 1770 was making his final tour of the area. Wilkinson fell in with a group of revivalist Baptists in Cumberland and began to comb through the Bible with strange intensity. She often meditated and sat alone in her room. Within a few years of her religious rebirth, Wilkinson showed signs of another wave sweeping the area: typhus fever.

On October 4, 1776, Wilkinson stumbled to her bed with a high temperature. She slipped in and out of delirium, returning to consciousness to describe dreams of heavenly realms and their angelic inhabitants. Her health worsened and she fell into a comatose state where her breathing grew faint and her pulse slowed. The end seemed imminent. But after thirty-six hours immobile in a near-lifeless state, she suddenly bounded from bed with a burst of renewed energy. Jemima Wilkinson had "passed to the angel world," she told her family. And the girlish form before them was now "reanimated by a spirit" destined to "deliver the oracles of God." This new entity told visitors and family that she would respond to no other name than *Publick Universal Friend*.

On the Sunday following her recovery, though still skinny and pale from her illness, the Publick Universal Friend went to a local church that was a center of the area's Baptist revival. The congregation was taken aback at the reappearance of the young woman who had been written off as dead. After services, surprise turned to shock when Wilkinson walked out to a shady tree in the churchyard and began preaching. It was probably the first time any of them had seen a woman deliver a homily in public. Her message—repentance from sin, humility, the Golden Rule—was little more than warmed-over Quakerism. But it electrified listeners, who marveled at the confidence and eloquence of the formerly bedridden girl who now claimed to be a supernatural channel.

The Friend soon began traveling around New England and down to Philadelphia—not exactly seeking converts to a religion but followers of her as an avatar of God. While in Philadelphia, the Friend came under the influence of at least one close admirer with ties to the mystical commune at Ephrata in Lancaster County. The commune had been founded in 1732 by Johann Conrad Beissel, a dynamic successor to the Rhine Valley mystic

Kelpius. Like the Ephratans, the Friend came to reject the formality of church services, liturgy, confessions of faith, and vows. She adopted the Ephratan practice of identifying the Sabbath on Saturday. Also like the German mystics from Lancaster, she encouraged—but stopped short of demanding—celibacy among her followers. If anything, the Friend's appeal was characterized by its almost total lack of hardened doctrine. She relied instead upon the lessons of Scripture and a simple do-unto-others ethic. Indeed, the Friend's teachings—in contrast to her fantastic claims about herself—could seem downright ordinary, extending to the virtues of punctuality and good-neighborliness.

Unlike the intense devotees around Mother Ann Lee, the Friend attracted a milder circle of landowners, merchants, and gentry. Shakerism, by contrast, was always running afoul of authorities as a migrant British movement whose converts came largely from the rear pews: kitchen maids, hired hands, and hardscrabble farmers. Followers of Mother Ann were once jailed simply on a rumor that they were driving sheep into British-held territory. The Universal Friend, on the other hand, moved freely around Rhode Island during the Revolutionary War, preaching to both American and English troops. Even when the Friend did end up in court after the war, the results were almost comical. In a dispute with an angry ex-follower, the Friend was dragged before a Central New York circuit court on charges of blasphemy, only to hear the presiding judge calmly inform the parties that blasphemy was not an indictable offense in the new republic. In a tale that would be dismissible as legend were it not on public record, Judge Morgan Lewis—later the governor of New York—then invited the Friend to preach before the court and applauded her "good counsel." It was a reception Mother Ann never could have dreamed of.

Pioneer Prophetess

After learning about the success of Ephrata, the Friend's followers began to discuss creating a colony of their own. By late 1788, a cluster of devotees journeyed from New England to the lakes of Central New York to break ground on a settlement to house the Universal Friend. In so doing, followers of the "pioneer prophetess," as Wilkinson's impeccable twentieth-century biographer Herbert A. Wisbey, Jr., dubbed her, became some of the earliest white settlers of Central New York. Their community of Jerusalem eventually grew near Crooked Lake—now called Keuka Lake. It continues to stand as an incorporated town today, a place in which family names belonging to the Friend's earliest followers still appear in the local telephone directory.

Many Central New Yorkers harbored conflicting attitudes toward their spirit-possessed pioneer, who cut a theatrical presence in her trademark cape and wide-brimmed hat. Their ambivalence resulted in a wide range of tall tales that depicted the Friend as a shrewd operator of slightly ill repute. One story of the Friend is as deeply ingrained in the folklore of New York State as is the legend of the Headless Horseman. Like many folktales, its location changes with nearly every recitation, the setting variously put at the banks of Seneca or Keuka Lake, or on bodies of water stretching as far north as Rhode Island or as far south as the Schuylkill River near Philadelphia. It gets repeated today on the tidy main street of the Central New York town of Penn Yan, near Jerusalem, where one teller sincerely placed the story at a canal at the end of the road. Based on prevailing versions, it goes this way:

> One morning, the Friend led a band of followers to a lakeshore, where she preached to them on the powers of faith. She built to a fiery conclusion and then proclaimed she was going to walk on water.
>
> "Have ye faith that I can do this thing?" she demanded of the crowd.
>
> "Yea, we believe!" followers replied.
>
> "Then if ye have faith," the Universal Friend said, "there is no need for any vulgar spectacle."
>
> And with that she turned around, got into her carriage monogrammed with her initials, U * F, and rode off.

The only confirmable part of the story is the monogrammed carriage, which still survives. Another apparent fiction surrounded the Friend's death. Her detractors claimed that the Friend said she was immortal and that, when she died in 1819, her deputies snuck her body out of her Jerusalem basement by night and secreted it to an unmarked grave. In fact, Wilkinson's body was interred with several others in a traditional burial vault on her property. It was not until several years later that her remains were moved, in Quaker fashion, to an unmarked plot.

Legal battles over township land emerged before and after the Friend's death, but by and large her followers and their families—similar in spirit to the Millerites—balanced within them both fantastical beliefs and the canny abilities and competences needed for a successful outer life. Following their teacher's death, these farmers, merchants, and tradesmen moved on to populate many of the region's liberal and experimental religious communities. The Friend's ministry, at once supernatural and down-to-earth, played a lasting if little-seen role in peopling the movements and attitudes that traveled the Psychic Highway and acculturated the nation to religious experiments.

The Lost Tribe

When Route 20 remained just a well-traveled carriage path, an ambitious, dreamy young man who grew up near its perimeter in the town of Palmyra—about forty miles north of the Universal Friend's settlement—became its most influential traveler. Raised on the folklore of the Burned-Over District and possessed of ingenious and extraordinary visions, he went on to establish one of the fastest-growing religions of the contemporary world: Mormonism.

As a teenage boy in the late 1810s and early 1820s, Joseph Smith of Palmyra was locally known as a clairvoyant guide who could track down hidden treasure using a "seer stone"—a smooth rock, variously opaque or marked with magic symbols, that he placed in his hat and gazed into to gain the power of second sight.

The manner in which Smith went about "peep-stoning" might be compared today with scrying or crystal-gazing. The area's buried-treasure hunters valued his talents. In the early nineteenth century, many Western and Central New Yorkers believed that ancient artifacts were squirreled away within Indian burial mounds or subterranean chambers under the region's hills and valleys. Legend told of buried ruins that belonged to a civilization older than the Indians.

Magic and myth were part of the firmament of the Smith household. According to historian D. Michael Quinn in his monumental study *Early Mormonism and the Magic World View,* Joseph Smith's family owned magical charms, divining rods, amulets, a ceremonial dagger inscribed with astrological symbols of Scorpio and seals of Mars, and parchments marked with occult signs and cryptograms popular in eighteenth- and nineteenth-century English and American folklore. In her 1845 oral memoir, the family matriarch, Lucy Mack Smith, recalled the Smiths' interest in "the faculty of Abrac"—a term that might have been lost on some. In fact, *Abrac,* or *Abraxas,* is a Gnostic term for God that also served as a magical incantation.* It forms the root of a magic word known to every child: *abracadabra.*

For his part, Joseph Smith venerated the powers of the planet Jupiter, which was prominent in his astrological birth chart. According to Quinn, Smith's first wife, Emma, reported that Smith carried a protective Jupiter amulet up to his death. The surviving silver amulet displays markings that derive from the work of Renaissance mage Cornelius Agrippa and that were spread among British and American readers by the English occultist Francis Barrett in his 1801 book *The Magus,* a popularization (and partial copycat) of Agrippa. Smith's occult interests closely reflected those that traveled through Central New York. Later in life, his theology suggested the existence of a male–female God, an idea found in Hermetic and Gnostic traditions, though one that Smith

---

* Gnostics were members of early Christian sects that had not been enfolded within the Church structure. Their literature and theology were a distinctly independent mixture of Christian, classical, and pagan thought.

may have imbibed locally through the teachings of Mother Ann Lee or Jemima Wilkinson. He also grew fascinated with the temple rites and symbols of Freemasonry, a movement of tremendous influence and controversy in the Burned-Over District, as will soon be seen.

The rebellious, spiritually adventuresome Smith began reporting divine visitations in the 1820s, which culminated in the angel called Moroni directing him to golden plates buried in the Hill Cumorah, near his home. It was the same place where local legend held that a lost tribe of Israel had made its last stand, a pillar of Smith's later theology. Like Smith, many early-nineteenth-century observers took seriously the existence of a highly developed, pre-Indian civilization in the area. In 1811, New York's Governor DeWitt Clinton told the New York Historical Society:

> There is every reason to believe that, previous to the occupancy of this country by the progenitors of the present nations of Indians, it was inhabited by a race of men, much more populous, and much further advanced in civilization. The numerous remains of ancient fortifications, which are found in this country . . . demonstrate a population far exceeding that of the Indians when this country was first settled.

Clinton and others reported discovering esoteric fraternities among the nineteenth-century Iroquois, which some considered a form of "ancient Freemasonry." These speculations were heightened when the Seneca leader Red Jacket and other New York–area Indians were seen wearing Freemasonic-style medals in the shape of the square and compass, a fact well documented in a 1903 New York State Museum monograph, *Metallic Ornaments of the New York Indians* by archaeologist William M. Beauchamp.

All of the area myths—the remnants of a lost civilization, the uses of peep stones, ancient buried treasure—formed tantalizing threads in Joseph Smith's expanding worldview. They wound together in the narrative of the golden plates Smith discovered at

Cumorah—written in "reformed Egyptian hieroglyphics" and translated by the young seeker through a pair of ancient seer stones. In 1830, he revealed the testimony as the Book of Mormon. Smith's record traced a vast alternate history, involving a tribe of Israel fleeing the Holy Land for the American continent, experiencing the gospel directly from Christ, and later suffering fracture and vanquish in a "great and tremendous battle at Cumorah . . . until they were all destroyed" (Mormon 8:2). The scale and scope of the Book of Mormon were extraordinary— seen by followers as buttressing the lore of Smith's home district rather than built upon it.

Yet Smith's theology found little influence within the Burned-Over District, where he was often seen as a former "peep-stoner" peddling himself as a prophet. Like Israel's lost tribe, Smith and his followers would have to journey west to live out their destiny. But the ideas and loyalties that the prophet developed in Central New York converged with profound consequences over the lives of Smith and the small band that followed him down the Psychic Highway.

"Our New Order of the Ages"

Smith was fascinated with Freemasonry, and for a time the religious–civic brotherhood was widely popular in the Burned-Over District and many parts of America. Early American Freemasons held a sense of breaking with an Old World past in which one overarching authority regulated the exchange of religious ideas and sought to position itself as an intermediary between the individual and the spiritual search. Both American and European Freemasons professed ecumenism and religious toleration. In so doing, they may have taken a cue from the so-called Rosicrucian manuscripts that had aroused the imagination of radical Protestant reformers. Beginning in 1614, Europe had marveled over cryptic manuscripts produced by the Rosicrucians, an "invisible college" of adepts who extolled mysticism and higher learning while prophesying the dawn of a new era of education and enlightenment. There is question about whether a secret fraternity of Rosicrucians actually existed. Regardless, the manuscripts, laced with symbolism and parable, gave powerful expression to the principle of ecumenism—a nearly unthinkable ideal at the time and one that may have influenced the religious pluralism espoused by Freemasonry as it took shape in seventeenth-century Europe and then in America.

In another apparent echo of the Rosicrucian texts, Freemasonry drew upon arcane imagery as codes for personal and ethical development. As members rose through the fraternity's ranks, their achievements were marked on ceremonial badges and aprons by rising suns, luminous eyeballs, pentagrams, and pyramids. This practice informed one of the greatest symbols of Masonry, or at least those influenced by it: the all-seeing eye and incomplete pyramid of the Great Seal of the United States, familiar today from the back of the dollar bill. The Great Seal's initial design began, appropriately enough, on July 4, 1776, on an order from the Continental Congress and under the direction of Benjamin Franklin (himself a Mason), Thomas Jefferson, and John Adams.* The Latin maxim that surrounds the unfinished pyramid—*Annuit Coeptis Novus Ordo Seclorum*—can be roughly, if poetically, translated as: "God Smiles on Our New Order of the Ages." It is Masonic philosophy to the core: The pyramid, or worldly achievement, is incomplete without the blessing of Providence. In its symbols and ideas, Masonry saw this polity of man and God as a break with the sectarianism of the Old World and a renewed search for universal truth as it existed in all the great civilizations. Renaissance occultists had viewed ancient Egypt as the source of a primal, ageless wisdom transcending nation or dogma. The eye and pyramid of the Great Seal expressed a tantalizingly similar ideal.

---

* As will later be explored, the Great Seal did not actually appear on the back of the dollar bill until 1935. Until then the seal was an instrument of official government business, of little familiarity to the general public. In a stroke that would make the arcane image instantly recognizable, the Great Seal was placed there on the initiative of a president and vice president who also happened to be Masons: Franklin Delano Roosevelt and Henry A. Wallace.

In the laboratory of religious experimentation that was the Burned-Over District, Freemasonry—this cryptic religious order with liberal values—should have enjoyed a long and fruitful influence. But there the secretive brotherhood ran into a scandal that nearly threatened its existence in America. It began in the mid-1820s, sparked by a violent episode that played out not far from Joseph Smith's home and would leave its mark on Smith's life—and death.

The Widow's Son

In 1826, a disgruntled Mason living in Batavia, New York, William Morgan, threatened to expose Masonry's secret rites in a manuscript he was readying for publication. Morgan soon suffered a variety of persecutions, ranging from his arrest on specious charges to an attempted arson at the print shop that held his manuscript. He was eventually kidnapped and never seen again—possibly murdered at the hands of Masonic zealots. Residents of the Burned-Over District certainly believed as much.

The presumed homicide and the dead-end legal investigation that followed raised suspicions about Masonry's influence on law enforcement and the courts. The episode let loose a torrent of anti-Masonic feeling, first in the Burned-Over District and soon throughout America, stoked by a general mood of discontent over corruption in high places. In time, fifty-two anti-Masonic newspapers sprang up in the nation, and dozens of anti-Masonic representatives were sent to state legislatures. While the waters soon calmed, Freemasonry would never again command the same level of prestige in American life. But the brotherhood's influence spread in unexpected ways.

The victim William Morgan left behind an attractive widow, Lucinda. She eventually met a new husband, George Harris, with whom she traveled west as part of a dawning religious order: Mormonism. But Lucinda was fated to be more than an ordinary convert. Around 1836, the blond, blue-eyed ex–New Yorker, though since remarried, became one of many "spiritual wives" of the prophet himself, Joseph Smith. Smith had lived about fifty miles east of the Morgans in Palmyra, but it is unlikely he and Lucinda met until Mormonism began its westward trek. As a younger man, Smith was initially swept up in the Burned-Over District's wave of anti-Masonry, but an older Smith became an enthusiast of the secret society that had once widowed his new bride.

As the Mormons wandered the nation in search of a safe home, Smith founded a Freemasonic lodge at his large community at Nauvoo, Illinois. According to his compatriots, Smith believed that the priestly rites of Freemasonry represented a degraded version of the lost rituals of Hebraic priests. Such rites, he reasoned, were a precious thread to the ancient tabernacle. And Smith determined he would take that thread and, weaving it through with divine revelations of his own, restore the ceremonies of the Hebrews.

In the early 1840s, he introduced into Mormonism the symbols of Masonry, such as the rising sun, the beehive, and the square and compass. Using adapted Freemasonic rites—which included ritually bathing neophytes, clothing them in temple garments, and giving them new spiritual names and instruction in secret handgrips and passwords—Smith conducted initiation ceremonies in a makeshift temple over his Nauvoo store. Smith also studied Hebrew and possibly elements of Kabala with a French–Jewish scholar and Mormon convert named Alexander Neibaur. It was a period of tremendous innovation within the nascent movement. But it reached a sudden end.

In 1844, Smith turned himself over to authorities at Carthage, Illinois, where he sat in a jail cell to await trial on charges arising from the destruction of an opposition newspaper at Nauvoo. Smith had directly sanctioned the burning and sacking of a critical news sheet. Though his act was indefensible, it served merely as an excuse for the state government to finally get its hands on the religious leader. Illinois's frontier towns were increasingly fearful and suspicious of the Mormon newcomers, who maintained their own militia and formed a political power bloc in the state. While the prophet and his closest colleagues waited in the second floor of the two-story jailhouse in Carthage, they found themselves without the protection that the state's governor had promised. The days turned tense as armed bands circled the area. During the early evening of June 27, a mob—including state militiamen with soot-disguised faces, who were supposed to be protecting Smith—stormed the jail.

Before diving from a window in a vain attempt at escape, Smith was reported by witnesses to issue the Masonic distress signal, lifting his arms in the symbol of the square and beginning to shout out, "Oh, Lord my God, is there no help for the widow's son!" Musket balls tore through his falling body. On his corpse, descendants claimed, appeared his old protective amulet marked with the astrological symbol of Jupiter, now just a cold piece of silver. At thirty-eight, the most famous son of the Burned-Over District was dead—a man driven by the strange alliances and esoteric philosophies that seemed to grow from the very soil of his upstate New York home.

Paradise Found

The people of the Burned-Over District believed in the redemptive power of ideas—whether political or spiritual. Rare was the person with a foothold in a mystical sect who didn't also have one in a social sect, and vice versa. For many, the two worlds naturally blended.

The area hosted some of the New World's earliest utopian religious communities, including the nation's most long-lived and economically successful commune at Oneida. From about 1848 to 1880, under the leadership of John Humphrey Noyes, the Oneidans thrived in the manufacture of animal traps, cutlery, and other high-quality goods, while experimenting with sexual liberation, biblical communism, and attempts at human "perfectionism." By the mid-nineteenth century, the Burned-Over District housed about twenty villages or active societies based on agrarian socialist ideas. Most were short-lived.

A dizzying range of reformist, civic, and spiritual movements shared members and melted into one another in the Burned-Over District. Suffragism, temperance, and abolitionism each had deep footholds in its terrain. Through the flow of people and ideas heading west from New England, the region spread Transcendentalism, or "Yankee Mysticism," whose influence will be explored. It hosted some of the earliest American branches of Freemasonry and anti-Masonry. And it eventually gave birth to one of the strangest and most influential of American religious innovations: Spiritualism.

Spiritualism shared a common trait with the utopian movements of the area. Spiritualists harbored the Yankee attitude that religion rested not just on faith but on proof. Like William Miller poring through Scripture to pinpoint the date of Armageddon, Spiritualists found tantalizing "facts" to back up their belief in the physical reality of the afterworld: spirit raps, table tilting, and communication through mediums. In a similar vein, the utopians maintained that they, too, were simply following a process of logic, in their case the cause-and-effect of better styles of living making for better men and women. In the Burned-Over District, mystics and radicals felt a shared stake in the prophecy of progress. They believed that spiritual and social forces, if properly discovered and used, could remake a person, inside and out. And a prophet was about to enter their midst who would herald the dawning of the Spiritualist movement and unify the reformist and religious passions that traveled the Psychic Highway.

As Miller was foretelling the dawn of a glorious new world, as Noyes was forecasting an earthly utopia, as Smith was spreading a new testament, further downstate, in the Hudson Valley region, a seventeen-year-old half-educated cobbler's apprentice experienced cosmic visions of his own as he ambled across moonlit fields and meadows. His name was Andrew Jackson Davis—or, as he was called in the press after his hometown, the "Poughkeepsie Seer." His influence did more than any other's to shape the occult and alternative religious traditions of a growing nation.

The Poughkeepsie Seer

Andrew Jackson Davis was born in 1826 to an upstate New York family that scarcely fit his high-sounding name. The four-day-old infant was named "Andrew Jackson" by a boozy uncle who wept with sentiment over the future president and hero of the Battle of New Orleans—"the greatest man a livin' in the world!"

Davis's Hudson Valley home life was dreary: His mother spent most of her time bent over housework, and his cobbler father was an on-and-off drinker who could barely keep his family fed and clothed. Andrew, his older sister, and their parents were forced to pick up odd jobs and harvest chores at local farms to survive. With money short, there was little time for education. Davis's young mind took to local influences: Tales of spooks and witchcraft ran up and down the Hudson countryside. Neighbors showed a sharp interest in strange signs and omens. And Davis's mother—a dignified and honest woman in the face of both near-poverty and physical frailty—told of prophetic dreams and visions.

But Davis was no superstitious yokel. As though possessed of some finer instinct of the mind, he chafed against the hellfire-and-fury ramblings of the itinerant ministers who crisscrossed the Burned-Over District and Hudson Valley. He took careful notice that some of the most outwardly pious men neglected their debts at the country store where he clerked. His neighbors often felt sheepish and tongue-tied before well-practiced preachers who seized upon unsuspecting "sinners" on local lanes and at store counters, commanding them to repent or face hellfire. But Davis would argue back. "I ain't afraid to meet my God," he once told a local firebrand, sending the pastor into spasms of indignation. *Be—calm!* an inner voice reassured Davis. *The—pastor—is—wrong; you—shall—see!*

When the Davis family moved to the growing town of Poughkeepsie in 1839, things began to look up, at least a little. The family was able to enroll its fourteen-year-old son in an inexpensive experimental Quaker school. It was inexpensive because there were no teachers to pay: Founder Joseph Lancaster's "experiment" was to have its children teach one another. Soon, Davis was placed in charge of his own class, which he recalled in his memoirs as a "miscellaneous band composed of about twenty snarly-haired, bad-odored, dirty-faced, ragged-dressed, comic-acting, squinting, lisping, broad-mouthed, linkum-slyly, and yet somewhat promising urchins."

By age sixteen, Davis was apprenticed to a shoemaker, presumably set to follow in his father's career path. The boy's new employer considered him kindly and honest—though he wrote in a letter that the lad's learning "barely amounted to a knowledge of reading, writing and the rudiments of arithmetic." Nonetheless, if Andrew could avoid his father's attachment to liquor, life seemed to promise him a stable, if humdrum, existence. But humdrum was the last thing in store for the polite young man. News of a strange practice had begun spreading through the Hudson Valley, one by which men could be induced into a half-conscious condition called a "trance." Teachers from Europe had begun carrying it to America, laying the events for a wildly unexpected turn in Davis's life.

Mesmer's Children

Like many things American, this one began in Paris. In 1778, a Viennese physician and lawyer named Franz Anton Mesmer arrived in the French capital with a controversial and exotic method of healing. Mesmer theorized that unseen ethereal matter—what he termed "animal magnetism"—animated all of life. Mesmer enthralled members of Europe's aristocracy with a method of entrancement through which he purported to manipulate this substance and cure ailments. News of his practice began to reach the New World.

In a letter to his friend and fellow Freemason George Washington, the Marquis de Lafayette wrote from Paris on May 14, 1784: "A German doctor called *Mesmer* having made the greatest discovery upon *Magnetism Animal*, he has instructed scholars, among whom your humble servant is called one of the most enthusiastic—I know as much as any conjuror ever did . . . and before I go, I will get leave to let you into the secret of Mesmer, which you may depend upon, is a grand philosophical discovery." On a visit to America that summer, the French Revolutionary War hero not only discussed the inner workings of Mesmerism with Washington but gave Washington a personal letter from the magnetic healer. Washington replied to Mesmer with polite caution on November 25, 1784, explaining that the marquis had described his theories and if "the powers of magnetism . . . should prove as extensively beneficial as it is said it will, must be fortunate indeed for mankind, and redound very highly to the honor of that genius to whom it owes its birth."

The marquis continued his explorations in America that fall, walking ten miles on foot from Albany to the Shaker colony at Niskayuna several weeks after Mother Ann Lee's death. He hoped to inquire firsthand whether the Shaker trances had anything in common with Mesmerism. A colleague of the marquis noted that the Shakers seemed able to spin on one leg with "surprising rapidity," perhaps suggesting some kind of spirit control. The marquis also attempted to entrance one of the Shaker followers, apparently with little effect.

While the marquis and Washington were considering Mesmer's theories from America in 1784, another American statesman was across the sea tearing them apart. In Paris that same year, Benjamin Franklin sat on a committee of the French Academy of Sciences that blasted Mesmer's ideas as illusory. The highly anticipated report, commissioned by Louis XVI, turned French public opinion against the once highly feted Mesmer, and he was soon run out of Paris. But history granted the self-styled healer a final victory: His trance-inducing technique began to spread throughout Europe and was soon practiced in America, where its influence touched religion, medicine, and the modern quest to understand the human mind.

Mesmerism began its climb to popularity in America through the efforts of two displaced Frenchmen. Joseph Du Commun, a language instructor at the military academy at West Point, delivered the first widely attended lectures on the topic in New York

City in 1829. He lamented that the great American Benjamin Franklin had signed the report against Mesmer, insisting that the scientist–statesman had been "sick" at the time. The practice began to spread in earnest through another lecturer, Charles Poyen, who had received magnetic treatments for anxiety and digestive problems as a medical student at the French Academy. While visiting his family's plantations in the French West Indies, Poyen discovered that both whites and African slaves were equally susceptible to Mesmeric trances. This formed in him a deep belief in commonality among the races and an aversion to slavery. Disgusted with living in a slave-based society, the nineteen-year-old Poyen journeyed to New England in late 1834, soon taking up residence in Lowell, Massachusetts. He became involved in abolitionist circles and scraped together a living by giving French lessons to the daughters of local mill owners.

The topic of Mesmerism struck a deep chord with Lowell's mayor, a Brown-educated medical doctor. With the mayor's encouragement, Poyen began delivering lectures on the practice. He proved a poor stage presence: Poyen's appearance was boyish, his English was halting, and half of his face was covered by a dark red birthmark. Despite mixed reactions in the press and among audiences, Poyen's stage demonstrations planted a seed. By the end of the decade, a coterie of self-taught Mesmerists was traveling New England and the Burned-Over District, like so many circuit-riding preachers.

While practitioners used different methods, a stage Mesmerist would typically begin by gently waving his hands around the head and face of the subject, bidding him to release his conscious thoughts and drift into a more relaxed state. It was believed that once a subject was enthralled, the Mesmerist could manipulate the subject's life substance, or animal magnetism, exercise uncanny powers to heal him of physical ailments, order him about, or even command him to speak in unknown foreign tongues. In the most popular displays, a subject might awaken to the laughter of friends who said he'd barked like a dog or obeyed commands to make love to a broomstick. More seriously, a Mesmerist might—in a forerunner to hypnotism—suggest to a subject that a certain pain or ailment was relieved. And many did report healings in this way.

A New Light

When a traveling Mesmerist rode through Poughkeepsie in 1843, Andrew Jackson Davis at first could not be entranced. But Davis good-naturedly agreed to the experiment again with a local tailor who had begun practicing Mesmerism. With his new magnetizer, the youth discovered that he was actually an easy subject—someone who could enter a trance quickly and deeply. At first, Davis was terrified by the loss of bodily control and the feeling of falling through space. But soon, like many subjects, he found that the trance experience aroused pleasure and even ecstasy. As the hands of his tailor–Mesmerist made their passes over him, Davis recalled a warm, shimmering sensation throughout his body. He felt plunged into a great inner darkness and experienced a sense of weightlessness and loss of mobility. His body glowed with lightness.

Davis was not the first to describe this kind of experience. In his *Journal of Dreams,* the eighteenth-century Swedish scientist–mystic Emanuel Swedenborg fondly recalled one of his early trance states: "I had in my mind and body the feeling of an indescribable delight, so that had it been in any higher degree, the whole body would have been, as it were, dissolved in pure joy." In early drawings, Mesmerists and their subjects are sometimes seated closely enough for limbs to be touching or interlocked, conveying an unmistakable sensuality. Indeed, the French report that rebutted Mesmer in 1784 included a confidential rider— intended for the eyes of Louis XVI alone—warning of the sexual undertones to Mesmerism and the possible liberties taken under its effects.

For Davis and Swedenborg, as for many others, however, the experience did not end at physical sensation. After his feeling of dissolution, Davis discovered that his mental acuteness remained intact—and seemed to expand into higher realms. He had an inner vision of standing on a pitch-dark shore with waves crashing about him. He remained still but with a sense of brilliant alertness, as though poised to receive some great message. "Ain't this exceedingly strange?" he marveled to himself.

On one "chilly, fitful, disagreeable" winter night in 1844, Davis found that after a particularly deep Mesmeric session he had trouble returning to ordinary consciousness. He stumbled back to the room where he was staying, at the home of his tailor–trance master. Davis dropped onto his bed and immediately fell asleep. Later he awoke at the beckoning of a voice outside that sounded like his recently deceased mother. He ran outdoors and on the road beheld a vision: It was a flock of unruly sheep being led by an overcome shepherd; the shepherd seemed to need his help. At this point Davis embarked on a kind of vision quest—or what he called a psychical "flight through space"— traveling in either mind or body (and possibly both, as he vanished until the next day) over the wintry New York terrain.

He said he traversed west across the frozen Hudson River, scaled steep hills in the Catskills, slept on a pile of tree branches resembling an altar, and beheld incredible visions of nature: mountains caked with snow and ice; dark, forbidding valleys; a thunder-and-lightning torrent of rain. He eventually found his way to a fenced graveyard, where he encountered the spirits of Galen, the legendary Greek physician, and none other than Emanuel Swedenborg himself. "By thee will a new light appear," the Swedish scientist and seer told him.

Davis returned to the tailor's home the next day, shaken but possessed of a sense of mission. The bearded youngster no longer seemed an apprentice cobbler ready to perform stage tricks. "No more time upon wonder-seekers," he insisted. Instead, Davis began delivering lectures on religious or metaphysical topics while in a trance, or magnetized, state. His ideas, he claimed, came from higher regions that he could visit in his psychical flights. Davis determined that he would dictate an entire book this way: It would be the vehicle for the "new light" Swedenborg told him to deliver to humanity.

The Seer Emerges

In 1845, the nineteen-year-old Davis decided to leave his tailor friend and his hometown. Accompanied by two new collaborators—a doctor of "botanic remedies" from Bridgeport, Connecticut, and a Universalist minister from New Haven—the Poughkeepsie Seer moved to Manhattan. From a series of low-rent downtown apartments, Davis entered a trance day after day for months. He dictated visions of other planets, heaven, angels, afterlife realms, and the spiritual mechanics of the entire universe, all recorded by his minister friend for the pages of a massively swelling book.

The trance sittings were open to witnesses—one of whom was a pallid, no-nonsense journalist named Edgar Allan Poe. While Davis was living on Vesey Street in Manhattan's financial district, Poe sojourned from his Greenwich Village apartment to make a survey of the seer's work. Poe was fascinated by Mesmerism, placing it at the center of some of his most famous stories, including "The Facts in the Case of M. Valdemar," a tale completed in New York that same year. Poe's story involves the sickly Valdemar, who agrees to be suspended in a Mesmeric trance at the moment of his death. For seven months, the trance master, called P__, keeps Valdemar's consciousness—or magnetic fluid—separated from the man's physical form, suspending him in a state of semilife. The body can move only the "swollen and blackened tongue" in its open mouth, from which issues a horrifying, hollow voice that begs the Mesmerist to set him free. When P__ finally releases Valdemar from the trance, the body "within the space of a single minute, or less, shrunk—crumbled—absolutely *rotted* away beneath my hands. Upon the bed, before the whole company, there lay a nearly liquid mass of loathsome—of detestable putrescence."

It was one of Poe's most widely read tales. Never explicitly billed as fiction and written like a medical case study, the story was initially taken as literal reportage by some in the United States and Britain. The *Sunday Times* of London reprinted it without comment in January of 1846 under the banner *Mesmerism in America: Astounding and Horrifying Narrative*. Whatever the author's intent, "The Facts in the Case of M. Valdemar" served to popularize and lend credibility to the mysterious art.

Whether Poe was equally fascinated with the facts in the case of Andrew Jackson Davis was another matter. The one public reference Poe made to the young medium was a brusque aside in *Graham's Magazine* in 1849: "There surely cannot be more things in Heaven and Earth than are dreamt of (Oh, Andrew Jackson Davis!) in *your* philosophy." In one of Poe's last short stories, "Mellonta Tauta," he opened with an obviously satirical letter that parodied Davis's name and called the story "a translation, by my friend, Martin Van Buren Mavis, (sometimes called the 'Toughkeepsie Seer,')."

Regardless, when Davis's boldly titled tome, *The Principles of Nature, Her Divine Revelations, and a Voice to Mankind*, appeared in its nearly eight hundred pages in 1847, it became an instant sensation, selling nine hundred copies in a single week. (Poe soon followed with his own cosmological tract, "Eureka," in which some noted more than a little more similarity with Davis's grand vision. Humorously or not, Poe read from his work in an apparent trance state before an audience.) Although dense, repetitive, and ponderous, Davis's *Principles of Nature* attempted grand heights, setting forth its new creation myth: "IN THE BEGINNING, the Univercoelum was one boundless, undefinable, and unimaginable ocean of LIQUID FIRE!" Davis described the making of the great universe and all its spiritual dimensions—of which life on earth was just one.

He recorded journeys to other planets and provided details of the afterlife and the creative workings of the Eternal Mind. To some critics, the book was an obvious pilfering of Swedenborg. Indeed, some of Davis's passages—such as his flights through the planets and discourses on the extraterrestrial beings of Saturn and Jupiter—are direct echoes of the Swedish mystic, who produced his own massive treatises on interplanetary dimensions and higher realms before he died in 1772. These volumes by Swedenborg appeared in their first widely circulated English translations in America in 1845, about the same time that Davis embarked on his trance dictations. Davis openly acknowledged his "debt" to Swedenborg—but, he insisted, strictly as a student to a spirit guide. Davis maintained that he had read next to nothing in his young life, and certainly not the formidable works of Swedenborg. A preacher who had befriended Davis while the seer was still a local Poughkeepsie boy recalled that the lad displayed a ravenous appetite for "controversial religious works . . . whenever he could borrow them and obtain leisure for their perusal." Rather lamely, Davis countered that he had merely *borrowed* his preacher friend's books "for others who wished to read but who did not sufficiently know the pastor to borrow for themselves."

Some influential observers didn't know what to think. A prominent Davis supporter named George Bush, a professor of Hebrew at New York University—and a first cousin, five times removed, to President George W. Bush—told the *New York Tribune*: "I can solemnly affirm that I have heard him correctly quote the Hebrew language in his lectures and display a knowledge of geology which would have been astonishing in a person of his age, even if he had devoted years to the study."

The Church of the New Jerusalem, the ecclesiastical body founded in North America on the principles of Swedenborg, kept its distance from the controversial medium. Indeed, the Swedenborgian Church already had its own American icon: He was a curator of apple nurseries from Ohio named John Chapman—or, as the world would come to know him by legend, Johnny Appleseed. According to the 1817 minutes of a Swedenborgian society meeting in Manchester, England:

> There is in the western country a very extraordinary missionary of the New Jerusalem. A man has appeared who seems to be almost independent of corporeal wants and sufferings. He goes barefooted, can sleep anywhere, in house or out of house, and live upon the coarsest and most scanty fare. He has actually thawed ice with his bare feet. He procures what books he can of the New Church Swedenborg, travels into the remote settlements,

> *and lends them wherever he can find readers, and some-*
> *times divides a book into two or three parts for more ex-*
> *tensive distribution and usefulness. This man for years*
> *past has been in the employment of bringing into culti-*
> *vation, in numberless places in the wilderness, small*
> *patches (two or three acres) of ground, and then sowing*
> *apple seeds and rearing nurseries.*

By the time of John Chapman's death in 1845 and the advent of Davis's fame, the Church of the New Jerusalem was on a quest for acceptance and respectability. The last thing it needed was the backcountry mystic Davis claiming to be the protégé of its ghostly founder and quite possibly lifting ideas from the theologian's texts. Johnny Appleseed was apostle enough for the Swedenborgians.

Davis's controversial reputation served only to fuel public interest. He would never again dictate a book in a trance state, but—in an unusual feat for a cobbler's apprentice—he began writing his own cosmic treatises, which would number more than thirty by the time he died in 1910. They continued to be based on his psychical visions, now freely entered. Davis discovered that he could go into a "Superior Condition" on his own, without a Mesmerist, and return to consciousness with fresh insights. Up until this point, trance writers or spirit mediums were considered mere channels of otherworldly forces, passive vessels for communication from higher powers. Not any longer in America. "In the land of democracy," wrote nineteenth-century English historian and psychical researcher Frank Podmore, "we are confronted with a singular development unknown to the older monarchies. The transatlantic seers constantly tend to be independent; they assume the authority of the prophet. . . ."

And to a growing body of readers, Davis's trance-induced writings were a divine revelation. Davis wrote reassuringly of heaven—or the Summer Land, as he called it—which sounded a lot like an idyllic version of the Burned-Over District and the Hudson Valley: "Its streams, rivers, fountains flitter with their own immortal radiance. Its mountains and undulating landscapes are ever green, beautiful with diamond effulgence, more 'delectable' than any pilgrim dreams, while the firmament glows with suns and planets, clusters within clusters, constellations within universes, far beyond mind's conception. High thoughts visit us from the Heavenly alps."

The landscape, metaphysics, and reformist ideals of Central New York formed the model for Davis's cosmology. His Summer Land included people of all races and creeds—Africans, American Indians, Jews, and followers of "Mahomet." The Hudson Valley prophet went further still, declaring the existence of "a Mother as well as a Father in God," echoing Mother Ann Lee and Jemima Wilkinson. He proclaimed a social gospel "of freedom equally to man and woman, young and old, lord and serf." For many, the true magic of Davis's message was in its liberalism: sexual and racial parity, religions on equal footing, and a universal faith based on reason.

In the philosophy of Andrew Jackson Davis, the ideas of utopianism, Mesmerism, and Swedenborgianism were becoming joined. The concept of entering a trance state to reach the afterworld was playing on the public imagination. And the notion that higher dimensions were open to an everyday American— an uneducated cobbler's apprentice, no less—made the possibilities all the more enticing. If mystical visions were no longer the exclusive domain of biblical prophets but were in reach of ordinary people, what splendors might lie in store for inhabitants of the American Israel?

CHAPTER TWO

MYSTIC AMERICANS

✦ ✦ ✦

*The world is infested, just now, by a new sect of
philosophers, who have not yet suspected themselves of
forming a sect, and who, consequently, have adopted
no name. They are the Believers in Everything Old.*

—EDGAR ALLAN POE, "FIFTY SUGGESTIONS"

Today, Manhattan's West 47th Street—a narrow strip of soot-stained office towers, honking traffic, and sidewalks lined with cut-rate jewelry stalls—seems an unlikely birthplace for a spiritual revolution. But in the late nineteenth century, the grimy thoroughfare was every bit as much a staging ground for a flowering of occultism as the marbled palaces of the Renaissance had been four centuries earlier.

It was there in the summer of 1876 that a bearded lawyer and former Civil War officer whom people still called "the colonel" turned a crucial page in his life. The respected jurist had recently divorced his religiously conservative wife, the daughter of an Episcopal minister. In the process he effectively severed his relationship with two teenage sons, who could not follow, much less understand, the new life their father had chosen. His name was Henry Steel Olcott. Decades later, the Buddhist nation of Ceylon would enshrine his image on a postage stamp and mark his death with a national holiday. Hindus in India would celebrate his birthday. And if there were a Mount Rushmore of American occultism, his visage would be carved on it. But instead, in his home country, his name was quickly forgotten.

A tall, bespectacled man whose muttonchop beard made him look older than his forty-four years, Olcott outwardly appeared the product of his conservative Presbyterian upbringing in Orange, New Jersey. But beneath his respectable exterior lay a passion for the arcane that he had harbored since he was young. As a boy of twelve, he made a pilgrimage to Poughkeepsie. There he climbed the stairs of a two-story building to witness Andrew Jackson Davis, still a teenager himself, hold in his hand the lock of a sick man's hair, from which Olcott said the seer made a complete medical diagnosis. The memory never left him. After entering New York University at fifteen, Olcott was forced to drop out following his first year, when his businessman father went broke. On his own, he traveled to relatives in Ohio to try a career in farming. When fieldwork was done, his relatives cultivated an unusual set of interests: séances, Spiritualism, and table-rapping—trends that were just winding their way down the Psychic Highway of New York's Burned-Over District into the farm country of the West.

The fields of Ohio were not enough for Olcott's ambitions. Within a few years he returned home to work at an agricultural school in Newark, New Jersey. A relative soon left him an inheritance, which he used to open a research farm near Mount Vernon, New York. And here the winds of fate lifted him. The young agriculturalist had developed expertise in a strain of Chinese sugarcane that seemed promisingly adaptable to the climes of the American North. As the threat of war loomed over the Mason–Dixon Line, Northerners grew anxious to loosen their dependence on the South's sugar crop. Not yet twenty-five, Olcott wrote a widely read monograph in 1857 on the benefits of his imported cane, called "sorgho" (which Americans still consume as a sweetener today). In a short time, Olcott went from being an ex-collegiate Ohio farm boy who dabbled in séances to a wunderkind of scientific agriculture, his advice sought by state legislatures and even foreign governments.

When the Civil War broke out, Olcott's reputation took yet

another turn. Originally commissioned as a signals officer, the still-young man displayed a talent for research, numbers, and money trails. He was placed in charge of a team of auditors and detectives to investigate fraud and forgery among military contractors, and was promoted to staff colonel to lend weight to his investigations. Exposing a racket of fake provisions sales, Olcott saved the Union army enough money for Secretary of War Edwin M. Stanton to write him that his efforts were "as important to the Government as the winning of a battle." His reputation as an investigator grew. When Lincoln was assassinated in 1865, Olcott volunteered his services. Stanton telegraphed him in New York to "come to Washington at once, and bring your force of detectives with you." During the twelve days that John Wilkes Booth remained a fugitive, Olcott and his investigators made the first arrests and interrogations of suspected coconspirators.

Rich in government contacts following the war, Olcott studied for the bar and opened a legal practice in New York City. Settling into family life, he could have expected the secure if somewhat ordinary prospects of Sunday suppers, gentleman's clubs, a lawyer's paycheck, and maybe even a run for local office. But he grew restless. He took a break from law by writing cultural reviews and investigatory pieces for some of the larger New York dailies, a career he had dabbled in before the war. His interest in Spiritualism began to reemerge—especially upon reading press reports of strange happenings at a Vermont homestead.

In the fall of 1874, Olcott made several trips as a correspondent for the *New York Daily Graphic* to a gloomy farmhouse in Chittenden, Vermont. There a spirit medium named William Eddy, with the help of his brother Horatio, had been treating witnesses to a nightly parade of ghostly beings, ranging from American Indians to figures draped in costume and couture from faraway lands and eras. The ghostly forms emerged from a wooden cabinet that seated William Eddy and that credulous visitors swore had no trick doors or openings. It was here at the Vermont "ghost farm" that Olcott had a fateful encounter—one that would send tremors not only through his own life but across other continents.

On the sunny midday of October 14, Olcott stepped onto the

Eddy porch to light the cigarette of a new visitor: a strange, heavyset Russian woman with whom he grew quickly enchanted. She showed him flesh wounds she said she had suffered fighting beside the revolutionary hero Giuseppe Garibaldi in his campaign to unify Italy; she told tales of travels in exotic lands; and she hinted at far deeper truths about the nature of the spirit world than were revealed to the nightly gawkers at the Eddy home. Olcott was perplexed—and utterly fascinated. The college dropout in him seemed somewhat awed by "the arrival of a Russian lady of distinguished birth and rare educational and natural endowments." He marveled over her tales of "traveling in most of the lands of the Orient, searching for antiquities at the base of the Pyramids, witnessing mysteries of Hindoo temples, and pushing with an armed escort far into the interior of Africa."

His growing, and soon very intense, friendship with this mysterious lady led him on a late summer's day in 1876 to the bustling corner of Manhattan's West 47th Street and Eighth Avenue. His destination was a weathered five-story apartment building, a structure that stands largely unnoticed today as a budget hotel and that possessed little more prestige then. It was there that the colonel rented an eight-room apartment—effectively a salon and headquarters—for himself and his lady friend. In a joking reference to the monasteries of Tibet, the *New York World* dubbed their home the "Lamasery." It was a cramped Neverland of a place where, amid stuffed baboons, Japanese cabinets, jungle murals, mechanical birds, and palm fronds, New York's spiritually adventurous—ranging from inventor Thomas Edison to Major-General Abner Doubleday—huddled to discuss, argue over, and marvel at arcane ideas.

The young Edison told Olcott about an elaborate instrument he had constructed—with one end attached to his forehead and the other to a pendulum—to test the kinetic powers of the mind. By 1920, Edison told a reporter that he had "been at work for some time building an apparatus to see if it is possible for personalities which have left this earth to communicate with us." If Edison ever completed the device, it was not unveiled to the public. The baseball popularizer and Civil War commander Doubleday discoursed among his new acquaintances about karma, which he said had given him courage under fire. Doubleday also began producing the first English translation of French magician Éliphas Lévi's nineteenth-century occult classic *Ritual and Dogma of High Magic*, better known as *Transcendental Magic*.

To Olcott's family and friends, the whole arrangement would have been bizarre enough if Henry's new roommate was merely one of the sundry mediums he had taken to writing about. But this was odder still. His lady cohabitant—with whom he grew passionately close but never shared a bed—was the rotund, hypnotic-eyed Russian officer's daughter named Helena Petrovna, or, as she would become famously known in *fin de siècle* culture, Madame Blavatsky: a magic-making, myth-weaving high priestess of the occult. After years of far-off travel, the eccentric, chain-smoking noblewoman had reached American shores in 1873, shortly before she and Olcott met at the Eddy farmhouse. Many said she could conjure up mediumistic or psychical phenomena at will—such as the ringing of invisible bells, the appearance of magical paintings, or the bump-in-the-night mischief of poltergeistlike "elemental spirits." On a typical day at the Lamasery, Blavatsky materialized—or, in Olcott's lexicon, "phenomenally produced"—a set of phantom sugar tongs when no pair could be found for the couple's after-dinner coffee.

But this was child's play. Blavatsky said she was dispatched to America by a secret order of religious masters—"Mahatmas," or the "Great White Brothers," she would later call them. (She didn't mean *white* in any racial sense but in a sense of inner purity.) Her mission was to expose the limits and fallacies of Spiritualism and point the way to higher truths. While she admired the cosmic visions of Andrew Jackson Davis, Blavatsky hinted at secret teachings that the Poughkeepsie Seer and the trance mediums who trailed after him could only begin to guess.

Soon after they met, Olcott began to receive peculiar gold-inked letters from some of Blavatsky's Eastern Masters, or Mahatmas, signed with pyramidlike cryptograms or the name *Tuitit Bey, Observatory of Luxor*. Olcott later claimed that one of the turbaned masters materialized before him in their West Side apartment. Addressing Olcott as "Brother Neophyte," one of the Mahatma letters directed him to stay at Blavatsky's side and "not let one day pass away without seeing her." He listened—and the two worked together days into nights. They collaborated on Blavatsky's epic-in-the-making, *Isis Unveiled*—a dense, sprawling, and ultimately extraordinary panoply of occult subjects. Blavatsky told of a hidden doctrine that united all the world's ancient religions and cosmic laws but that was unknown to materialist science and modern religion. Most fatefully, she and Olcott transformed their salon of fellow seekers into a nascent organization dedicated to rediscovering *theosophia,* or "divine wisdom." It was called the Theosophical Society. It was not a religion itself but rather aimed to plumb the inner depths of religion, to promote religious universality, and—in a goal that would become increasingly important as time passed—to encourage and defend the Eastern faiths, especially Buddhism and Hinduism, from being chipped away by missionaries and colonialism. In the typically blunt fashion that made her a favorite of the New York press, Madame Blavatsky publicly declared, "The Theosophical Society means, if it cannot rescue Christians from modern Christianity, at least to aid in saving the 'heathen' from its influence." *The New York Sun,* never wearying of the Russian madame, dubbed her the "famous heathen of Eighth Avenue."

The Journey East

For all the heat it generated in the press, the early Theosophical Society was active only briefly during Blavatsky and Olcott's few years together in America. By December 1878, the pair moved to India, uprooting the organization with them. Their mission to rescue the religions of the East from the Goliath of colonialism, Olcott and Blavatsky reasoned, would be best engaged on the soil from which those traditions sprang. For Blavatsky and Olcott, America had already served its purpose: It was a staging ground where the eccentric couple and their nascent following could formulate their ideas unmolested, except for the occasional gibe in the papers. Blavatsky even departed as an American citizen.

Once replanted in India, the story of Theosophy belonged less and less to America or to any nation. Olcott, Blavatsky, and their successors allied themselves with India's independence movement and encouraged the spread of literacy in Hinduism's holy texts, endearing themselves to countless Hindu worshippers. Starting in 1880, Olcott, often with a gouty leg and nothing but an oxcart to carry him over muddy roads, traveled throughout the nation of Ceylon (now Sri Lanka). He spoke in temples and open squares, where he urged youths and their families not to relinquish their Buddhist–monastic tradition and to argue against colonialist missionaries. An Anglican bishop groused in a letter home that "the Secretary of an obscure society" had been encouraging Buddhist monks, "hailing them as brothers in the march of intellect." Olcott used the missionaries' own methods against them: He wrote *A Buddhist Catechism*—still read in Sri Lankan classrooms today—to codify the native faith as missionaries had the Christian one. He successfully lobbied English authorities to permit the national celebration of Buddha's birthday, during which worshippers rallied around an international Buddhist flag Olcott helped to design. He raised money for schools and educational programs. The Buddhist revival ignited. Within twenty years of Olcott's first visit, the number of Buddhist schools in the island nation grew from four to more than two hundred.

Had any of his former friends in the law or newspaper business inquired as to what became of old Henry, they might have chortled over the spectacle of a retired military investigator with an eagle eye for fraud now traveling throughout the Orient with this Russian magician lady. But that would be far too shallow a reading of Olcott's character. With Madame Blavatsky at his side—the two like Don Quixote and Sancho Panza, each interchangeably occupying either role—the colonel understood himself to be on the mission of a lifetime. It was a mission whose influence touched Hindu and Buddhist cultures so deeply that

Olcott may be the single most significant Western figure in the modern religious history of the East.

And if there were any hidden Mahatmas who had sent Blavatsky to America and then with Olcott to India, they might have had reason to be proud of their neophytes on other counts. Back in the United States and Europe, Blavatsky's book *Isis Unveiled* popularized the word *occultism* and made the concept a matter of passionate interest among artists, authors, and spiritual seekers of the Western world—more than it had been any time since Renaissance scholars had marveled over the magical writings of Greek–Egyptian sage Hermes Trismegistus.

Transcendental Magic

The American public's fascination with Blavatsky, and its ability to make any sense of her aims and background, was assisted by an earlier intellectual movement that would have wanted little truck with so histrionic a figure: New England Transcendentalism. The ideas and interests of Ralph Waldo Emerson, Henry David Thoreau, Bronson Alcott, and the venerable Yankee Mystics played a decided role in introducing magical philosophies into American thought.

In 1851, the Boston-based Transcendentalist writer and teacher Alcott made the mythical Hermes Trismegistus the opening subject in a program of literary salons. "Few persons to hear and discuss Hermes, in consequence of the rain," Alcott remarked in his journals. "But we had a very good time of it." Alcott's interest in the magico-Egyptian writings of Hermes probably arose from Emerson, whose influence touched the circle of Transcendentalists more deeply than any other. Emerson mentioned Hermes in his journals as early as 1834, challenging pedants to "strengthen the hearts of the waiting lovers of the primal philosophy." He admiringly quoted the seventeenth-century philosopher Sir Thomas Browne, who, chin out, declared: "The severe Schools shall never laugh me out of the Philosophy of Hermes, that this visible World

is but a Picture of the invisible wherein . . ." The Transcendentalists wouldn't be laughed out either, and they embraced the Hermetic concept of man as a microcosm of the universe. "The
world," wrote Emerson in his essay "Compensation," "globes itself in a drop of dew." It was an American sounding of the great
Hermetic dictum: "As above, so below."

As seen through his journals, Emerson was among the first serious American writers to carefully consider topics such as the
Persian prophet Zoroaster (1822), Hindu mythology (1823), the
Greek mage Pythagoras (1832), Confucius (1836), Buddha
(1838), the Vedas (1839), Hermes and the Neo-Platonists (1841),
and reincarnation (1845). He familiarized the reading public
with esoteric ideas in a way that later made it possible for Theosophy and other occult movements to be understood in America.
"It may seem ludicrous to suggest that Emerson was the chief
forerunner of Madame Blavatsky, her John the Baptist," wrote
religious scholar Alvin Boyd Kuhn in his 1930 study, *Theosophy.*
"Yet, seriously, without Emerson, Madame Blavatsky could
hardly have launched her gospel when she did with equal hope of
success."

Mystical Europe

Some of Blavatsky's earliest and closest followers harbored a secret hope, discussed in letters and lodge conversations. It was that
the mysterious madame had arrived to replace a fallen heterodox
hero—the renegade Freemason and occult seeker Cagliostro, who
had perished in the prisons of the Inquisition in Central Italy in
1795. First arrested in Rome in 1789 for the "heresy" of Freemasonry and other antipapal activities, the mysterious, widely traveled Cagliostro was probably the last man to die under the
penalties of the Inquisition. But in the 1870s, antimonarchists
and papal foes were riding on high hopes that history had finally
turned their way, as conservative monarchies and Church influence waned throughout the decade. In 1870, Rome itself had
fallen as an independent state, disbanding its military and stub-

bornly joining a unified Italian republic. It was weakened after years of assault by the democratic revolutionary Garibaldi— himself a committed Freemason and reputed confederate of Madame Blavatsky. "For admirers of the martyred Cagliostro," wrote historian K. Paul Johnson, "events in Italy that decade were long-awaited retribution for the Church's savage persecution of Masonry."

In Europe, the occult experimentation that had been cut short by the Thirty Years' War seemed everywhere to flourish anew. What came to be seen as a European occult revival touched America's burgeoning occult culture and mixed with it. But the two movements soon divided into different channels, each with its own distinct aims and styles of thought. To understand how these sister movements converged and then split requires a brief look at how Europe's revival emerged.

Napoleon's disastrous military campaign in Egypt at the end of the eighteenth century had the strange by-product of giving birth to the field of modern Egyptology. The would-be conqueror brought with him an army of sketch artists, naturalists, and scribes, whose findings ignited a renewed fascination with the symbols and monuments of the lost civilization. Napoleon's soldiers chanced upon the Rosetta Stone, which in decades ahead unlocked the hieroglyphic wording—if not the underlying meaning—of the Black Land's rites, gods, and customs.

In France, a highly speculative and widely influential interpretation of the Tarot cards—which had appeared, with little obvious antecedent, in early-fifteenth-century Italy—identified ancient Egypt as the source of their beguiling imagery. The self-styled historian Antoine Court de Gébelin produced a string of subscription volumes on ancient history, *Monde primitif* (*The Primitive World*), which in their 1781 series deemed Tarot a secret book of primeval Egyptian wisdom. Closely following de Gébelin was an antiquary and fortune-teller who went by the single name Etteilla (the not-terribly imaginative backward spelling of the surname of Jean-Baptiste Alliette). Etteilla embraced the Egyptian connection and designed the first Tarot deck used expressly for divination.

Translations of Far East mystical literature, such as the mysterious source of Taoist philosophy *Tao Te Ching* and the divinatory masterpiece the *I Ching,* also began to emerge from the West's reencounter with China. Hindu literature, such as the allegorical wisdom book *Bhagavad Gita* and the magisterial epic *Mahabharata,* were translated and read in Europe and America for the first time.

In Europe as in America, the theories of Darwin had the dual effect of undermining old ecclesiastical certainties while creating a new hunger for mystery in a biologically ordered world. And there existed, perhaps, a troublesome sense that Europe's material progress and scientific reason had failed to resolve the inner and outer perplexities of life, particularly as the squalor of industrialization and the bleakness of William Blake's "dark Satanic mills" became increasingly evident.

For avant-garde artists and intellectuals who had lost faith in old-line religion, a new light began to shine. In 1855, Éliphas Lévi, in his *Transcendental Magic,* proclaimed the existence of an occult philosophy hidden at the base of:

> all the hieratic and mystical allegories of ancient doctrines, behind the darkness and strange ordeals of all initiations, under the seal of all sacred writings, in the ruins of Nineveh or Thebes, on the crumbling stones of old temples and on the blackened visage of the Assyrian or Egyptian sphinx, in the monstrous or marvelous paintings which interpret to the faithful of India the inspired pages of the Vedas, in the cryptic emblems of our old books on alchemy, in the ceremonies practised at reception by all secret societies.

In Lévi's vision, occultists discovered a new sense of mission and drama.

The European occult revival attracted formidable intellects and earnest seekers, though with a peculiar twist: European occultists often adopted airs of secrecy and pageantry, as if mimicking the outer appearances of ancient temple orders and mysterious sects would assist their quest to revive lost or fragmentary knowledge. Sometimes on the thin pretext of concealing hallowed doctrine, they cloaked their study groups and fraternities in mystery. They used—or, more often, invented—the names of antique cults, such as the Hermetic Brotherhood of Luxor or the Hermetic Order of the Golden Dawn. In turn, they employed ceremonies and costumes that aped incredibly old, only dimly understood rituals. These groups drew hasty connections between the divinatory arts, such as Tarot and modern number mysticism, and the civilization of ancient Egypt. Indeed, Europe's leading occultists typically—and often fatuously—claimed lineage to mythical or underground brotherhoods in which the old teachings were said to be preserved.

As a result, the European avant-garde's laudable efforts at translating and reinterpreting ancient and esoteric doctrine, from alchemical manuscripts to the works of Hermes, gave way to the gloomy prospect that occultism had survived so many storms and buffets only to be lathered over with modern-day fantasy and theatrics. And our story might simply end there—were it not for a young nation across the sea that was feeling the influence of the occult to its very foundations.

The Spiritualist Tide

Madame Blavatsky explained that she approached America, the land of Spiritualism, "with feelings not unlike those of a Mohammedan approaching the birthplace of his Prophet." The opening created by Spiritualism made the young nation into a magnet for every kind of spiritual experiment. And like many cultural openings, this one appeared so quickly and dramatically that it could leave observers unsure of what was even occurring.

The Shakers had prophesied that spirits would "visit every city and hamlet, every palace and cottage in the land." And that prophecy began coming to pass in March of 1848, directing us once more to the American occult's equivalent of Mount Sinai: the Burned-Over District of upstate New York. In a small wood-framed house outside Rochester, in a village named Hydesville, lived two attractive young girls: Kate, who had just turned eleven, and Margaret, fourteen. Weird things had been happening in the Fox home; strange cracklings and noises ripped through the darkened rooms, coming, it seemed, from nowhere. The girls told their Methodist parents that the bangs and knocks were "spirit raps." Soon, in front of baffled neighbors, the young sisters made a display of asking questions and receiving replies in the form of ghostly raps, worked out in a language so that knocks corresponded to letters of the alphabet. Local tales told of the murder of a traveling peddler in the area, and, sure enough, bones were discovered in the Fox basement. They were considered the earthly remains of the rapping spirit whom the Fox girls eerily called "Mr. Splitfoot." Within weeks, curiosity seekers, clergy, and newspaper reporters converged on the little hamlet. The girls were tested, talked about, and looked over by newspaper editor Horace Greeley, New York Supreme Court Justice John Edmonds, and a variety of religious and scientific examiners—many of whom publicly attested to the genuineness of the phenomena. Americans were transfixed, and by the end of the 1840s the Spiritualist era was born.

Why did the relatively modest event grip people so? Hauntings, ghosts, and belief in an afterlife had touched every culture and civilization. And news from the spirit world was hardly unknown in America: The Publick Universal Friend had claimed to speak as an avatar from the heavens; the Poughkeepsie Seer had already produced his first massive volume of trance writing; and the Shakers had reported that spirits were visiting them ten years prior to Rochester. So spirit communiqués were nothing new. But the story told by the Fox sisters provided something of a different order. It fulfilled what was implicit in the career of Andrew Jackson Davis: that spirit communication was open to anyone, anytime. If two teenage girls could reach the otherworld, it stood to reason that *everyone* could. It was a completely egalitarian take on the supernatural, with newspapers and publicity-hungry investigators ready to spread the word.

And the spirit raps heard in Rochester could strike at the

deepest emotions of American homes in an era when children were constantly lost to disease. In New York City in 1853, nearly half of all reported deaths were children under five. "And oh! mother that reads this," wrote Harriet Beecher Stowe in *Uncle Tom's Cabin,* "has there never been in your house a drawer, or a closet, the opening of which has been to you like the opening again of a little grave? Ah! happy mother that you are, if it has not been so." For many, the hope of contact soothed the agony of loss.

As the news from Rochester spread, grieving parents, widows and widowers, or those simply pursuing otherworldly thrills gathered together in clubs and parlor rooms, schoolhouses and churches, to reach out to the dead. And many avowed that such contact came. In darkened rooms, tables lifted and rocked, disembodied knocks cracked through the night air, and trance mediums spoke in otherworldly voices: *I-am-here-Mother,* a medium might intone, as a listener sobbed and squeezed the hands of those on either side of her.

Americans like organizing things, and the supernatural was no exception. Within a decade of the Fox sisters, the nation saw the growth of Spiritualist clubs, lecture societies, and séance circles. Modeled on the instructions developed by Andrew Jackson Davis in his 1851 book *The Philosophy of Spiritual Intercourse,* three hundred distinct "circles" emerged in Philadelphia alone during that decade. According to a survey, the Burned-Over District was home to eighty-nine trance mediums and Spiritualist lecturers by 1859. And those numbers probably failed to capture the full range of "hobbyist" mediums. In 1850, journalist E. W. Capron counted in Auburn, New York, "fifty to one hundred" mediums "in different stages of development," including those who could induce unseen hands to strum guitars and pound drums.

In the 1850s and beyond, believers and enthusiasts were served by dozens of newspapers specifically devoted to Spiritualist phenomena and ideas. Among the largest were *The Banner of Light* and *The New Era* in Boston, *The Spiritual Telegraph* in New York, *The Better Way* in Cincinnati, *The Carrier Dove* in Oakland, and *Spiritual Republic* and *Religio-Philosophical Journal* in

Chicago. Most were ardently progressive, espousing suffragism and abolitionism alongside news of the spirit world. The *Religio-Philosophical Journal,* which began publication just after the Civil War, launched its maiden issue with an editorial against capital punishment for Confederate leaders, urging Spiritualists to "heal the breach" of war and begin "the *regenerative* work of enlightening and spiritualizing the masses."

There soon emerged Spiritualist churches, summer camps, and—again at the instigation of Andrew Jackson Davis—Sunday schools, the first of which opened in New York in 1863. It was based on Davis's description of teaching methods in the heavenly realm of Summer Land. Aiming to cultivate the wisdom of the "imperishable and perfect" soul of the individual child, Davis's Children's Lyceums anticipated future trends in progressive education by emphasizing the personal needs of each pupil.

In the minds of many Spiritualists, their movement held a special place for children. Oakland's *Carrier Dove* featured a "Children's Department," which offered stories of "little angels coming to converse with wee Willy and Maud." In 1886, the paper covered a children's séance where a motherly trance medium:

> placed the little stand into the center of the room and took her seat beside it, then called the children, six at a time, to come and put their hands upon it, while it danced to the tune of lively music. Then came the raps, and each child received some little message. It was indeed a beautiful picture to see the sweet, animated faces of the little ones as they heard for the first time the signals from the spirit land.

Mysterious Numbers

While the numbers were large, it is difficult to say precisely how many Americans considered themselves Spiritualists in the nineteenth century. The figure of 1.5 million, out of a total population of about thirty million, appears repeatedly at the movement's initial flush of excitement in the 1850s—sometimes attributed to surveys, other times not attributed at all.

Works of history, both old and new, report figures upward of that amount. As a rule, the higher the number, the thinner the attribution: 2.5 million from the pen of a sympathetic Reverend W. R. Hayden in 1885 (and repeated in an influential British study); three million reported in several early Spiritualist journals; nine million claimed in 1874 by the movement's preeminent theologian Davis (confirmed while in a clairvoyant trance); and Boston's *Banner of Light*, hitting the all-time record, reported eleven to thirteen million the same year. It was, claimed *The Banner*, a figure encompassing the many secret believers who were afraid to formally step forward.

Given Spiritualism's nationwide range of clubs and publications—including a peak of sixty-seven newspapers—it is reasonable to estimate that the population ran into hundreds of thousands and, depending on how stringently one defines a follower, possibly a million or higher. In a nation that counted its overall population at thirty to thirty-five million in the mid-nineteenth century, it is likely that almost one in ten free adults considered themselves believers, of one degree or another. The numbers were so large that, by the close of the 1850s, the Burned-Over District had become eclipsed by the movement it spawned and would no longer serve as the laboratory of mystical religion in American life. Chicago, Boston, New York, Philadelphia, and many towns and cities had Spiritualist societies, newspapers, and congregations and soon produced innovations of their own. Spiritualism was not a regional sensation but a national movement.

"He Was Too Good for This Earth"

When facing the tragedies of death, many families were remarkably alike. In this sense, the Spiritualist experience was typified by the household of the most famous family in the nation: the Lincolns. Several months after occupying the White House in

March of 1861, Abraham and Mary Todd Lincoln experienced the nightmare of so many mid-century parents: Their eleven-year-old son, Willie, was gripped by a serious fever, probably from typhus. A sensitive, precociously religious child with a keen mind and a love for adult company, Willie was the family favorite. He was seen holding hands with his father, whom he sometimes accompanied on official trips, the two sharing a room together. After illness struck, weeks of struggle and bedside vigils did no good. In February of 1862, the boy died late one afternoon.

"My poor boy," Lincoln said at the bedside. "He was too good for this earth. God has called him home. I know that he is much better off in heaven, but then we loved him so. It is hard, hard to have him die!" For Mary Todd, the loss was too great. She began to frequent trance mediums in desperate hope of contact. And, in the aggrieved mother's heart, contact did occur. One evening she rushed into the room of her half sister, who had served as a nursemaid to Willie. "He lives, Emilie!" the first lady exclaimed. "He comes to me every night and stands at the foot of my bed, with the same sweet, adorable smile he always had." Mary Todd's was the kind of story told time and again, repeated in newspapers and letters by people from every walk of life who eloquently, if agonizingly, testified to the reality of another world. For those Americans who ardently believed, Spiritualism provided some of the most moving and deeply affecting experiences of their lives.

Mary Todd Lincoln, Spiritualist

For Mary Todd Lincoln, Spiritualism was a lifelong interest—and sometimes a public embarrassment. Seven years after her husband's assassination, she was the subject of bruising articles in February 1872 in both the *Boston Herald* and *The New York Times*. Each reported that the veiled widow clandestinely sought out the mediumistic services of the older Fox sister, Margaret. *The New York Times,* in "A Curious Story About Mrs. Lincoln Reiterated," obliquely called Margaret Fox "a well-known lady

medium on Washington-street" in Boston. Knowledgeable readers immediately understood the reference to the Spiritualist pioneer. Margaret was a no-longer-young woman suffering family
fissures and heated charges and countercharges of fraud, and
now earning her living at the séance table. Mrs. Lincoln had
made the insufficient effort of disguising herself on a Boston hotel
registry as a "Mrs. Linder." The most famous widow in America
joined others at a public sitting in Margaret's parlor, where, reported *The Times,* "the spirit of her lamented husband appeared
and, by unmistakable manifestations, revealed to all present the
identity of Mrs. Lincoln, which she had attempted to keep secret." In 1875, Mary Todd's one surviving son, Robert, had her
briefly committed to a sanitorium, claiming—spuriously—that
she was squandering her estate on Spiritualist hoo-ha such as that
in Boston.

And this, at last, is the image with which most historians are
comfortable: the widow Lincoln, famously nervous and often
depressed, her mind loosened from too much loss, seeking final
solace in the darkened séance room. But less understood is that
President Lincoln himself may have taken more than a passing
interest in Spiritualism. In April of 1863, in the presence of a reporter from the *Boston Gazette,* Lincoln hosted a séance in the
Crimson Room of the White House. Attending were Mary
Todd, two cabinet secretaries, and a trance medium, Charles E.
Shockle, who seemed more nervous than anyone else during the
whole affair (twice during the evening he fainted and had to be
revived). Once everyone was seated at the table, according to the
Gazette's correspondent, Prior Melton, Lincoln gamely pitched
political questions to Shockle, the "spirit visitors" who spoke
through him, and the two cabinet members, while Mary Todd
looked on silently.

As with all such episodes in Spiritualist history, this one raises
the question of which sources to believe. Historian John B.
Buescher noted that no trance medium named Charles E. Shockle
appeared in any of the Spiritualist newspapers of the day, which
suggests the *Gazette's* correspondent may have invented the
whole affair. Several days after the *Gazette* article's publication,

however, *The New York Herald* reprinted the evening's account ("which we presume to be true," stated an adjunct note) and added its own news analysis about Spiritualism's popularity. Several other newspapers followed suit in reprinting the piece. There is no record of the White House ever disputing the report. Lincoln biographer Carl Sandburg took note of the affair and wondered why the president permitted a reporter to be present at all. The likelihood is that the White House séance served a shrewd political end. Lincoln used the encounter to show the public that, even in the midst of the Civil War, the commander in chief could sit back and sample the same kind of parlor-room novelty that other Americans were marveling over. The *Gazette* story presented Lincoln as relaxed, good humored, and not excessively encumbered by wartime command. In something of a White House propaganda coup, at least one paper of the Confederacy, Georgia's *Macon Daily Telegraph and Confederate*, reprinted the *Gazette* piece in full.

Whether elements of the story were fabricated—such as the mysterious, possibly pseudonymous Mr. Shockle—the dialogue does suggest vintage Lincoln. When the medium told the president that an Indian spirit wished to convey a message, Lincoln replied: "Well, sir, I should be happy to hear what his Indian Majesty has to say. We have recently had a visitation from our red brethren, and it was the only delegation—black, white or blue—which did not volunteer some advice about the conduct of the war." In other settings, the president had often—and humorously—complained of how visitors liked nothing better than to bestow advice about the war, when what he needed were victories.

When Shockle's spirits did get around to giving their inevitable military advice—through the channeled words of no less than Henry Knox, secretary of war to George Washington—Lincoln was unimpressed: "Well, opinions differ among the saints as well as among the sinners. They don't seem to understand running the machine among the celestials much better than we do. Their talk and advice sounds very much like the talk of my Cabinet." Lincoln then asked his discomforted cabinet secretaries whether they agreed that the spirits knew little better how to proceed than the mortals—which elicited stammering assurances from Navy Secretary Gideon Welles that, uh, well, sir, he would certainly consider the matter.

Supernatural Politics

If the *Gazette* had intended to expose Lincoln as a Spiritualist, it more fully captured him as a good-humored skeptic. But there exists another remembrance of the Civil War era that depicts a different Lincoln from the one teasingly subjecting his cabinet members to spirit counsels.

An 1891 memoir by a trance medium named Nettie Colburn Maynard, *Was Abraham Lincoln a Spiritualist?*, stands apart from some of the era's hackneyed literature in its vividness of style and even verisimilitude. At the end of 1862, wrote Maynard, as the Civil War passed into a second Christmas season, with hopes for peace at a dreary low, she was, at the instigation of Mary Todd Lincoln, ushered into the private quarters of the White House and asked to give a spirit reading to the exhausted commander. At the time, Lincoln had drafted but not yet signed the cornerstone measure of his presidency: the Emancipation Proclamation. There was enormous tension in the nation over when or whether he would put his signature to it.

"For more than an hour I was made to talk to him," Maynard reported. During the course of her unconscious transmission from the spirit realm, Maynard wrote, Lincoln was assured that if he acted to sign and enforce the Emancipation Proclamation, it would be the primary achievement for which he would be remembered. As Maynard emerged from her trance, she found that a grave hush had fallen over the room. "Mr. President," asked Congressman Daniel E. Somes of Maine, an onlooker at the séance, "would it be improper for me to inquire whether there has been any pressure brought to bear upon you to defer the enforcement of the Proclamation?" Yes, Maynard reported Lincoln saying, "*It is taking all of my nerve and strength to withstand such a pressure.*" Lincoln then turned to the teenage medium. "My child, you possess a very singular gift; but that it is of God, I have no doubt. I thank you for coming here tonight. It is more important than perhaps anyone present can understand."

Whether any part of the account is true cannot be known. But it underscores a distinct and misunderstood quality among many American Spiritualists. And this was the desire to associate supernaturalism with the social good.* Here is the impulse of Andrew Jackson Davis and his vision of heaven as a place containing all of the world's peoples; of the Shakers to whom spirits spoke of the need to end slavery and the tragedy that settlers had visited upon the Indians; and of the Freemasons and their ideal of a religious nation that eschewed sectarian division. Maynard, whatever her veracity as a witness, sought not to convince the public that she counseled Lincoln on how to conduct himself in war, how to exercise power, or how to deal with the Confederacy, but rather that, through her trance reading, she advised him to do the greatest thing a leader could do, in the eyes of social reformers.

In this way, Spiritualism was both an occult movement and a political one. It attracted the interest and participation of utopians, suffragists, and radicals, because, among other things, it provided a setting in which women—for the first time in American history—could regularly serve as religious leaders, at least of a sort. Most spirit mediums were women, with many voting-rights activists among them. Spiritualist thought-leaders included the formidable Anglo-American religious thinker Emma Hardinge Britten—an early Theosophist and political reformer who had stumped for Lincoln's candidacy and who saw Spiritualism as the basis of a new religious order. Andrew Jackson Davis's second wife (the seer married thrice) was the suffragette–activist Mary Fenn Love, who in 1853 coconvened the first New York State Women's Rights Convention. "Spiritualism has inaugurated the era of woman," Love announced.

---

* Maynard's account, and particularly her record of Lincoln's remarks, also shows Spiritualism's continued emphasis on the Christian underpinnings of mediumship.

In 1872, the Equal Rights Party, a consortium of suffragists and abolitionists, named trance-medium Victoria Woodhull the nation's first female presidential candidate. Woodhull had gained national prominence the previous year in a historic voting-rights speech before the congressional Judiciary Committee. She was the first woman to appear before a joint committee of Congress. She later told supporters that the Woodhull Memorial, as her testimony was known, had been dictated to her in a dream by a ghostly, tunic-wearing Greek elder—a spirit guardian who had guided all of her public utterances ever since she was a little girl. Woodhull's presidential campaign was quixotic and short-lived, quickly eclipsed by her twin passions for publicity-mongering and political chicanery. The medium–activist selected Frederick Douglass as her running mate—but without asking him. "I never heard of this," the abolitionist hero later said.

Another Spiritualist voice in Congress belonged to U.S. Senator James Shields. In 1854, the Illinois Democrat rose on the Senate floor to present a petition signed by fifteen thousand American Spiritualists. Shields begged senators to take seriously the petitioners' request to fund a "scientific commission" to investigate the possibility of talking to the dead—perhaps, Shields offered, even looking into "establishing a spiritual telegraph between the material and spiritual world." For most Spiritualists, science and religion were not at odds but were natural allies in the march of progress. Many considered communiqués from the spirit world to be as scientifically provable as the electrical current or the telegraph signal—faculties that only strengthened their belief in unseen forms of communication. Shields's Senate colleagues were having none of it, and in short order they hooted down the former general, one guffawing that his proposal should be dispatched to the Committee on Foreign Relations.

Some of the nation's better-respected political reformers also counted themselves as believers in the Rochester rappings. They included the liberal congressman and Lincoln confidant Robert Dale Owen, who participated in dozens of nightly sittings that summoned up a voluptuous female spirit named Katie King. King "materialized" in physical form and received gifts and doting gazes from the aging activist. When Owen learned he was being tricked by an actress, it so broke him that he spent time in a sanitorium. The reformist newspaper editor Horace Greeley invited the younger Fox sister, Kate, to live for four months in his dark, rambling home in Chappaqua, New York. With Greeley and his wife, Kate attempted to contact the couple's departed five-year-old son. So heavily did the lines between progressive politics and Spiritualism intersect in the nineteenth century that it was rare to find a leader in one field who had not at least a passing involvement in the other.

Spirit Journeys

Spirit rappings had a peculiar way of spreading. Soon they were being heard at séance circles in the drawing rooms of Paris and London, where the fashionable classes took a deep interest in things that went bump. Spiritualism became, in effect, the first spiritual movement that America exported abroad.

In France in the late 1850s, a stout, bearded writer and lecturer named Allan Kardec crafted "Spiritism" into a full-blown religion, complete with its own cosmic theology, liturgy, and doctrine of redemptive, or karmic, reincarnation. Determined to appear as no one's imitator, Kardec displayed little fondness for his American counterparts—or, it seemed, for anyone. His English friend and translator Anna Blackwell recalled Kardec as possessing such a "habitual sobriety of demeanor that he was never known to laugh." Regardless, after his death in 1869, the French theologian became venerated as a kind of Spiritualist saint in Latin America, where his writings had been spread by Portuguese traders. To the current day, Kardec's image—depicted not as stout but firm and angular—appears on devotional candles and amulets from Peru to the *barrios* of North America. In Brazil, where *Espiritismo* is an officially recognized faith, the government placed Kardec's image on a postage stamp in 1957 to celebrate the *First Centenary of Organized Spiritism*.

And Spiritualism traveled still farther, inspiring a vast supernatural religion in the nation of Vietnam. It began in the late 1920s, when a Vietnamese civil servant working for the French colonial administration conceived of the faith he called *Caodaism* (roughly, "religion of the high palace"). It was a mélange of Eastern traditions—from Taoism to Buddhism to Hinduism—combined with the ideas of Allan Kardec and other French Spiritists, including poet and novelist Victor Hugo, himself a habitué of séances. To communicate with the otherworld, Caodaism relied upon American Spiritualism's most popular innovation: the Ouija board. Ouija proved surprisingly adaptable to the Latinized version of the Vietnamese language that had begun under the influence of Catholic missionaries. So closely was Ouija associated with Caodaism that novelist Graham Greene in *The Quiet American* lampooned the Vietnamese faith as "prophecy by planchette," using the French name for the little platform that slides around the board.

Caodaism had a defiant politics. It was militantly anticommunist and maintained a private army that sided with American forces against the Vietcong as late as 1975. After the war, the religion fled underground. Newly emergent in the twenty-first century, Caodaism claims up to eight million followers worldwide and ranks as Vietnam's third-largest faith, after Buddhism and Catholicism. Though unknown to most Americans—whose primary association with Vietnam is war and loss—Caodaism is by far the largest organized religion to emerge from the Spiritualist age. And its origins can be traced back to the ghostly rappings heard one winter night at a cottage in the Burned-Over District. The "cradle of Modern Spiritualism," as Madame Blavatsky once called America, had sent its children on a long journey. And they would find still stranger games to play along the way.

CHAPTER THREE

DON'T TRY THIS AT HOME

Ouija and the Selling of Spiritualism

❖ ❖ ❖

*. . . these creepy things; there may be great truths in
them, but they have nearly destroyed us.*

—SWAMI VIVEKANANDA, *COMPLETE WORKS*

More than a century after the dawn of the Spiritualist era,
three teenage girls, who'd probably never heard the word
Spiritualism uttered in their 1960s suburban homes, huddled
over an object nearly every teenager recognized: the Ouija board.
Giggling nervously, they asked about their futures: "Will we all
get married?" They rested their fingers with no more than the
weight of a whisker on the molded plastic pointer, or planchette,
waiting for the little tripod to slide across the board's lettered surface. And it did, first in a slight jerk and then smoothly, as though
guided by some unseen force. As the board's eerie faces of the sun
and moon grinned back at the girls, the pointer slid over the
word: YES. "Will there be divorce?" they asked. The pointer
moved again: YES: THREE. It was not until years later that the
anxious girls, grown into middle-age women, could look back
and laugh: All had married, but only one had divorced—thrice.

By the time youth culture had become big business, when the
Beach Boys sang about T-Birds and having "Fun, Fun, Fun" at

hamburger stands—developments that would have been as un-recognizable to the Fox sisters as life on Mars—Ouija reigned supreme as the nation's most intriguing novelty. The game board's mysterious movements and beguiling communications made it a staple of slumber parties and toy-cluttered basements. By the late 1960s, its sales rivaled those of the best-selling board game in the world, Monopoly.

Though patented and sold as entertainment, Ouija was no or-dinary fad. It was, in fact, a homemade device concocted by nineteenth-century American Spiritualists who, from the earliest days of their movement, yearned to make talking with the dead as natural as dinnertime conversation. Whether the object of fear or fascination, Ouija proved the most enduring symbol of their success.

Spiritual Telegraphs

Among nineteenth-century believers, Spiritualism was a practice of deep intimacy. Acolytes squeezed hands around séance tables, felt the quickened breath of those on either side of them, and heard raps and voices in a way that could make the dead seem close enough to embrace. Profoundly touched by their experi-ences, Spiritualists determined to find ever better and easier ways to communicate with the beyond. Acting from the best American instincts, they demanded a do-it-yourself approach to the matter. Their homespun efforts at reaching the afterlife led to what is called Ouija, or what its earliest users called "talking boards" or "spirit boards." But such devices did not appear until early Spiritualists and inventors worked through several other methods.

One involved a form of table-rapping in which questioners solicited spirit knocks when letters of the alphabet were called out, thus spelling a word. Many Spiritualists in the 1850s, however, found this a tedious and time-consuming exercise. A faster means was "automatic writing," in which spirit beings could communicate through the pen of a medium, but some complained that this produced many pages of unclear or meandering prose.

Another invention directly prefigured the heart-shaped pointer that moves around the Ouija board. The planchette—French for "little plank"—was a three-legged writing tool with a hole at the top for the insertion of a pencil. The planchette was designed for one or more people to rest their fingers upon and allow it to "glide" across a page to write out a spirit message. The device originated in Europe in the early 1850s; by 1860, commercially manufactured planchettes were advertised in America.

Two other items from the 1850s are direct forebears to Ouija: dial plates and alphabet paste boards. In 1853, a Connecticut Spiritualist invented the Spiritual Telegraph Dial, a roulettelike wheel with letters and numerals around its circumference. Dial plates came in various forms, sometimes of a complex variety. Some were rigged to tables to respond to "spirit tilts," while others—like planchettes—glided beneath the resting hands of questioners.

Alphabet boards further simplified matters. In use as early as 1852, these talking-board precursors allowed seekers to point to a letter as a means of prompting a "spirit rap," thereby quickly spelling a word. It was, perhaps, the easiest method yet. And it was only a matter of time until experimenters and entrepreneurs began to see the possibilities.

Baltimore Oracles

The conventional history of American toy manufacturing credits Ouija to a Baltimore businessman named William Fuld. Fuld, we are told, "invented" Ouija around 1890. So it has been repeated in articles, books of trivia, reference works, and "ask me" columns in newspapers. For many decades, the manufacturer itself—first Fuld's company and later the toy giant Parker Brothers—insinuated as much by running the term *William Fuld Talking Board Set* across the top of every board.

The conventional history is wrong.

The patent for a "Ouija or Egyptian luck-board" was filed on May 28, 1890, by Baltimore resident and patent attorney Elijah J. Bond, who assigned the rights to two city businessmen, Charles W. Kennard and William H. A. Maupin. The patent was granted on February 10, 1891, and so was born the Ouija-brand talking board.

The first patent reveals a familiarly oblong board, with the alphabet running in double rows across the top and numbers in a single row along the bottom. The sun and moon, labeled respectively YES and NO, adorn the upper left and right corners, while the phrase GOOD BYE appears at the bottom center. Later on, instructions and the illustrations accompanying them prescribed an expressly social—even flirtatious—experience: Two parties, preferably a man and woman, were to balance the board between them on their knees, placing their fingers lightly upon the planchette. ("It draws the two people using it into close companionship and weaves about them a feeling of mysterious isolation," the box read.) In an age of buttoned-up morals, a toe-to-toe Ouija session could be a tempting dalliance.

True Origins

The Kennard Novelty Company of Baltimore employed a teenage varnisher who helped run shop operations, and this was William Fuld. By 1892, however, Charles W. Kennard's partners removed Kennard from the company amid financial disputes, and a separate patent—this time for an improved planchette—was filed by a nineteen-year-old Fuld. In years to come, it was Fuld who would take over the novelty firm and affix his name to every board.

After Fuld took the reins of Ouija manufacturing in America, business was brisk—if not always happy. Fuld formed a volatile business alliance with his brother, Isaac, which landed the two in court battles for nearly twenty years. Isaac was eventually found to have violated an injunction against creating a competing board, called the Oriole, after being forced from the family business in 1901. The two brothers would never speak again. Ouija, and anything that looked directly like it, was firmly in the hands of William Fuld.

So went the business history of Ouija. But the board had a still deeper set of roots. Contrary to the many conflicting claims of ownership, talking boards of a homemade variety were already a popular craze among Spiritualists by the mid-1880s. And here we encounter Ouija's lost link to the Spiritualist movement. In its Sunday supplement of March 28, 1886, the *New York Daily Tribune* ran an article on "A Mysterious Talking Board and Table Over Which Northern Ohio Is Agitated." The short piece featured a matchbox-size illustration of a rectangular alphabet board—the spitting image of Ouija, a full four years before its first patent was filed.

"I know of whole communities that are wild over the 'talking board,' as some of them call it," an Ohio man was quoted. "I have never heard any name for it. But I have seen and heard some of the most remarkable things about its operation—things that seem to pass all human comprehension or explanation." And best of all: "Anyone can make the whole apparatus in fifteen minutes, with a jack-knife and a marking brush."

The 1886 eyewitness described how to use the "witching thing" as clearly as later instructions on a Ouija box top: "You take the board in your lap, another person sitting down with you. You each grasp the little table with the thumb and forefinger at each corner next to you. Then the question is asked. . . . Pretty soon you think the other person is pushing the table. He thinks you are doing the same. But the table moves around to 'yes' or 'no.' "

Covering the spate of Ouija patent litigation, the *New York World* asked in 1920: "Who shall own the cable line to the spirit-land?" Well, if trial judges had been clearer on the history of the matter, it is possible that the question of who "owned" Ouija might have been tossed out of court, and the original patent with it. Obviously Bond, Kennard, and their associates were capitalizing on a Spiritualist sensation—not inventing one.

Ancient Ouija?

Another oft-repeated but misleading claim is that Ouija or talking boards have ancient lineage. In a typical example, Frank Gaynor's 1953 *Dictionary of Mysticism* states that primeval boards of different shapes and sizes "were used in the sixth century before Christ." In a wide range of books and articles, everyone from Pythagoras to the Mongols to the ancient Egyptians are said to have possessed Ouija-like devices. But these claims rarely withstand scrutiny.

Ouija collector and chronicler Eugene Orlando points out that the primary reference placing Ouija in the premodern world appears in Lewis Spence's widely reprinted 1920 *Encyclopedia of Occultism:* "As an invention it is very old. It was in use in the days of Pythagoras, about 540 B.C. According to a French historical account of the philosopher's life, his sect held frequent séances or circles at which 'a mystic table, moving on wheels, moved towards signs, which the philosopher and his pupil, Philolaus, interpreted to the audience as being revelations supposedly from the unseen world.'" It is, Orlando notes, "the one recurring quote found in almost every academic article on the Ouija board." But the story presents two problems: The "French historical account" is never identified, and the Pythagorean scribe Philolaus lived not in Pythagoras's time but in the following century.

While successive generations of Pythagoreans produced a wide range of mathematical and mystical treatises, precious little is known today about the philosopher and his original school. No writings of Pythagoras survive, and the historical record depends upon interpretive works—some of which were written centuries after his death at the end of the sixth century B.C. Hence, commentators on occult topics are sometimes tempted to project backward onto Pythagoras all sorts of arcane practices, Ouija and modern numerology among them.

Still other writers, when not repeating claims like the one above, tend to misread ancient historical accounts and mistake other divinatory tools, such as pendulum dishes, for Ouija boards. Oracle methods were rich and varied from culture to culture—from Germanic runes to Chinese pictograms to African cowrie shells. But the prevailing literature on oracular traditions supports no suggestion that talking boards were in use before the American Spiritualist era.

And what, finally, of the beguiling name *Ouija*? Alternately pronounced *wee-JA* and *wee-GEE,* its origin raises another question mark. Baltimore's Charles W. Kennard at one time claimed it was Egyptian for "good luck" (it's not). William Fuld later said it was simply a marriage of the French and German words for "yes." One early investor claimed the board had spelled out its own name. As with other aspects of Ouija history, the board seems determined to withhold a few secrets of its own.

Ouija Boom

By 1920, the Ouija board was so well known that artist Norman Rockwell painted a send-up of a couple using one—the woman dreamy and credulous, the man fixing her with a cloying grin—for a cover of *The Saturday Evening Post.* For manufacturer Fuld, though, everything was strictly business. "Believe in the Ouija board?" he told a reporter. "I should say not. I'm no Spiritualist. I'm a Presbyterian—been one ever since I was so high." In 1920, the Baltimore *Sun* reported that Fuld, by his own "conservative estimate," had pocketed an incredible $1 million from sales.

Whatever satisfaction Fuld's success may have brought him was soon lost: On February 24, 1927, he fell to his death from the roof of his Baltimore factory. The fifty-six-year-old manufacturer had been supervising the replacement of a flagpole when an iron support bar gave way, and he fell three stories backward.

Fuld's children took over his business, and they generally prospered. While sales dipped and rose—and competing boards came and went—only the Ouija brand endured. And by the 1940s, Ouija was experiencing a new run of sales.

Historically, séances and other Spiritualist methods have proliferated during times of war, when families struggled with uncertainty and loss. "People have had to bear so many things they had not thought possible," wrote Thomas Mann on an upsurge of Spiritualism after World War I, "and to undergo such dramatic events, that the indignation we are still struggling to feel . . . is combined, in a not negligible proportion, with a tendency to make concessions." During World War II, many American families "made concessions" to unseen powers and looked toward Ouija for news of loved ones, or to reach those who had died. In a 1944 article, "The Ouija Comes Back," *The New York Times* reported that one New York City department store alone had sold fifty thousand Ouija boards in a five-month period.

For all its commercial reach, Ouija remained essentially a family-operated business. But after the war, novelty manufacturing shed its slightly disreputable, carnival-style reputation and became a more mainstream line of business. And American toy giants began looking more closely at the enduring curio. In a move that would place an instrument from the age of Spiritualism into playrooms all across America, the manufacturer Parker Brothers bought the rights to Ouija for an undisclosed sum in 1966. With the Fuld family out of the picture, Ouija was poised for its biggest success ever.

The following year, Parker Brothers is reported to have sold more than two million Ouija boards—topping sales of its most popular game, Monopoly. An occult vogue that rode the countercultural tides of the late 1960s, as astrologers adorned the cover of *Time* magazine and witchcraft became a fast-growing "new" religion, fueled the board's sales for the following decades. A Parker Brothers spokesperson reports the company has sold more than ten million boards since 1967.

The '60s and '70s saw Ouija's reinvention as a fad among adolescents. For some it was a mere diversion, while for others its secret messages and intimate communiqués became a youthful rite of rebellion. Ouija circles sprang up in college dormitories, often with young women at their helm, unconsciously reprising the role of spirit medium that women had held in the Spiritualist days. A onetime teenage experimenter recalled an enticing atmosphere of danger and intrigue—"like shoplifting or

taking drugs"—that allowed her and a girlfriend to bond together over Ouija sessions in which they reached the spirit of
"Candelyn," a nineteenth-century girl who had perished in a
fire. Sociologists suggested that Ouija sessions were a way for
young people to project and work through their own fears. But
many Ouija users claimed that the verisimilitude of the communications was reason enough to gather around the board. Not all
sessions were titillating or adventurous, however. As will be
seen, some were tragically, terribly frightening.

Ouija in Winter

While officials at Parker Brothers (today a division of Hasbro)
do not disclose the ebb and flow of sales, there's little question
that Ouija declined commercially as it neared the twenty-first
century. In 1999, the company brought a tradition to an end
when it discontinued the vintage Fuld-era design and switched
to a smaller glow-in-the-dark version of the board. In consumer
manufacturing, the redesign of a classic product often indicates
an effort to reinvigorate shaky sales. In the first decade of the
twenty-first century, Ouija retailed at $22.99, about sixty per-
cent more than old favorites like Monopoly and Scrabble, further suggesting its transformation into a specialty item.

Today, the "Ouija Game" (*ages 8 to Adult*) merits barely a
mention on Hasbro's Web site. The company posts no official
history for Ouija, as it does for its other storied brands, such as
Twister and Yahtzee. And the claims from the original 1960s-era
box—*Weird and mysterious. Surpasses, in its unique results,
mind reading, clairvoyance and second sight*—are now significantly toned down. Given the negative attention the board
sometimes attracts—both from frightened users and religionists
who smell a whiff of Satan's doings—as well as the fact that its
sales are likely on the wane, Ouija seems like a product that
Hasbro would just as soon forget.

And yet Ouija has a way of hanging on. It receives more
customer reviews—alternately written in tones of outrage,

fear, delight, or ridicule—than most other "toys" for sale on Amazon.com: "DANGER—YOU CAN BE POSSESSED." "I wouldn't even consider using it without deep and sincere prayers for protection." "This IS a TOY, made by Parker Brothers, NOT a Satanic Board Game!" Even in its September years, Ouija polarizes opinion among those who dismiss it as a childhood plaything and others who condemn or extol it as a portal to the other side. Just as it figured in *The Exorcist* in the 1970s, Ouija saw new life in the early-twenty-first-century fright films *What Lies Beneath* and *White Noise*. A Ouija-based movie entered the early stages of production in 2008. And its urban mythology remains a ubiquitous presence online. There seems little doubt that Ouija—as it has arisen time and again—awaits a revival in the future. But what has made this game board and its molded plastic pointer so resilient in our culture and, some might add, in our nightmares?

"An Occult Splendor"

One of the most notable characteristics of Ouija lore is the vast—and sometimes authentically frightening—history of stories reported by users. A common story line involves communication that is at first reassuring and even useful—a lost object may be recovered through the board's counsel—but eventually gives way to threatening or terrorizing messages. One group of Ouija enthusiasts reported ghostly knocks on their apartment doors after contacting the spirit of a serial killer. Others claimed physical and sexual assaults from unseen hands after a night of Ouija experimentation. One famous murder trial in 1933 involved claims that Ouija had "commanded" an Arizona girl and her mother to kill the girl's father. Hugh Lynn Cayce, the soft-spoken son of the famous American psychic Edgar Cayce, once cautioned that his researches found Ouija boards among the most "dangerous doorways to the unconscious."

For their part, Ouija enthusiasts respond that influential spiritual teachings such as the "Seth material," channeled by writer Jane Roberts in the 1970s, first emerged through the board. In the

World War I era, a St. Louis housewife used Ouija to record a remarkable range of novels, plays, and poems from a seventeenth-century English spinster named Patience Worth. Some were hugely ambitious in scale and written in a Middle English dialect that the St. Louis homemaker (who didn't finish high school) would have had no obvious means of knowing. Ouija writing also produced a posthumous full-scale "novel" by Mark Twain in 1917, pulled from store shelves after a legal outcry from the writer's estate. While such works won brief popularity, they failed to retain enduring readership. Further up the literary scale, poets Sylvia Plath and Ted Hughes wrote haunting and dark passages about their experiences with Ouija. ("Fame will come," the board tells Sylvia in Ted's 1957 poem, "Ouija," ". . . And when it comes you will have paid for it with your happiness, your husband, and your life.") Though darkly prophetic, such works are not generally counted among either poet's finest efforts.

Given that this mysterious object has, in one form or another, been on the American scene for over 120 years, it's natural to wonder: Can anything of lasting value be attributed to Ouija? The answer is yes, and it has stared us in the face for so long that we have nearly forgotten it is there.

In 1976, the American poet James Merrill published—and won the Pulitzer Prize for—an epic poem that recounted his experience, with his partner, David Jackson, of using a Ouija board from 1955 to 1974. His work, *The Book of Ephraim,* was later combined with two other Ouija-inspired epic poems and published in 1982 as *The Changing Light at Sandover.* "Many readers," critic Judith Moffett wrote in her penetrating study *James Merrill,* "may well feel they have been waiting for this trilogy all their lives."

First employing a manufactured board and then a homemade one—with a teacup in place of a planchette—Merrill and Jackson encountered a world of spirit "patrons" who described for them a sprawling and profoundly involving creation myth. In Merrill's hands, it became poetry steeped in the epic tradition, in which myriad characters—from W. H. Auden, to lost friends and family members, to a ghostly Greek muse/interlocutor called Ephraim—walk on and off stage. The voices of Merrill, Jackson, and those who emerge from the teacup and board alternately offer theories of reincarnation, worldly advice, and painfully poignant reflections on the passing of life and ever-hovering presence of death.

The Changing Light at Sandover is nothing less than a new mythology of world creation, destruction, resurrection, and the vast, unknowable mechanizations of God Biology (GOD B, in the words of the Ouija board) and those mysterious hosts who enact his will: bat-winged creatures who, in their cosmological laboratory, reconstruct departed souls for new life on earth. And yet we are never far from the grounding human voice of Merrill, joking about the selection of new wallpaper in his Stonington, Connecticut, home, or from the moving counsel of voices from the board, urging: *In life, stand for something.*

"It is common knowledge—and glaringly obvious in the poems, though not taken seriously by his critics—that these three works, and their final compilation, were based on conversations . . . through a Ouija board," wrote John Chambers in his 1997 analysis of Merrill in *The Anomalist.* Critic Harold Bloom, in a departure from others who avoided the question of the work's source, called the first of the *Sandover* poems "an occult splendor." Indeed, it is not difficult to argue that, in literary terms, *The Changing Light at Sandover* is a masterpiece—perhaps *the* masterpiece—of occult experimentation. In some respects, the book challenges the cautionary moral of Mary Shelley's *Frankenstein,* as its two protagonists, Merrill and Jackson, successfully pierce the veil of life's inner and cosmic mysteries. But, as with Victor Frankenstein, did the revelation they found also destroy them?

Creepyville

Merrill and Jackson acknowledged that their social contacts with friends withered as they became more engrossed in their nightly readings. Their sometime friend and neighbor Truman

Capote drifted away, branding Stonington as "Creepyville." One of their closest friends, novelist Alison Lurie, even suggested that the Ouija-channeled spirit Ephraim sanctioned the couple's pursuit of multiple sex partners outside their domicile, contributing to the sixty-eight-year-old Merrill's death in 1995 from heart failure linked to HIV. All of this leaves hanging the question: Can Ouija be a tool, psychological or otherwise, for hidden knowledge and ideas—or is it merely a disastrously distracting toy?

An academic survey of Ouija buffs in the 2001 *International Journal of Parapsychology* found that one half "felt a compulsion to use it." An eighteen-year-old male offered researchers this chilling account:

> There have been many interesting [ones] but the best would be with a spirit named Kyle. He was a sixty something year old child molester. I don't remember how he died but he seems to have some kind of connection to me. Every time I use the Ouija board Kyle's name comes up. Most of the time the people playing know nothing about him. Even sometimes I'm not even playing when he comes up. I think I've seen him twice in spirit form and he once threatened to kill my half sister. He's a complete psycho. He scares me. Strange things happen the nights we speak to him. He likes to switch lights on/off.

More than two centuries earlier, the mystic Emanuel Swedenborg, who inspired so many American spiritual visions, would not have been surprised by such accounts. While Swedenborg recorded his own flights to heavenly realms, he often warned that spirit communications should never be attempted casually. In what may have been the first application of the don't-try-this-at-home disclaimer, the seer cautioned in his 1758 opus, *Heaven and Hell:* "At the present day to talk with spirits is rarely granted because it is dangerous . . . evil spirits are such that they hold man in deadly hatred, and desire nothing so much as to destroy him both soul and body, and this they do in the case of those who have so indulged themselves in fantasies as to have separated from themselves the enjoyments proper to the natural man."

Sounding a different but not unrelated note, twentieth-century authorities in psychic research made the contention that Ouija is a gateway for the gremlins of the unconscious. For years J. B. Rhine, the veritable dean of psychical research in America, worked with his wife, Louisa, a trained biologist and well-regarded researcher in her own right, to bring scientific rigor to the study of psychical phenomena. Reacting to Ouija's popularity, Louisa wrote in the winter 1970 newsletter of the American Society for Psychical Research: "The very nature of automatic writing and the Ouija board makes them particularly open to misunderstanding. For one thing, because [such communications] are unconscious, the person does not get the feeling of his own involvement. Instead, it seems to him that some personality outside of himself is responsible. In addition, and possibly because of this, the material is usually cast in a form as if originating from another intelligence."

For his part, the poet Merrill took a subtler view of the matter. "If it's still *yourself* that you're drawing upon," he said, "then that self is much stranger and freer and more far-seeking than the one you thought you knew." And at another point: "If the spirits aren't external, how astonishing the mediums become!"

In the end, Ouija confounds. This oddly magnetic toy—the one device from the age of Spiritualism still used in the twenty-first century—evokes nostalgic memories of pajama parties for some and for others nightmares they would sooner forget. It also left an indisputable mark on the work of one of the greatest American poets of the last century. Whether Ouija is a mysterious instrument, a harmless entertainment, or a "dangerous doorway" lies in the experience of the user. But the words *caveat emptor* inevitably hang over the history of this strangest of American curios.

CHAPTER FOUR

THE SCIENCE OF RIGHT THINKING

The mind is its own place, and in itself
Can make a Heav'n of Hell, a Hell of Heav'n.

—JOHN MILTON, *PARADISE LOST*

It began as the bleakest of Christmases at the Wattles home. In the Indiana winter of 1896, the family patriarch, Wallace, a rake-thin Methodist minister with a passion for Christ's defense of the poor, had been away in Chicago at a conference of social reformers. A Christian socialist, Wallace D. Wattles was already irritating the more-conservative members of his episcopate, some of whom were eyeing his dismissal. Back home in LaPorte, Indiana, his family had no money for a Christmas tree; all they could muster was an evergreen branch decorated with a few smudgy tallow candles and strung with popcorn. Gifts were meager—the family had spent the last of its holiday savings on a cuff box that waited for Wattles under the branch.

"Finally Father came," his daughter Florence recalled. "With that beautiful smile he praised the tree, said the cuff box was just what he had been wanting—and took us all in his arms to tell us of the wonderful social message of Jesus." It was a critical turning point for Wattles. In Chicago, he had met a radical minister named George D. Herron. An ardent purveyor of the "social gospel," Herron had gained national prominence using the message of Christ to condemn the cruel mechanisms of an economic system that sent children to work in cotton mills. He impressed upon Wattles that Christ's vision of social justice must be at the heart of the pastorate's mission.

For Wattles, it was the final stroke in a spiritual philosophy he was developing himself. The minister had been imbibing metaphysical ideas that were bubbling up around him and combining them with his own experiments into the creative powers of the human mind. As Wattles saw it, man was a prisoner to outer circumstance only to the degree that he was a prisoner of inner circumstance. *Free the mind,* he concluded, and outer circumstance would follow. If the mind—this magical, ethereal "thinking stuff" that molded the surrounding world—could be properly harnessed, there was no limit to what a man could achieve.

A Science of God

America in the late nineteenth century was suffused with influences from Spiritualism, Mesmerism, and Theosophy. Each, in its own fashion, imbued the nation's spiritual culture with the conviction that divine mysteries existed not at the top rung of a cosmic ladder but within the settings of ordinary life.

And ordinary life was undergoing remarkable changes. As the nineteenth century closed, the fruits of modern science appeared everywhere: telegraphs, motor engines, electricity, and automated production. In medicine, Pasteur's germ theory was explaining illnesses that for years had resisted understanding. In biology, Darwin had theorized a gradual order in the development of all forms of life. In politics, Marx had classified economics as a matter of "science," in which inevitable outcomes could be foreseen. In psychology, Freud had begun to codify childhood traumas that triggered adult neuroses, and hypnotists (more-respectable versions of Mesmerists) claimed the power to alter behavior through autosuggestion and conditioning. Caught in this onrush of currents, intellectual leaders from all walks of life—academia, clergy, business—reasoned that scientific principles were applicable to every aspect of existence. Why couldn't there be a "science" of success, or even a "science" of religion—that is, a protocol of definable, rational steps that would produce a desired result?

Inspired by the possibilities, a group of religious thinkers and impresarios formed a loosely knit spiritual movement around this "scientific" religious concept. Thoughts, they argued, could be seen to manifest into actual events, such as health or sickness, wealth or poverty. They claimed Ralph Waldo Emerson as their founding prophet: "We know," the Concord mystic wrote in 1841, "that the ancestor of every action is a thought." The Bible, in their reading, seemed to agree, particularly in the Proverb: "As a man thinketh in his heart, so is he." In an enthused leap of reasoning, the movement that came to be known as New Thought maintained that the individual's creative mind was one and the same as the creative force called God. As such, a person could literally think his dreams to life. It was America's boldest—and most influential—attempt at what religious scholar John B. Anderson called "a practical use of the occult powers of the soul."

Healthy Thinking

Like most religious movements, New Thought had its earliest beginnings in the experience of a single individual. In the early 1830s, a clockmaker named Phineas P. Quimby noticed that his tuberculosis seemed to ease whenever he took a rejuvenating carriage ride in the Maine countryside. A small man with intense, piercing eyes, Quimby discovered that when his spirits lifted, so did his illness. He began hearing news of Mesmerism as it was spread by the young Frenchman Charles Poyen, who visited Bangor, Maine, in 1836. Two years later, Quimby attended another Mesmerist lecture, delivered in Belfast, Maine, by a Massachusetts physician named Robert Collyer. Where Poyen's style had been hesitant and retiring, in a language that was never fully his own, Collyer came across as a formidable and convincing presence. Quimby grew fascinated with the similarities between Mesmerist healings and his own experience. He began to study the practice and soon developed the ability to Mesmerize subjects of his own.

Like Andrew Jackson Davis before him, Quimby possessed little in the way of formal education. He was self-schooled and gave no appearance otherwise. One Belfast citizen wrote in admiration to a friend, "Mr. Quimby is not an educated man, nor is he pretending or obstrusive; but I think if you should take occasion to converse with him you will discern many traces of deep thought and reflection. . . ." Quimby's lack of formal schooling, while a mark of his genuineness to some, later became a point of harsh criticism.

In another parallel to the life of the Poughkeepsie Seer, Quimby toured New England in the early 1840s with a seventeen-year-old boy named Lucius Burkmar, whom Quimby would put into a trance state. From this state, Burkmar diagnosed and prescribed folk cures for diseases. Stories abounded of Burkmar's abilities. But Quimby eventually grew convinced that it was neither Burkmar's powers to mentally scan the human body nor his herbal-tea remedies that were curing people: rather, it was the boy's ability to change their *beliefs* about their illnesses. The mind itself was where the actual cause—and cure—seemed to rest. Disease, Quimby reasoned, "follows an opinion." By 1859, Quimby developed a philosophy of "mental healing" and began using it to treat patients himself, without a Mesmeric trance or clairvoyant intermediary. When a man was sick, he explained, "I affirm that the disease is in his belief and his belief is in error." While Quimby focused primarily on the mind's curative abilities, he increasingly came to view the subconscious as an extension of the Divine power, through which a person could, with the proper training and understanding, create outer circumstance. "Man's happiness," he later wrote, "is in his belief." And he meant it in the most literal sense.

Quimby's ideas quickly found influence. One of his earliest followers was religious thinker and writer Warren Felt Evans. When the men met in around 1864, Evans had already left the Methodist ministry to pursue the ideas of the Swedish mystic–scholar Emanuel Swedenborg. Evans was one of the first American metaphysical writers to use the term "New Age" to herald a dawning era of mystical awareness, as he did in his 1864 book, *The New Age and Its Messenger*. The "messenger" was Swedenborg.

Quimby's ideas made innate sense to people who had studied Swedenborg's theory that cosmic laws corresponded to and affected the qualities of the human soul. For Quimby, these cosmic laws were Christian laws, their action was summoned through one's thoughts, and their power extended to all forms of experience. Like Evans, some of Quimby's earliest supporters were American Swedenborgians willing to make the leap to this bold philosophy that they believed was implicit in the work of the Swedish seer. Evans's books, such as *The Mental Cure* in 1869, helped spread Quimby's ideas beyond New England. But a far greater apostle already sat at the master's feet.

In 1862, Quimby had begun to treat a patient named Mary Glover Patterson. She later remarried and took the name by which she is remembered in religious history: Mary Baker Eddy. Eddy proved an extraordinary, if contentious, proponent of spiritual healing. Far and above any of Quimby's other patients or students, Eddy codified a theology around the "doctor's" core ideas. She called it *Christian Science*—a term Quimby himself had used. Eddy's philosophy at once overlapped with Quimby's and sharply diverged from it. Rather than extolling the agencies of the human mind, she believed in the need for its eradication. The "mortal mind," steeped in malevolence and illusions, needed to be overcome by the universal "divine mind," the one true and absolute reality. Eddy denied the reality of disease, evil, and physical matter itself as mere human perversions, or "an illusion of material sense," as she later wrote in her masterwork, *Science and Health*.

After Quimby died in 1866 (the mind healer was just sixty-four), Eddy, whose own health had been suffering, briefly cast about for a new mentor. Finding none to answer the call, she soon decided to build her own spiritual-healing religion, with herself at its helm. With a degree of absolutism that she may have later come to regret, Mrs. Eddy (as followers called her) dismissed her old mentor Quimby as little more than a back-woods Mesmerist, at times depicting the unschooled man as one step above a carnival performer. Quimby's followers retaliated. They pointed out that Eddy had published articles heaping ado-ration upon the mental healer even after his death, when she eu-logized him in a Lynn, Massachusetts, newspaper as one "who healed with the truth that Christ taught." Eddy countered that, even if she had written such things, it must have been under the thrall of the "illiterate" Quimby's Mesmeric powers.

For every lash that Eddy directed at Quimby's memory, she was tougher on her own disciples. In the 1880s, Eddy cut off stu-dent after student who attempted innovations or referred to in-sights of their own. A wrong word in a pamphlet or journal could earn immediate dismissal. In this way, Eddy became the mother—or, as some came to see it, the stepmother—of New Thought, fostering an offspring that she never wanted. When Eddy's beautiful and articulate younger student Emma Curtis Hopkins made passing reference to her own intimacies with the Divine power in *The Christian Science Journal*, which she edited for Eddy in the mid-1880s, the church leader drummed her out of the movement.* Hopkins was locked out of the Christian Sci-ence ladies' dormitory in Boston where she had lived. Forced to rely on her own resources, Hopkins relocated to Chicago, where she hung out a shingle as an independent instructor of Christian Science. Widely read and strikingly intelligent, Hopkins became known within mental-healing circles as the "teacher of teach-ers," influencing an extraordinary range of the movement's key lights in the late nineteenth and early twentieth centuries.

But Mrs. Eddy would have no comparisons between Chris-tian Science and the more freewheeling Hopkins philosophy, with its openness to Theosophical and occult ideas. By the early

---

* The *Journal* is not to be confused with *The Christian Science Monitor*, which Eddy started in 1908 in response to the "yellow journalism" of the day and, in particular, its attacks on her. The *Monitor* remains one of Eddy's finest legacies as a sober and independent source of news.

1890s, after fighting off a range of factional splits and internal challenges, Eddy succeeded in copyrighting the term Christian Science, suing anyone who used it without her permission. Searching for alternate names, practitioners and teachers outside the Eddy camp used terms like *Divine Science, Mental Science,* and the *Science of Right Thinking.* The last term came from the nation's doyenne of inspirational poetry, Ella Wheeler Wilcox, who is best known for her 1883 lines: "Laugh and the world laughs with you; Weep and you weep alone." Wilcox, a combination of social-reform activist, occult explorer, and Hallmark-style homilist, was an early student of Emma Curtis Hopkins.

Eventually one term gained dominance: *New Thought.* It may have entered the culture through Emerson, who wrote in his essay "Success" in 1870: "to redeem defeat by new thought, by firm action, that is not easy, that is the work of divine men." In 1887, a capitalized reference to New Thought appeared in a pamphlet, "Condensed Thoughts about Christian Science," written by another Swedenborgian, William Henry Holcombe. By 1894, *New Thought* became the title of a Massachusetts mental-healing magazine. And in 1899, the gavel fell on a "New Thought Convention" in Hartford, Connecticut. The movement had found its name.

As for Eddy's Christian Science, it continued on its own way, attracting hundreds of thousands of members. Throughout the late nineteenth century, the nation had no standard system of medical licensing, and some doctors persisted in prescribing dangerous and painful treatments, like bloodletting or the ingestion of mercury. For many Americans, Eddy's message of spiritual healing represented a gentler (and ultimately safer) alternative. Flush with members, the Eddy movement purchased magnificent properties on which it built enormous, stately churches, many of which dot America's eastern cities today. But Eddy placed her metaphysical movement squarely within the folds of the nation's orthodox Christian congregations, much like the new religion of Mormonism. Christian Science would tolerate no individual experimentation, nor would it seek to move with the times. To guard against future heresies, in 1895 Eddy forbade sermons in her churches, instead requiring that weekly passages from Scripture and her 1875 *Science and Health* be uniformly recited from each pulpit on Sunday mornings, not by pastors but by rotating "Readers."

Although New Thought gave rise to its own thriving network of metaphysical churches—under the names of denominations such as Unity or Religious Science—it became a kind of antireligion, its borders porous and open to every idea and individual (including many who retained membership in mainline churches), and its philosophy adaptable to a wide range of viewpoints. Ironically, or perhaps inevitably, New Thought is a term that few Americans would hear after World War II. Its ideas were so widely adopted—a sociological study of the 1950s found that most inspirational literature published in America between 1875 and 1955 had some kind of New Thought bent—that the source itself became obscured. Secularized elements of the New Thought philosophy successfully vied for influence with the more religiously inspired variants. In the 1930s, nonreligious figures like Dale Carnegie (*How to Win Friends and Influence People*) and Napoleon Hill (*Think and Grow Rich*) rode the wings of New Thought to worldwide fame. The popularity of mind-power philosophy hit its peak in the Reverend Norman Vincent Peale's 1952 megaseller, *The Power of Positive Thinking*, which reached into churches and living rooms across America. As will be seen, Peale, an orthodox and politically conservative Protestant minister, brought an entirely mainline, Christian emphasis to what started as a mystical philosophy.

The Secret of the Ages

From a psychological perspective, New Thought's founders were shrewd observers of human nature. They intrinsically understood how to get along well in organizations and at work. Indeed, during the movement's rise, more and more Americans were taking jobs inside large companies—where they often struggled to find their way. New Thought literature displayed an innate grasp of the can-do, upbeat attitude required to succeed in the new world of corporate America. And to many Americans—at least, measured by book sales—it came as a help.

New Thought's popularity coincided with a time when the idea of "getting ahead" began to play on the American psyche. And if New Thought displayed one unmistakable aim in the twentieth century, it was success. Not necessarily the inner sort described by Ralph Waldo Emerson in his essay "Success," which extolled the quiet certainty of self-determinism. However much New Thoughters liked to cite Emerson as their founding prophet, they had more worldly priorities. Throughout the first half of the twentieth century, New Thought volumes—and fresh ones arrived by the bushelful—abounded, with subject headings like: "how to pray and grow rich"; "a success mind-set"; "why you cannot fail"; "your infinite power to be rich"; "the secret of getting well"; "the magic law of tithing"; and so on. Slowly and inexorably, New Thought replaced the clean-living credo of American success—*early to bed, early to rise makes a man healthy, wealthy, and wise*—with an enticing new principle: He who believes he can, *can*.

The metaphysical dimensions of New Thought could seem so magical, so unrestrained in their promise of limitless potential, that a 1920s best seller by publisher Robert Collier deemed New Thought *The Secret of the Ages*. Many of the movement's most popular writers and sermonizers reimagined worldly acquisition as the very exercise of God's will. In their hands, it was as if the entire object of Transcendentalism—that is, the transcendence of earthly bonds and distractions—had been turned on its head. And here New Thought's sense of ethics and seriousness as a religious movement fell open to question: What was to finally separate this philosophy from being anything other than a tool for pursuing one's most random drives and selfish wants? Was this the end point of American religious innovation—the vaunted "secret of the ages"?

On this question hung the dilemma of Indiana minister Wallace D. Wattles. Although his books became central to a twenty-first-century New Thought revival and served as the major influence behind the blockbuster book and movie *The Secret,* the social-gospel advocate had wanted the "occult powers of the soul" to serve a different end than worldly gain. It wasn't that he eschewed New Thought's emphasis on wealth-building—indeed, he embraced such aims in his 1910 guide, *The Science of Getting Rich.* But there was a critical difference in Wattles's approach, one overlooked by those who later embraced his work: Wattles believed in using mind power to wipe away barons of industry and overthrow the prevailing social order. In *The Science of Getting Rich*—which a century later rode a new wave of popularity to best-seller lists—he wrote the following, with his concluding emphasis in the original:

> *You are to become a creator, not a competitor; you are going to get what you want, but in such a way that when you get it every other man will have more than he has now. I am aware that there are men who get a vast amount of money by proceeding in direct opposition to the statements in the paragraph above, and may add a word of explanation here. Men of the plutocratic type, who become very rich, do so sometimes purely by their extraordinary ability on the plane of competition. . . . Rockefeller, Carnegie, Morgan, et al., have been the unconscious agents of the Supreme in the necessary work of systematizing and organizing productive industry; and in the end, their work will contribute immensely toward increased life for all. Their day is nearly over; they have organized production, and* will soon be succeeded by the agents of the multitude, who will organize the machinery of distribution.

If his more-careful readers detected a tinge of socialist language there, they were right. Wattles saw New Thought as a means to the kind of leisurely socialist utopia that enthralled readers of Edward Bellamy's futurist novel *Looking Backward.*

Writing in the same year in his lesser-known *A New Christ*, Wattles envisioned a marriage of New Thought—America's homegrown success philosophy—and Christian socialism:

> *As we approach socialism, the millions of families who are now propertyless will acquire their own beautiful homes, with gardens and the land upon which to raise their food; they will own horses and carriages, automobiles and pleasure yachts; their houses will contain libraries, musical instruments, paintings and statuary, all that a man may need for the soul-growth of himself and his, he shall own and use as he will.*

It was as though Karl Marx had imbibed the mother's milk of American metaphysics. Within Wattles there existed a struggle to unite two mighty currents that were sweeping early-twentieth-century America: social radicalism and mind-power mysticism. Was it possible, as Wattles dreamed, that these movements could be united into one radical whole? Could there be a revolution by mental power?

"Do Not Talk About Poverty"

By the time he emerged as a New Thought leader, Wattles had already been forced to resign from the Methodist pastorate. He had gone too far in his social radicalism, at one point insisting that churches should refuse monetary offerings from businessmen who profited from sweatshop labor. After 1900, he became active in the more liberal environs of Quakerism. And while Wallace gained allies in mind-power circles—particularly his trailblazing publisher, Elizabeth Towne, a Massachusetts suffragist who ran his work in her New Thought magazine, *Nautilus*—he suffered conflict in that world too.

New Thought emphasized the idea of action *from within* and discouraged emphasis on politics or the travails of outer life. Too much notice of tragedy, poverty, or injustice, so went the New

Thought gospel, served only to perpetuate such things. Hence, Wattles could sound at war with himself. In one stroke he urged readers, "Do not talk about poverty; do not investigate it, or concern yourself with it," and at other times he spoke passionately before audiences of the squalor of Chicago tenements and the hopelessness of immigrant children living there. He admiringly quoted from the social-reform journalism of Elbert Hubbard, who had exposed child-labor abuses in turn-of-the-century cotton mills. Hubbard, as it happened, was another success prophet with a taste for social protest.

Hubbard was famous for his 1899 motivational essay, "A Message to Garcia," in which he extolled the can-do heroics of a U.S. soldier during the Spanish–American War. Business leaders loved it. Yet Hubbard lost his life while hoping to end another war. In 1915, Hubbard and his wife, Alice, a suffragist and New Thought enthusiast, died with nearly 1,200 civilians when a German U-boat torpedoed the passenger ship *Lusitania* in the waters off Ireland. Hubbard had boarded the ship in New York on a self-styled peace mission to Europe, where he had declared plans to interview the German kaiser and inveigh against the carnage of the Great War. "Big business is to blame for this thing," wrote the motivational hero before he left, "let it not escape this truth—that no longer shall individuals be allowed to thrive through supplying murder machines to the mob."

Even the most popular New Thought prophet of the day, Ralph Waldo Trine, harbored a passion to unite mysticism and social reform. Trine gained a legion of followers through his 1897 mind-power book, *In Tune with the Infinite*. It was the book that every New Thought minister and writer seemed to have read and borrowed from. Industrialist Henry Ford kept copies in his office and would press it on guests. But beneath Trine's placid, almost priestly exterior beat the heart of another social radical. A 1902 profile in the New Thought magazine *Mind* said Trine believed in the cooperative ethos of socialism and that he planned to write a book "from the viewpoint of a socialist who is such because of his New Thought philosophy."

It is not clear that Trine ever wrote such a book, but

something very close appeared under his byline in 1910: *Land of Living Men*. While Trine's *In Tune with the Infinite* had assumed a gentle, folksy tone emphasizing gratitude and generosity, *Land of Living Men* showed surprisingly different colors. In it, the New Thought pioneer called for "a great people's movement to bring back to the people the immense belongings that have been taken away from them." Trine advocated busting up monopolies, striking for higher wages, and placing essential utilities and industries into public hands. This was one book that Henry Ford didn't give to his friends. Indeed, *Land of Living Men* seemed to make little impact at all on Trine's followers. By 1928, Trine was an honored guest in Ford's office, where he engaged in an almost fawning interview with the automaker. Their conversation was turned into a popular book, *Power that Wins*, which ranged from Ford's love for avocados to his belief in reincarnation. Whatever Trine's innermost commitments, he would never again be seen—nor succeed as—a political Jeremiah. But Wattles went in the opposite direction and became ever more public about his political passions.

"We Were Robbed"

In 1911, in what was to be Wattles's last book, *The Science of Being Great*, he offered tribute—probably the only one in all of motivational literature—to the Socialist Party of America leader Eugene V. Debs, a fellow Hoosier who later went to federal prison for opposing U.S. entry into World War I. "Debs loves men," Wattles explained. "It is a great thing to love men so and it is only achieved by thought." Taking inspiration from Debs's presidential campaigns, Wattles embarked on a journey almost unheard of in New Thought circles: He made upstart bids for public office, each time on the Socialist Party ticket. In his home state of Indiana, he first campaigned for Congress in 1908, and, after losing, he ran the next year for mayor of the town of Elwood. During his 1909 mayoral campaign, the delicate-framed man stood before 1,300 striking workers during a heated show-down at a local tin mill and pledged them his support. Though he made only a token showing in the congressional race, he ran a surprisingly close second for mayor.

Wattles's daughter, Florence, a budding socialist orator in her own right, insisted that the mayoral vote was rigged and the election had been stolen. "They voted not only the dead men in the cemeteries, but vacant lots as well," twenty-three-year-old Florence said in her 1911 address to a socialist convention in Kokomo, Indiana. "We were robbed of the election, but in 1912 we will carry the election. Mark that. And we'll get the offices too. We mean to do it through a thorough and completely effective organization."

On the stump, Florence exuded the same sense of biblical justice as her father—the man who told of the social gospel and the metaphysical powers of the mind. With Florence at his side, her spirits fresh and ready for a fight, anything seemed possible. Yet within a week of Florence's speech, Wattles was dead. Though his writings had extolled the curative powers of the mind, he had always been physically frail. His health collapsed on February 7, 1911, when he died of tuberculosis at age fifty while traveling to Tennessee.

The Fort Wayne Sentinel, knowing the local author and organizer mostly as a political figure, noted "he was one of the best known socialists in Indiana." And, almost as an afterthought, "He also wrote several books on scientific subjects."

The Reluctant Organizer

Though Wattles and his contemporaries never succeeded in joining metaphysics to social protest, the question lingered whether New Thought could become a morally convincing movement. After Wattles's death, there emerged one unique figure who seemed to hold the answer. Ernest Holmes, a short, rotund Yankee, journeyed from Maine to Los Angeles to spread his version of the New

Thought gospel. For a time, his Religious Science, or Science of Mind, movement held the promise of growing into the great American metaphysical faith for which many yearned.

In actuality, the last thing Holmes wanted was to start a religion. From his early days on the metaphysical speaking circuit in the 1910s until his death in Los Angeles in 1960, Holmes mounted a plaintive resistance against enthusiasts who transformed his mind-power philosophy into a network of churches replete with textbooks, rule-making bodies, and enough factional splits and infighting to fill a New Thought version of *I, Claudius*. At the founding ceremonies of an ornate church in Los Angeles months before his death, Holmes looked out over the crowd and said, "This church was not my idea."

Whatever the reluctance of its founder, the Science of Mind movement, known more formally as the United Church of Religious Science, became the last—and in some ways the most influential—of all New Thought denominations. Other ministries had come earlier and claimed more members, such as the Unity School of Christianity based in Kansas City, Missouri. But none had a figurehead like Ernest Holmes. Not only did Holmes devise a fully fleshed-out theology, but he also inspired the most formative self-help philosophy of the twentieth century: the "power of positive thinking" of author–minister Norman Vincent Peale. In the end, Holmes proved a mighty catalyst, though his fame would trail far behind his influence.

The Problem of Evil

Born in 1887 in a dingy Maine farmhouse and never formally educated, the young Holmes devoured works on religious philosophy, physics, and the writings of Ralph Waldo Emerson. He grew particularly enamored of Emerson's "Self-Reliance," which stoked Holmes's belief in the creative potential of the human mind.

Moving from New England to Venice, California, the vibrant Holmes and his brother and intellectual partner, Fenwicke, began filling lecture halls as early as 1916 with their metaphysical lectures. California was experiencing boom times, and its residents, migrants from all parts of the nation, were ready to take in new ideas. Roundish and twinkle-eyed, Holmes exuded an unlikely charisma—as well as a shrewd command of different spiritual philosophies and religious systems. He spoke with clarity and total confidence, rarely using notes. "As a speaker, a lecturer," Norman Vincent Peale recalled, "he was able to put together spontaneously a talk as airtight as a lawyer's brief, no loopholes, no perceived errors. It all held together."

The young metaphysician's following grew as he performed "treatments"—or mind-power healings—on guests at the office where he worked as a purchasing agent for the city of Venice. After travels to New York and other cities, where Holmes tested his message among different listeners, he molded his ideas into a philosophy called Religious Science. (This proved an ill-fated choice of words that in later decades served to confuse his movement with the more visible and entirely unrelated religion of Scientology.)

Holmes's command of Scripture and Yankee foursquare style seemed, at least in his person, to nudge New Thought away from its fixation on personal gain. The greater struggle for Holmes, in his writings and lectures, was to consistently wed what was fundamentally a success-driven philosophy to a Christian ethic. Like his contemporaries, Holmes believed that the human mind was at one with what is called God and that it possessed the same creative power. As such, he reasoned, this power was intrinsically good. "Evil," Holmes wrote in his 1929 *The Bible in Light of Religious Science,* "... has no reality behind it or actual law to come to its support." It was similar in approach to the Unity writer H. Emilie Cady, who claimed, "Apparent evils are not entities or things of themselves. They are simply an absence of good.... But God, or Good, is omnipresent, so the apparent absence of good (evil) is unreal."

Most purveyors of New Thought described evil as darkness in a room once the light—or the God Law—had been closed out. But, unlike the Transcendentalists in their study of the cycles of nature, these enthusiasts made no allowance for the inevitability of night following day. They made no room for the balance of life and death, illness and health, that Emerson depicted in the essays they claimed as their inspiration. Nor did New Thought acknowledge Emerson's disdain for self-centered prayer. ("Prayer as a means to effect a private end is meanness and theft," he wrote in "Self-Reliance.") Hence, the movement embraced those portions of Transcendentalism that spoke to affirming mental power, and ignored other complexities.

And here we reach the ultimate dilemma of this most popular of American metaphysics. Unable to come to terms with questions of tragedy or catastrophe in what believers considered a self-created world, New Thought lapsed into circular reasoning or contradiction. In one beat, Holmes described evil or illness as illusory. Yet in the next he cautioned: "The law [of mental creativity] is no respecter of persons and will bring good or evil to any, according to his use or misuse of it."

Even the movement's central concept—the Law of Attraction—could appear jerry-rigged. This spiritual "law" had its origins in the work of Andrew Jackson Davis, though he never quite intended for how it came to be used. In 1855, writing in Volume IV of another of his massive treatises, *The Great Harmonia*, Davis coined the term *Law of Attraction* to describe the human soul's affinity for different spheres of the afterlife. Remade by New Thoughters—and later resurfacing as the catchphrase of *The Secret* and numerous motivational best sellers—the Law of Attraction meant that whatever a person or group of people dwelled upon in their thoughts would manifest in events good or bad, joyous or catastrophic, in their earthly lives, presumably whether one was a slave or a wealthy slaveholder, a person of robust health or a sickly child. Coming from a movement based in hope and limitless potential, such thinking could seem like a naively cruel calculus. While outcroppings of New Thought would appear in other nations, including South Africa and Japan (*The Secret* was made in Australia), this way of reasoning confined the philosophy largely to an American middle class, where the security of life was a relative given.

In what may have been a bitter irony of his life, the intellec-

tual Holmes was on surer ground in carrying out the practical-
ities of building a ministry than in confronting the ultimate
questions of human suffering. By the time of Holmes's death in
1960, his robust movement encompassed more than a hundred
congregations with more than one hundred thousand formal
members. Indeed, Holmes's legacy is considerable: His text-
book, *The Science of Mind,* continues to sell thousands of
copies a year; acolytes of his ideas number among the nation's
most popular inspirational writers and speakers (such as Tony
Robbins and Marianne Williamson); and his United Church
of Religious Science—along with a closely related offshoot called
Religious Science International—actively ordains new ministers
and practitioners.

Holmes did successfully bridge the gap between New Thought
as a loosely conceived idea and an organized religion. Yet he also
lived long enough to see his movement marred by factional splits
and infighting, and he often seemed happier delivering a lecture
or completing a book than contending with the demands of organizational life. Just before Holmes's death, a student and protégé, Obadiah Harris, whom Holmes had handpicked to preach
at some of his leading churches, came to the mentor's bedside.
Harris had to confess that he was leaving the movement to find
his own path. "I wish I could go with you," the teacher replied.

Behind the Power

That might be the coda of Holmes's career but for his broadest,
if least known, achievement. The driving principle behind all the
self-help movements of the late twentieth and early twenty-first
centuries appeared in the title of Norman Vincent Peale's 1952
The Power of Positive Thinking. Raised in the Midwest, Peale
was placed in charge of an ailing and shrinking congregation on
Manhattan's East Side during the Great Depression. Within
twenty years, however, the Protestant minister reached into every
corner of America—and many corners of the world—with his
manifesto proclaiming the transformative power of positive

imagery and self-affirmation. His philosophy was core New Thought, though couched in terms to which the churchgoing public could easily relate. Peale eschewed references to "magic laws" or "secrets of the ages," instead emphasizing traditional prayer, Bible reading, and a healthy self-image. Nevertheless, careful readers might have wondered at the Mesmeric tone of the minister's ideas about "the emanation of prayer power," specifically that "the human brain can send off power by thoughts and prayers. The human body's magnetic power has actually been tested."

In his thousands of articles, lectures, books, and homilies, Peale shared innumerable stories from his life, but he revealed relatively little about his influences or how he related to the spiritual and intellectual trends around him. He went further, however, in a remarkable and overlooked interview given in 1987, six years before his death, to the magazine Ernest Holmes had started, *Science of Mind*. In it, the best-selling minister recounted the direct influence he found in his older contemporary. Peale recalled that when he worked as a cub reporter at a Detroit daily newspaper in the early 1920s, a tough-talking editor spotted his "paralyzing fear of inadequacy." As the minister recounted, "He took me aside and handed me a book, *Creative Mind and Success,* by Ernest Holmes." It was Holmes's second book, written in 1919.

"Now I want you to read this," the editor told him. "I know this fellow Holmes. I've learned a lot from him, and so can you." And what did Peale learn? "Love God, love others, you can if you think you can, the proper control and use of the human mind, drop your limited sense of self and gain true Self-Reliance." Holmes's slender volume of essays and affirmations changed everything for Peale, who entered Boston University's School of Theology soon after finding it. "There is no question in my mind that Ernest Holmes's teachings had helped me on my way," he said.

Three decades later, the ideas that Peale had discovered in that short book—clearly broadened by his own life experiences— formed the basis for the most influential self-help philosophy of the twentieth century. While Peale was gracious in tone and lavish in praise when asked about Holmes in 1987, the minister otherwise appeared to go little out of his way to credit the California mystic. Biographies of Peale, including his personal memoirs, make no mention of Ernest Holmes. Ten years after Peale's death, a staff member conducting a tour of the minister's headquarters in upstate New York had never heard the name.

CHAPTER FIVE

THE MAIL-ORDER PROPHET

✦ ✦ ✦

What is whispered in your ear, shout from the roof tops.

—MATTHEW 10:27

A vast range of figures professed their own versions of the New Thought gospel, and many succeeded in attracting readers and audiences. But a man called Frank B. Robinson holds a special place. From the onset of the Great Depression to the years immediately following World War II, this solidly built Idaho druggist used ads in newspapers, in magazines, and on the radio to craft nothing less than his own mail-order religious faith.

He named it Psychiana, and its ideas were bedrock New Thought, packaged and sold to an audience of unprecedented proportions. Indeed, by the time of Robinson's death, he had amassed enough subscription-based followers—estimates ran as high as two million, with his lesson plans circulating through the hands of many more—to be able to claim stewardship over the eighth-largest religion on the planet. "And the best thing about it," he bragged to a wire-service reporter, "is that we guarantee results or your money refunded. I guess it's about the only 'money-back' religion in the world."

For all the sensation Robinson caused when he was alive, the man and his movement are found in virtually no major work of

American religious history written in the last forty years. And the college town of Moscow, Idaho, where Robinson began his rise to religious fame and ran his mail-order empire, now marks his memory only on the sign of a park he donated to the county.

But Robinson's pioneering techniques as a media evangelist—particularly his early grasp of mail-order marketing and his ability to popularize mystical ideas—touched the nation in ways that have far outlived his organization. Indeed, the success of Psychiana revealed many Americans' hunger for practical and therapeutic religious thought during a period in which traditional congregations were shrinking. And his well-attended speaking campaigns emphasized themes of social equality and religious pluralism in an era when many American churches remained racially segregated.

This is a story of triumph gained and quickly lost at the hands of a remarkably able and remarkably flawed religious leader. Within the folds of his successes and failures lies the history of the mystical religion that once swept America.

"I Talked with God"

Robinson's method was disarmingly simple—so much so that advertising executives doubted it could ever work. Beginning in 1928, he began taking out a series of ads in American magazines. *I talked with God*, they boldly proclaimed. *Yes I Did—Actually and Literally . . . You too may experience that strange mystical power which comes from talking with God, and when you do, if there is poverty, unrest, unhappiness, ill-health or material lack in your life, well—the same Power is able to do for you what it did for me.*

Twenty dollars in cash bought twenty staple-bound lessons in the power of affirmative thought, one arriving every two weeks. Within several years of his initial ad, Robinson had sold more than a half-million lesson plans. Mainstream clergy had no idea what to think. Here was a heterodox teaching sweeping the American landscape, insisting that "God Power" existed inside every man and woman and was available at each moment through the harnessing of thought. By contrast, many Americans found mainline pulpits unable to provide help or guidance during the Depression, when churchgoing continued a slide that had begun in the 1920s. The promise of Psychiana was open to all—no services, no confessionals, and no strict dogma. The sole commitment was to follow Robinson's densely packed, exclamation-marked lesson plans—which taught that through a focused thought you could satisfy "every right desire."

Word of mouth went Robinson's way, as many vowed that his mind-power system helped them find new jobs, sell or buy a home, or alleviate debt. "It's so simple and easy," one Robinson student reported. "If it doesn't work, you can get your money back," another enthused. As for the Psychiana theology, "I just take what helps me," one said.

Robinson kept up with thousands of correspondents who wrote him with personal questions or requests for prayer. Moscow's tiny post office was flooded with letters—sometimes addressed to only *Psychiana, U.S.A.,* or *Doctor Robinson, Idaho,* or even *The Man Who Talked with God, Idaho.* He proudly escorted journalists on tours of his Moscow headquarters, showing them correspondence from towns and cities all over America. From random mounds, he would pull letters ranging from the touching tribute of a West Virginia homemaker who reported that she had purchased a new typewriter and refrigerator—"your wonderful teaching has blessed me with a typewriter maching i don't know much about typeing so please excuse all unspelt words"—to heartfelt telegrams from men who had found work or recovered from illnesses.

Several years before World War II, Robinson received a note of tribute from the Italian fascist dictator Benito Mussolini. After the start of the war, Robinson publicly responded to the ruler, urging that he "refrain from joining Hitler in his crusade of madness." There came no reply. As war clouds thickened, Robinson—ever adaptable to the needs of the moment—reconfigured Psychiana as a spiritual army for Allied victory. Rallying his flock to what he termed "A 'Blitzkrieg' for God," the Idaho prophet mailed followers buttons with Hitler's image coupled with the vow: *I am helping to bring Hitler's defeat by repeating hourly: the power of Right (God) will bring your speedy downfall.*

In 1939, Robinson cabled Finland's Prime Minister Risto Ryti with a plan for using mental affirmations to help repel Axis forces, proposing that Psychiana members—along with the Finnish cabinet and army—spend fifteen minutes daily affirming: *The power of God is superior to the powers of war, hate, and evil.* The embattled premier replied that he would enact Robinson's plan as soon as "practicable."

In the mail, in advertisements, in the news—everywhere one looked, it seemed—there was Frank B. Robinson.

The Gathering Storm

For all the love of his followers, Robinson attracted equal invective from his critics. They called him a "religious racketeer," a "Mail Order Messiah," and "a doctor of Bunk." Indeed, Robinson's "doctorate" was from the College of Divine Metaphysics, an Indianapolis correspondence school. He claimed other diplomas but could abruptly cut off questioners who dared to ask about them. "That's none of your business," he told one student in the question-and-answer column of *Psychiana Weekly* in 1941.

On the national stage, the postmaster general hit Robinson with two unsuccessful investigations for mail fraud. The federal government even began deportation proceedings after a rival publisher accused Robinson of lying about his birthplace on a passport application. But the ensuing hearings served only to build Robinson's reputation as a fighter. "If you want to make anyone—persecute them," he wrote in his 1941 memoir, *The Strange Autobiography of Frank B. Robinson.* Indeed, with every assault from the press and pulpit, his presence seemed only to grow.

By the 1940s, Robinson turned out articles, newsletters, books, and pamphlets at an incredible pace. Between direct-mail solicitations and print advertising, his Psychiana pitches reached an estimated twelve million homes a year, roughly a third of all American households. His lectures ran on more than eighty radio stations. It was, observed religious journalist Marcus Bach, as though "a prophet had spoken in his own country." Whether a prophet, Robinson didn't quite have "his own country." In fact, Robinson's murky origins formed the basis of a deeply troubled childhood and of problems that would haunt him later in life.

A Wandering Prophet

Nothing about Robinson's birth is quite clear, except for the agreed-upon year: 1886. He was born to a hard-drinking English minister, though whether in England or America—where his parents were traveling—is a matter of dispute. Regardless of his native land, Robinson and his three younger brothers grew up in ice-hard circumstances. At eight years old, Robinson watched his mother, Hannah, die of pneumonia in the bedroom of their row house in Halifax, England. After Hannah's death, Robinson's father—a Baptist firebrand with a bad temper and a taste for liquor—turned on his sons with a vengeance. Punishments were frequent and brutal. But it was when the Reverend J. H. Robinson remarried, Robinson wrote in a rare understatement, that "the real trouble began."

The Robinson boys fought so bitterly with their stepmother that arguments exploded into physical fights. Robinson's father decided to enlist thirteen-year-old Frank in the British Navy—a fiasco that lasted about six months, when the youth jumped ship and fled back home. Determined to push him from the house, the elder Robinson then packed up fourteen-year-old Frank and his twelve-year-old brother, Sydney, put the equivalent of $5 in their pockets, and sent them off on a steamer to Canada. The only arrangement the minister made for them was a letter of introduction to a Baptist preacher who lived eight hundred miles from where the boys docked. Upon reaching their intended sponsor's home one Sunday morning, the penniless, bedraggled boys were shooed away, left to sleep in a hayloft.

Eventually, Frank and Sydney found jobs in farming and live-stock. When Sydney fell ill with the same disease that had killed their mother, the boys wired back home to their dad—and were told they were on their own. Sydney survived, but the years that followed were no easier. As time passed, Frank Robinson dis-covered a crippling habit: binge drinking. In what must be a record, the young Robinson earned the distinction of being kicked out of the British Navy, the Royal Canadian Mounted Police, and eventually the U.S. Army *and* Navy for drunkenness and bad conduct.

But friends and employers detected the spark of something un-usual in the young Robinson: He was strikingly handsome and articulate, and came across as surprisingly educated for someone who had never made it beyond grade school. In his early twen-ties, Robinson captured the attention of a Toronto millionaire, who offered to put him through Baptist seminary. Under the sponsorship of a group of local businessmen, Robinson entered McMaster University's Bible Training School in Toronto. But the Bible student immediately clashed with teachers and ministers. During a meeting with his benefactors, Robinson insisted that Eastern and pre-Christian religions had their own stories of humanity's fall from grace and even of a crucified savior. Why, he asked them, should any one religion hold a monopoly on truth?

> Other religions had their bibles too. They had a differ-ent "crucified god." Some of these "crucified gods" were so similar to the Christian's "crucified god" that logic and reason must admit that the story of the later "god" was either stolen or copied from the older "god." I did not want the Christian "god." I wanted the God of the entire universe.

When the meeting ended, Frank B. Robinson was once again on his own.

A Search Bears Fruit

Always a quick study, Robinson became a registered druggist and found steady work for the first time behind a pharmacy counter in Klamath Falls, Oregon. He married the well-regarded daughter of a circuit-court judge, and his new wife guided him into sobriety and a stable home life. In order for Robinson to accept a better job, the couple moved to Los Angeles, where they had a son. By age forty-two, Robinson finally seemed to be calming down. But his search for God had left him with a lasting sense of emptiness.

Then, one Sunday morning, everything changed. Robinson attended a Methodist service on Wilshire Boulevard. In the massively ornate church, with its plush carpets and oaken pews, he counted only twenty-six worshippers. Something in mainstream religion was dying, he thought. He returned home and sat alone in his room. Dejected with the Baptist faith of his youth and uninspired by the religious offerings of the present, the no-longer-young man felt his search for meaning had been a waste. On that day, he pleaded to be shown something more—challenging God to reveal himself.

"Oh, God," he cried, "if I have to go to hell, I'll go with the consciousness that I went there earnestly trying to find you, God." Rather than feeling hopeless, however, Robinson found that a strange sense of peace settled over him. He felt powerful yet relaxed—as though lifted to some higher place. He later said that he sensed the spirit of God pulsing within him, as though it filled his veins and arteries. Robinson came to reason that, through the right exercise of thought, this holy power could be tapped as a limitless resource. He determined to spread his vision of "a workable, usable God." It was do-it-yourself thinking taken to the furthest extreme—an audacious, heretical, and profoundly American approach to religion. And, however the jacket-and-tie-clad druggist viewed himself, his belief in harnessing the forces of an unseen world placed him, like other practitioners of mind-power metaphysics, directly in the steps of America's occult tradition.

With plans bursting in his head, he moved with his wife and young son to the five-thousand-person town of Moscow, Idaho, near Spokane, Washington. Moscow's nineteenth-century settlers had called it "Hog Heaven" for its abundance of flora favored by pigs. But by the time the Robinson family arrived, it was a bustling community with a neatly ordered main street and served as the home to the University of Idaho. Robinson's sole purpose in moving there was to accept a job at a pharmacy that closed at six P.M. Punching out early allowed the Corner Drug Store's new counter clerk to begin writing out the concepts of his "new psychological religion." Beginning one Saturday night, Robinson sat at a borrowed Corona typewriter and pecked the keys for thirty-six hours straight. When he stopped, he had the lesson plan that would deliver the "God law" into the hands of ordinary people. But he needed a way to reach them. Now a family man, Robinson's roustabout days were behind him; he could no longer pick up and roam the nation. National advertising was a new enough medium to still seem revolutionary, and it struck him as the perfect vehicle: His would be a mail-order faith.

Approaching everyone from a local highway commissioner to a grocery clerk, he pulled together $500 and visited an advertising agency in Spokane, the nearest city. They told him not to waste his money. So, on his own, Robinson spent $400 and placed a single ad in *Psychology Magazine*: *I TALKED WITH GOD—SO CAN YOU—IT'S EASY.*

Even Robinson was surprised when the one notice attracted five thousand replies and ultimately netted $13,000 in cash. He wasted no time in seizing the momentum: In newspapers, magazines, and radio stations all over America, Robinson proclaimed Psychiana a "money-back religion," promising unlimited potential—or a full refund—to any who tried it. Within the first decade, he secured six hundred thousand paying subscribers spanning sixty-seven nations. His direct-mail ads, consisting of detailed pamphlet-length espousals of Psychiana theology, began entering two to three million households a year. So was born a mass movement.

The Psychiana Method

Robinson took a bold tack on religion, insisting that its results should be measurable and provable. Hence, hopeful students and more than a few critics wondered: Did Robinson's ideas *work*?

Religious historian Charles S. Braden knew Robinson and wrote about him in the 1940s. One of the few scholars to take any note of Psychiana, Braden remarked on how Robinson's lessons had a way of "awakening, through the power of suggestion, a lively sense of expectancy in the student." Enthusiasm, as Carl Jung once noted, is the hidden key to the effectiveness of any belief system. In his classic study *The Varieties of Religious Experience,* William James found that a dramatic conversion could alter a person's character, objectively changing the circumstances of his outer life. On a similar scale, Psychiana, like other positive-thinking philosophies, could awaken new thoughts, ideas, and options, with the results seeming veritably magical at times.

Even in the twenty-first century—surrounded by an endless stream of self-help programs and practical spiritual ideas—it is still possible for a sympathetic reader to get swept up in the tone of portent and certainty that permeates Robinson's first lesson. In it, he encouraged the repeated use of his key mantra: "I believe in the power of the living God." Other affirmations quickly followed—"I am more and more successful"—and Robinson prescribed simple, specific methods, such as closing one's eyes at night before falling asleep and meditating on a "white spot"—the veil that he told students separates humanity from the Divine.

Although he would claim his ideas were wholly original, he stood on the shoulders of an already well-established spiritual philosophy: American-style New Thought. While freshly articulated, Robinson's techniques were the same as those that had been attracting American seekers to the philosophy of affirmative thinking since the late nineteenth century. And, like New Thought, Psychiana had difficulty providing ethical depth.

"If just any need can be met," asked the historian Braden, "does not that open the way to selfishness, which is the antithesis of the Christian ideal?" Indeed, Robinson tended to dodge most moral questions, insisting that if someone is in touch with the "God Power," that person will naturally do what is good. Yet Robinson never defined his concept of the good life, at least not beyond Sunday-school injunctions toward "clean living" and general fair play. In so doing, he often sounded much like the mainstream religionists he had vowed to overthrow.

Of Money and Spirit

At times, Robinson's own life begged questions of not only his ethics but of his ability to understand how critics saw him. In his autobiography, Robinson launched into a gleeful description of how he once snookered a drugstore client into purchasing gallons of useless mineral oil. He had related the same story several years earlier to a *Time* magazine reporter. The lack of moral embarrassment with which Robinson reported this petty con job could only leave a reader to wonder.

In the final analysis, did Robinson really believe in "the power of the Living God," or was he, as the evangelical *Bible Banner* charged in 1941, "a pious fraud" out "to sell the gift of God for money?" There is no question of Robinson's love for things material. Heavyset and more than six feet tall, he cut a dramatic figure on the streets of Moscow, Idaho, in mink coats, fancy suits, broad-brimmed Stetson hats, a chain watch, and a pipe. He proudly posed for photographs standing beside the latest-model cars. But surviving financial records reveal a subtler story than most critics understood.

Psychiana never made millions. Most of its receipts (which were in the hundreds of thousands annually) flowed back into the business for the constant postage and print and radio advertising needed to keep the operation afloat. While financial documents show bountiful growth early on, Psychiana sustained a cycle of boom-and-bust years and was losing money toward the end. *Time* magazine reported in 1938 that Robinson's operation had amassed record sales of $400,000 in 1934—more than doubling receipts from two years earlier, according to records archived at the University of Idaho. But by the end of that decade, sales had dipped to about one quarter of their high mark. A 1939 profit-and-loss statement reproduced in *The Sunday Oregonian* showed receipts dropping to a modest $46,331 for the first seven months of that year, exceeded by expenses, mostly in advertising, of $54,556.

Robinson himself never collected more than a good white-collar salary. Records show that his compensation rose significantly between 1932 and 1939, when it climbed from $500 to $750 a month. For 1939, the last year that partial figures are available, his annual pay would have amounted to $9,000, the equivalent of $130,000 today. By contrast, many times that amount flowed yearly to another religious controversialist and quasimystical figurehead named Arthur Bell, known to followers in the 1930s as "The Voice." Bell founded the California-based Mankind United, a prosperity cult and conspiracy club that foretold the rise of a social–spiritual utopia in which all chosen men and women—Mankind United members—would live in material comfort and bliss. Bell told of being directed by a council of unseen "Sponsors," who secretly waged war against "Money Changers" and "Hidden Rulers," who would enslave humanity. Thousands of lonely, directionless, and often elderly folk took his bait and plied Bell with membership fees, life savings, and often free labor in his roster of businesses. In the process, the handsome Bell, a frequenter of nightclubs and owner of multiple apartments and mansions (outfitted with swimming pools, wet bars, and draped Oriental love seats), amassed millions in assets, tax free. Nothing like that existed for Robinson, who lived with his wife and two children in an understated brick colonial in Moscow.

So, if Robinson was not profiting at quite the level detractors suggested, what drove him? Did the man derided as a "doctor of Bunk" believe in his own message? There is good reason to conclude that he did. The sheer volume of Robinson's writing—

a mixture of unmitigated passion and arguments over fine points of theology—suggests a figure motivated by deep conviction. In his twenty-three books and thousands of pamphlets, flyers, and articles, Robinson was constantly on the lookout for new ways to verify his ideas, searching for ever-sharper means of codifying his system.

Robinson was unafraid of showing emotion. He wept openly in front of visitors to his Moscow home while playing them his favorite gospel hymns on his personal pipe organ. He argued intensely about the shortcomings of the mainline faiths, one night debating a living room filled with ministers to a standstill for a full three hours. Among the most moving testaments to Robinson's convictions came from his son, Alfred, an Ivy League student and Navy bomber pilot in World War II. Journalist Marcus Bach remembered their encounter:

> I met Alfred, Robinson's son, after his graduation from Stanford. When he told me he was joining his father in the Psychiana movement, I asked him if he would be using the affirmations in his own work. "I was brought up on them." He smiled. "One of my earliest recollections is that of my father taking me for a walk in the woods." He went on intently: "When we reached a secluded spot Father would stop and say, 'Let's be still. Listen! You can hear the presence of the Almighty.' Often when he was alone he would shout in a loud voice, 'I believe in the Power of the Living God!'"

The critics were wrong, at least on this count: Robinson really did seem to believe in his ideas. And his way of thought went beyond Psychiana theology alone. At a time when Hitler's blitzkrieg threatened to engulf the world, Robinson—in a short-lived collaboration with Science of Mind founder Ernest Holmes—displayed a deeply felt and even prophetic instinct for religious tolerance and plurality. It would become the New Thought movement's finest hour.

American Spiritual Awakening

There is one known surviving photograph from an event now forgotten in the annals of American religion. It shows two men—Ernest Holmes seated on the left, Frank Robinson seated on the right—smiling gently at each other across the stage of the Philharmonic Auditorium in Los Angeles. A packed crowd of 3,500 looks on. While not visible from the photograph, a banner draped across the stage proclaims Robinson's key aphorism: *I Believe in the Power of the Living God.* The year was 1941, and the two spiritual teachers were rallying the faithful for a series of five meetings that Robinson called the "American Spiritual Awakening."

It was a kind of spiritual booster rally before America's entry into World War II. But the resulting program turned into something more: an affirmation of the universality of all religious beliefs and national backgrounds, moving one columnist for the West Coast African–American newspaper *The Neighborhood News* to write: "If it does for you what it has done for me, you would not take a hundred dollars for attending this meeting."

Looking back on a moment in history when ethnic hatreds and fascist ideology were plunging nations into war—and many American churches remained segregated—the message of plurality that pervades the surviving transcripts of the Robinson–Holmes mission seems pioneering. Ernest Holmes opened the first meeting on Sunday, September 21, 1941, leaving no mistake as to his feelings for his cospeaker:

> *Dr. Robinson calls his work "Psychiana," which means bringing Spiritual Power to the world. I happen to belong to a movement called "Religious Science," which means the same thing. Some of you may go to a Jewish Synagogue; you may be a Methodist, Baptist, Catholic, but there is but one God. We meet here today not on a theological background, but upon the foreground of a spiritual conception, the common meeting ground of*

every race, every creed, every color, every philosophy,
and every religion on the face of the earth.

Calling their racially mixed audience "Beloved," Robinson extended Holmes's remarks the next day:

> Now, Beloved, when the Almighty created the human
> race, He created black, white, yellow, and every other
> color which exists on earth, in one creation. He did not
> make three or four special jobs of creation, nor did He
> make several different attributes, one for each nation.
> He made them all flesh and blood—every human soul
> that has ever lived on the face of this earth. We are all
> brothers, regardless of our religious affiliation, our race,
> or nationality.

While known as a political conservative—Robinson ardently opposed the New Deal and supported each of the Republican challengers to Franklin Roosevelt—here was a religious leader who, together with Holmes, was making social statements that would not become common fare for at least another twenty-five years.

The five-day series was so popular that Robinson made a return engagement three weeks later. And he and Holmes drew up arrangements for Holmes's seminary, the Institute of Religious Science in Los Angeles, to offer graduate training to students who had already passed through the Psychiana lessons. It was the start of a plan to certify Psychiana teachers and practitioners for a nationwide congregational mission that would take Psychiana beyond its reliance on mail-order lessons or the pronouncements of its charismatic chief. Joint advertising literature was printed, featuring Robinson and Holmes together with the headline *When You Have Decided to Enroll for This Teacher's and Practitioner's Course, both Ernest Holmes and Dr. Robinson will Help You.*

In the end, however, the Holmes–Robinson partnership

became little more than a reminder of what might have been. Robinson showed little interest in the face-to-face management of a congregation, preferring instead to work privately on his books, lessons, ads, and radio addresses. Holmes had a growing flock and network of churches and was easily engulfed in his own organizational affairs. The two men drifted apart.

It is one of the more intriguing "what ifs?" of twentieth-century religious history to consider the possibilities had they remained together. Between Robinson's millions-strong reach and Holmes's well-established seminary and churches, it is possible that Psychiana might have survived the death of its founder, perhaps becoming the galvanizing force of New Thought's disparate flock. But by the time of Robinson's death—about seven years from the day that he and Holmes first spoke together—the organization foundered and then collapsed.

Remains of the Day

A large, athletic man, Robinson nonetheless had a weak heart. A series of cardiac failures in the mid-1940s caught up with him on October 19, 1948, when he died at sixty-two. Shocked followers flooded the Psychiana offices with telegrams of condolence, mourning the man who many said gave them a fresh start in life. Where, some wondered, would the movement find its new voice? Robinson's son, Alfred, stepped forward to run the operation, but he lacked the obsessive passion that drove his father. With new students dwindling and bills mounting, the family closed Psychiana's doors by the end of 1952.

The memories quickly faded. When the *Daily Idahonian*—which the Robinson family partly owned—ran a history of the town of Moscow in 1961, not one word appeared about Frank B. Robinson or Psychiana. It was as if neither had ever existed. What caused Psychiana's abrupt fall? Several factors seem paramount.

With the exception of his son, Robinson cultivated no deputies. And, in the absence of independent congregations, no leaders emerged naturally. He was a messenger without apostles.

Unlike figures such as Ernest Holmes and Wallace D. Wattles, Robinson had self-published all his own books and pamphlets. Hence, no outside organization stood to benefit from the sale and maintenance of his written work after he was gone.

And the last factor is perhaps the most important: Robinson succeeded to the extent that other, larger religious movements copied his outreach methods and self-help message and eclipsed his one-man operation. "It was no longer a sin," journalist Marcus Bach observed, "to personalize the faith and make it serve the needs and wants of man." In the end, the times had caught up with the "Miracle Man of Moscow."

Robinson, perhaps more than any other figure of his day, understood that mainstream Christian churches either had to address the problems of daily existence or risk irrelevance. Sounding a lot like Robinson, ministers and religious commentators of the late 1940s and early 1950s began to discuss the possibilities of advertising and the importance of serving the everyday needs of congregants. In 1946, Rabbi Joshua Loth Liebman published the first religious–therapeutic classic of the postwar era, *Peace of Mind*. Within a few years arrived Norman Vincent Peale's *The Power of Positive Thinking*. Where Robinson had called for "a workable, usable God," Peale wrote, "Christianity is a practical, usable way of life. . . ." And the trend was set. The American pulpit was now expected to address workaday concerns. Indeed, the books and sermons emanating from the twenty-first century's "megachurches" abound in the how-to appeal that marked the Robinson approach. Life coaching, prosperity lessons, marriage counseling, and even weight-loss programs are standard fare in the nation's largest congregations.

In his revolutionary use of radio, print, and mail-order marketing to spread a religious idea, Robinson was arguably the first media evangelist of the twentieth century. But he was more than just that. He was, perhaps, a figure possible only at a certain moment in American history—someone with a deeply held conviction, a few hundred dollars in ad money, and a fresh vision of spiritual life that spoke to a vast, neglected flock. Robinson believed—and lived out—his message, rising from decrepitude to achievement, providing not just a set of ideas but a personage in whom people from all walks of life could vest their hopes.

Writing in 1963, at a point by which Robinson's name had already faded, historian Charles S. Braden captured the heart of the mail-order prophet's work:

> *He used to advertise in the most unlikely places—on match covers, for example, which might be found in a saloon, or a brothel even. And many a man and woman found some new hope when they answered the ad of the man who had "talked with God." He more nearly followed the injunction of Jesus to "go out into the highways and hedges and bring them in" than probably any other man on the contemporary scene.*

CHAPTER SIX

GO TELL PHARAOH

The Rise of Magic in Afro-America

+ + +

> They came to Marah, but they could not drink the
> water of Marah because it was bitter. . . . And the
> people grumbled against Moses, saying, "What shall
> we drink?" So he cried out to the Lord, and the Lord
> showed him a piece of wood; he threw it in the water
> and the water became sweet.
>
> —EXODUS 15:23–25

Frederick Douglass had no use for fantasies or folklore. Born a slave, he was separated as a young child from his mother—a woman who walked miles from another plantation for the rare occasion of rocking him to sleep or giving him a handmade ginger cake. He grew to be a self-educated teenager determined not to play the role of whipped dog to a cruel overseer. But in January 1834, on the eve of his sixteenth birthday, Douglass found himself delivered into the hands of the worst of them, a Mr. Covey—known as "the breaker of Negroes."

A few years earlier, Douglass had been a domestic servant in Baltimore. There the burdens of slavery—the hunger, the beatings, the daily humiliations—were at least tempered by the surface civilities of city life. Indeed, his Baltimore mistress had taught him to read, until the lessons were stopped by his master. "If you teach that nigger how to read," the man told his wife, "there would be no keeping him." But Douglass discovered ways to keep educating himself through whatever books or newspaper scraps could be found. Soon, however, the Baltimore family rearranged its household, and Douglass was abruptly returned to plantation life. His new master in St. Michaels, Maryland, was suspicious: Could a young man who had tasted city living still work the fields? To be brutally certain, at the start of 1834 he "loaned out" Douglass for a year to Edward Covey—a petty, cruel farmer who used every opportunity to beat his new charge on trumped-up offenses. The beatings became so severe that, by August, Douglass sneaked back to his old St. Michaels master to beg for protection. His plea was rejected—and the youth, still bruised and caked with blood, was turned back to Covey's farm. Once there, he hid all day and into the night in the woods outside Covey's fields, not knowing what to do.

The days that followed, however, turned out differently than anyone could have imagined. To the shock of Covey, Douglass did return to the farm—and when beatings came, the youth stood up and fought back. For two hours one morning the men struggled, and Covey could not get the better of him. Embarrassed by his inability to control a teenager who finally said *enough*, the slave master was forced to back down. For Douglass, it was a moment of inner revolution from which he would never retreat: His act of self-defense had freed him in mind and spirit, leaving him to wait for the opportunity when he would finally be free in body as well. It is one of the most remarkable emancipation narratives in American history.

Yet tucked within the folds of Douglass's inner revolution there lies another, lesser-known drama. It arises from deep within African–American occult tradition—and it is an episode that Douglass would revise and downplay between the time when his earliest memoirs appeared in 1845 and when he published a more widely read account a decade later. It is a window on magic and slave life. And, to find it, we must return to the darkened woods outside Covey's farm.

The Magic Root

As Douglass hid in the woods on Saturday night, he was discovered by another man in bondage, Sandy Jenkins—someone Douglass described in his memoirs as "an old adviser." Sandy, he wrote in 1855, "was not only a religious man, but he professed to believe in a system for which I have no name. He was a genuine African, and had inherited some of the so-called magical powers, said to be possessed by African and eastern nations."

Sandy Jenkins was a root worker. He practiced an African–American system of magic and folklore that drew deeply upon Western and Central African religious tradition, Native American herb medicine, and sources as diverse as Jewish Kabala and European folklore. It was called hoodoo. White observers would often mistake it for the Afro–Caribbean religion properly called Vodou in Haiti and Voodoo in the American South, particularly in Louisiana, the home to Voodoo's nineteenth-century high priestess Marie Laveau. Reporters and anthropologists would routinely conflate Voodoo and hoodoo—but the two were very different.

The religion of Voodoo grew from the traditions of the Fon and Yoruba peoples who occupied the West African coastal states. These were the men and women of the "middle passage" who were hurled into slavery throughout America and the Caribbean. In the Fon language, the term *vodu* meant "deity" or "spirit." The Fon–Yoruba practices also morphed in the religion of Santeria, an Afro–Caribbean (and, today, increasingly American) faith that often associates ancient African gods with Catholic saints. In Santeria, for example, the great spirit Babaluaiye, guardian of health and sickness, is frequently associated with Saint Lazarus, a patron to the ill. This is the same "Babalu" that Cuban bandleader Desi Arnaz serenaded to the unknowing ears of *I Love Lucy* audiences.

Hoodoo was not a bastardized Voodoo or Santeria; it was something with roots all its own. "The way we tell it," wrote novelist and folklorist Zora Neale Hurston in her 1935 *Mules and Men,* "hoodoo started way back there before everything. . . . Nobody can say where it begins or ends."

In practice, hoodoo draws heavily upon botanical and household items—plants, soaps, minerals, animal parts, perfumes—objects that a displaced people adapted to find their way back to the old rituals and spirits. Sandy Jenkins and other root workers were so named for their virtuosity with herbs and roots, objects believed to hold hidden powers that could be tapped for protection, healing, love, money, and other practical needs. And here we return to the first narrative of Frederick Douglass. He receives advice—and something more—from Sandy in the woods:

> He told me, with great solemnity, I must go back to Covey; but that before I went, I must go with him into another part of the woods, where there was a certain root, which, if I would take some of it with me, carrying it always on my right side, would render it impossible for Mr. Covey, or any other white man, to whip me. He said he had carried it for years; and since he had done so, he had never received a blow, and never expected to while he carried it. I at first rejected the idea, that the simple carrying of a root in my pocket would have any such effect as he had said, and was not disposed to take it; but Sandy impressed the necessity with much earnestness, telling me it could do no harm, if it did no good. To please him, I at length took the root, and, according to his direction, carried it upon my right side.

There is no record to bear the matter out, but the object Sandy pressed upon Douglass was very likely a rock-hard, bulbous root known within hoodoo as John the Conqueror, or sometimes High John. *John de conker* is the pronunciation found in oral records and song. It is the ultimate protective object, used for everything from personal safety to virility, traditionally carried by a man rather than a woman. In the magical tradition of "like bestows like," the dried root is shaped like a testicle. There is historical conflict over the species of the root: Botanical drawings differ among the catalogs of old hoodoo supply houses. But the most careful observers and practitioners of hoodoo today agree that the likeliest source is the jalap root, which dries into a rough, spherical nub.

Armed with what he warily called "the magic root," Douglass set off for Covey's farm. Expecting God-only-knew-what fate, he received a strange surprise. It was now Sunday, and Covey—ever the upright Christian—was downright *polite*. "Now," wrote Douglass in his first memoir, "this singular conduct of Mr. Covey really made me begin to think that there was something in the *root* which Sandy had given me." But on Monday morning, things darkened. Mr. Covey, it seemed, was a Sunday Christian. Once the Lord's day of rest ended, the devil in him returned. "On this morning," Douglass continued, "the virtue of the *root* was fully tested." Covey grabbed Douglass in the barn, tied his legs with a rope, and prepared to beat him. "Mr. Covey seemed now to think he had me, and could do what he pleased; but at this moment—from whence came the spirit I don't know—I resolved to fight." Here began the historic turnaround in Douglass's life: "I now resolved that, however long I might remain a slave in form, the day had passed forever when I could be a slave in fact."

Ten years later, in 1855, Douglass—now a free man and internationally known as the voice of abolitionism—published his revised and expanded memoir, one that sold an extraordinary fifteen thousand copies in two months and helped galvanize antislavery feelings. Douglass's second memoir repeats, yet subtly alters, the episode involving Sandy, Covey, and the root. When grabbed by Covey, Douglass writes, with emphasis in the original: "I now forgot my *roots*, and remembered my pledge to *stand up in my own defense*." In a detail absent from his first memoir, Douglass notes that on the previous day he had made a personal vow to "protect myself to the best of my ability." Gone now was the observation, "from whence came the spirit I don't know."

Was Douglass some kind of a half believer in hoodoo, intent on covering his tracks? Not exactly. The greater likelihood is that the same man who served as the moral anchor of the abolitionist movement wanted no one to misunderstand the true nature of his life story: His was an *inner* triumph, a realization of personhood against inconceivable odds, a transcendence in thought that permitted him to see himself as a man of agency and as an actor possessed of rights under God. Indeed, Douglass—a proponent of education and self-improvement in the deepest senses—would almost certainly have considered hoodoo and folk magic as distractions at best and at worst as chains of delusion. In an 1845 footnote that he also repeated ten years later, Douglass distanced himself from the question of hoodoo and magic: "This superstition"—root work—"is very common among the more ignorant slaves. A slave seldom dies, but that his death is attributed to trickery."

But in both his earlier and later memoirs, Douglass proved resolute in his unwillingness to slam shut the door on the matter or to qualify the veneration he felt for Sandy. "I saw in Sandy," Douglass wrote in 1855, "too deep an insight into human nature, with all his superstition, not to have some respect for his advice; and perhaps, too, a slight gleam or shadow of his superstition had fallen upon me." Sandy, the "clever soul," the "old adviser," and the "genuine African," provided a rare measure of wise counsel in a chaotic and brutal world. His authority was grounded in an occult tradition that no slaveholder could enter. In this way, above all others, was Sandy a man of magic—a medicine man in the most profound sense.

Mojo Bags and Menorahs

By the early twentieth century, Americans were becoming widely accustomed to buying their household items from commercial catalogs or right off the shelf—and magic made for no exception. Where others would see rows of ordinary drugstore products, hoodoo practitioners saw the raw material for spells. For instance, Octagon bar soap—still marketed by Colgate as a budget cleanser—was scented with the all-important ingredient lemongrass, a key hoodoo formula for "spiritual cleansing" or exorcising homes of bad humors or maleficent spirits. The earthy scents of Florida or Kananga toilet waters were used for household protection, as fragrant altar offerings, or for the honoring of the dead. Hoyt's cologne was a favorite for gambling luck.

Richly illustrated "spiritual supply" catalogs came to sell items of a more specialized nature, such as lodestones (a favorite money-getting talisman), mojo bags (magical concoctions of herbs in small red flannel sacks to be carried on one's body), and a wide variety of roots, herbs, charms, and amulets. The commercial hoodoo supply houses, which included Keystone Laboratories of Memphis and the Valmor Products Company of Chicago, were operated by pharmacists and cosmetics dealers, often first- or second-generation Jewish immigrants to urban areas, who were among the few white retailers catering to a black clientele. In a spirit of *why not?*, the catalog dealers remarketed Judeo–Christian devotional items as occult supplies, such as menorahs (the traditional Jewish candelabra) and mezuzahs (encasements for prayer scrolls to be nailed at the front door of Jewish homes). Black and white customers gamely stocked their homes with Jewish, Catholic, Spiritualist, Hindu, and traditional hoodoo formulas, herbs, and candles.

In thousands of interviews with Southern hoodoo practitioners beginning in the 1930s, Episcopal priest and folklorist Harry Middleton Hyatt found that hoodoo mixed easily with other religious systems. In a sense, it was becoming America's first boundary-free faith. Hyatt's informants frequently spoke of petitioning Catholic folk saints—historically and theologically suspect saints barely tolerated by church doctrine but the subject of loving cults among the faithful. These included the legendary Saint Expedite—helper of those needing results in a hurry. "Well, St. Espidy, he's very good," related one subject, in the kind of dialect Hyatt faithfully captured:

> He have helped me. He helps me an when ah wants bread ah call on him an' he brings me a rap [answers by rapping]. Ah heard dat he was a man dat didn't believe in no evil work; an' he didn't fool roun' wit no kinda evil doin' when he was on dis scene an' he wus a true man an' when he died he went tuh heaven.

The books stocked by hoodoo supply houses encompassed Christian inspirational classics, such as *The Imitation of Christ* (again, repackaged as occult fare), or modern guides to hexes, spells, and folk cures. Folklore from the German–American community of Pennsylvania—influenced by the Rhine Valley mysticism of the Kelpius and Ephrata communes—proved especially popular among hoodoo readers. A favorite was German–Pennsylvanian Johann Georg Hohman's 1820 spell book *Pow-Wows or Long Lost Friend,* a volume that made its way into English in 1855. *Pow-Wows* was a haunting hodge-podge of myth, healing practices, and European folklore. The book referred to itself as a magic charm that would protect all who carried it. (So seriously was this belief held that soldiers of German–Pennsylvanian background were known to carry *Pow-Wows* on them in Vietnam.)

Far and away the most venerated book in hoodoo was another Germanic occult text, this one assembled from myriad sources in the mid-nineteenth century. Often considered the "hoodoo bible," it was a beguiling patchwork called *The Sixth and Seventh Books of Moses.* The grimoire, or manual of magic, served up a mixture of Kabala (and pseudo-Kabala), supernatural seals, the "spells" used by Moses against Pharaoh, and—most popular of all—instructions on the magical uses of the Psalms. For hoodoo practitioners, who discovered the book in its first English edition in 1880, it became a source of endless fascination. *The Sixth and Seventh Books of Moses* is cited more than any other single work in the interviews and oral records that survive of root workers. German–Pennsylvanian and Jewish influences grew so woven into hoodoo practice that a Louisiana-born conjurer living in Memphis in the 1930s told folklorist Hyatt about a love spell where: "Yo'd have to talk Hebrew-like. Yo' realize de Hebrew language—some of dat's in de 'Six' and Seven' Books of Moses' and den de balance is [in] de 91 Psalms of David."

Indeed, to many root workers, Moses himself was the great medicine man and conjurer of the ancient past—a savior from the African continent who used his divine powers to free and protect his flock. To hoodoo practitioners, Moses and Aaron's spells against Pharaoh revealed the true purpose of Africa's traditional esoteric crafts. A former Georgia slave named Thomas Smith put it this way in another dialect-faithful interview, which appeared in the Georgia Writers' Project guide: "Dat appen in Africa de Bible say. Ain' dat show dat Africa wuz a lan uh magic powah since de beginnin uh history? Well duh descendants ub Africans hab du same gif tuh do unnatchal ting."

"The Great Voodoo Man of the Bible"

The marriage of African cultural awareness, magic, and the emancipation brought by Moses found its greatest expression in the books of a man whose identity is lost to time. The 1930s and '40s saw the arrival of Henri Gamache, a pseudonymous author and literary man of mystery. His books were the finest original fare put out by the hoodoo publishers and supply houses. Gamache's works include an influential guide to candle magic called *The Master Book of Candle Burning*, as well as books of herb magic and protective spells. The centerpiece of the Gamache oeuvre is a little-known minor masterpiece. It is a work that has never gone out of print and that prefigured the African religious and cultural revival of later generations. Expanding on the themes of *The Sixth and Seventh Books of Moses*, it is called *Mystery of the Long Lost 8th, 9th and 10th Books of Moses*.

Published in 1945, Gamache's *8th, 9th and 10th Books of Moses* theorized the existence of lost Mosaic works, including those that might reveal the magical systems used by Moses, the Great Emancipator. Gamache depicted Moses as a figure born from within the magical ferment of Egyptian and African antiquity. In so doing, Gamache developed a cultural argument that all the great Western faiths were philosophies raised up from the cradle of Africa. Moses, he reasoned, was "The Great Voodoo Man of the Bible," a medicine man and miracle worker whose fingerprints could be found in the African-descended religious movements of Voodoo, hoodoo—and those that became Judaism and Christianity. "All across Africa and Egypt to the Sudan and thence to the Gold Coast is his influence manifest," Gamache wrote. "In Haiti, in the Western Hemisphere, the greatest of all the gods is Damballa Ouedo Ouedo Tocan Freda Dahomey who is none other than Moses himself."

It was a novel argument. In his analysis, Gamache previewed Afrocentrist and Garveyite perspectives that would begin to gain popularity twenty-five years later. And his perspective was not without subtlety. While anthropologists speculated over, and sometimes fiercely debated, the extent to which African cultural "retentions" could be found in America, Gamache—in an approach validated by later generations of ethnographers and religious scholars—showed an understanding that the most visible African retentions could be discovered in Haiti and the Caribbean, where older customs were more closely preserved.*

The person using the name Henri Gamache may have been the force behind other pseudonymous hoodoo-influenced books, including guides to magic and the occult under the bylines alternately spelled Lewis de Claremont and Louis de Clermont. Indeed, Gamache's own works emerged from companies owned by the same or related retailers who controlled the de Claremont titles and a variety of other works on dreams, spells, and numerology. But a liveliness and originality that is absent from the usual supply-house fare permeates Gamache's writing, suggesting the thought of a distinct, though unknown, individual. Gamache alone displays a broad interest in the religion, magic, and folklore of a vast range of cultures and belief systems, including Christian, Vedic, African, Judaic/Kabalistic, Voodoo, and Spiritualist. In an almost unheard-of device in hoodoo-oriented literature, Gamache

---

* Scholars generally attribute the greater retention of African religious traditions in the Caribbean and Latin America to the greater ratio of blacks to whites on comparatively vast plantations, as well as to the continual influx of new slaves. In America, by contrast, plantations were smaller, black-to-white ratios less, and by the start of the Civil War most North American slaves were native born. "In North America," writes historian Albert J. Raboteau in his classic *Slave Religion*, "a relatively small number of Africans found themselves enslaved amid a rapidly increasing native-born population whose memories of the African past grew fainter with each passing generation."

in each of his books supplied bibliographies and cited scholarly and journalistic sources—many of which were available at the New York Public Library. "He seems to have been a man of mixed race," notes Catherine Yronwode, the canniest contemporary observer of hoodoo history and practice, "possibly born in the Caribbean, who lived and worked in New York City."

There is one further literary connection to Gamache that begs scrutiny, and it involves yet another magician who associated himself with the wonders of Moses. The figure who authored the Gamache books is sometimes thought to have ghostwritten the memoirs of the most famous African–American stage magician of the first part of the twentieth century. He could neither read nor write but enthralled thousands of followers under the stage name Black Herman.

Professor Black Herman

"I am proud to introduce you to one of the greatest men of our time," the emcee would announce at the opening of Black Herman's stage shows,

> the President of the Colored Magicians Association of America, and the undisputed monarch of race magicians. All those present tonight are fortunate, because the territory he tours is so large that Black Herman only comes around once every seven years. This is the year for us all to remember. You will tell your grandchildren about this day. You know the legend of High John the Conqueror, now meet the legendary Professor Black Herman!

Although he had been born Benjamin Rucker in Amherst, Virginia, in 1892, the gangly, tuxedoed magician called Black Herman told his audiences a different story. He described a mythical childhood in a Zulu tribe and claimed great feats of magic and derring-do—including rescuing a child from a lion by hypnotizing the beast. In part of Herman's stage act, he invited audience members to tie him so he could show how, "If slave traders tried to take any of my people captive, we would release ourselves using our secret knowledge."

Unlike most stage magicians—who saw magic strictly as a hard-earned skill and disdained the claims of Spiritualists and psychics—Herman blended stagecraft and spellcraft, casting himself as both an entertainer and a master occultist. "I was born in the jungles of Africa," he intoned, "where I learned the secrets of roots from the greatest tribal witch doctors. I learned the language of the animals. When I first came to this country, if I became hungry, I would merely call to a rabbit; one would come—and I would have rabbit stew!" Herman would then commence with a part of his act that involved his famous animal impersonations and ventriloquism.

Like his stage show, Herman's 1925 memoir and guidebook, *Secrets of Magic, Mystery & Legerdemain,* was an unusual mixture of biographical myth-making, stage tricks, hoodoo formulas, astrology, and dream interpretation. It, too, framed magic as a way of resisting oppression: The cover showed a drawing of a caped Herman sitting astride a globe with a scroll marked *POWER* in his left hand; his right foot rested atop a pile of esoteric books with the names *The Missing Key, The Key to Success, The Key to Happiness,* and on the largest book the words, *Black Herman COVERS the WORLD.* Herman presented a dramatic anomaly in the field of professional magic, where a black performer—when employed at all—was typically cast as a clownish sidekick to a white magician. Black assistants often distracted the audience with pratfalls designed to conceal the headliner's sleight of hand.

There would be no such demeaning roles for Black Herman. He had apprenticed himself to another African–American magician ("Prince Herman") and entered the spotlight after his mentor died in 1909. But Black Herman aspired to be more than a lead performer. In true hoodoo fashion, Herman positioned himself in the footsteps of the great magician Moses—playing the part of a modern-day conjurer–emancipator. In his book, possibly ghostwritten by Henri Gamache, Herman noted:

Magicians have been in existence since the days of Moses. When Moses was commanded by the Lord to de- liver the Israelites from bondage, did he not come in touch with magicians? Did not the good Lord use magi- cians to prove to Pharaoh that he was God and beside Him there was no other? If magicians were needed in the days of Moses and Pharaoh, they are needed again at this time.

Offstage, Herman presented himself as a model of worldly achievement, appearing in an elegant Prince Albert coat, tuxedo, and tails, with a pyramid-shaped amulet around his neck. In the 1920s, he was a well-known figure in New York's Harlem, living in high style amid Oriental rugs, African masks, floor-to-ceiling murals, and antiques in his three-floor town house on West 136th Street. Herman claimed to readily loan money to neigh- bors and friends for rent and coal. He treated neighborhood kids to prizes in apple- and pie-eating contests. His stage shows and occult-product businesses provided full- and part-time work to dozens of people. Indeed, he could pack in crowds of four thou- sand a night at Marcus Garvey's Liberty Hall. His was not a "race act" but a rare integrated stage show, attracting both black and white audience members. Never one for small plans, Herman dreamed of fashioning his Harlem town house into the headquarters of a "New Negro Renaissance," and in the 1920s and '30s he presided over Sunday-night salons with local busi- nessmen, lawyers, and artists.

In a move of daring and self-confidence that rivaled any shown by Houdini, Herman one day revealed the peak of his personal powers. In his invaluable history of African–American stage ma- gicians, *Magical Heroes,* writer Jim Magus relates how Herman once outsmarted a group of thieves who were out for money— and blood. One afternoon while on national tour, Herman took his brother, Andrew, to go search for his missing stage assistant, Washington Reeves. Reeves had been dispatched to a local black cemetery to gather names and dates from tombstones—providing Herman with material for his "mind reading" act later that night.

But Reeves was a drinker and had long gone missing. "I am receiving a distinct psychic impression that he's drunk again," Herman told his brother. "Let's go find him."

Herman and Andrew went to the local cemetery, where they were quickly approached by four menacing men carrying large sticks. "This is our turf," one said. "You cross it, you got to pay a tax." Herman brushed right past the men, declaring: "The Great Black Herman is exempt from any such tax." The men smiled. They knew who the famous magician was and smelled big money. Gripping their clubs, they tightened around Herman and his brother. "If you're such a great magician," said one, "make us some money, now!" Herman shot back: "I do not deal with materialistic matters such as money. I do, however, occasionally practice the necromantic art of raising the dead!" Before the men could say anything, Herman shouted at the top of his stage voice: "Washington Reeves! Arise! Arise now!" Leaves rustled, and from behind a tombstone a figure struggled to its feet. The thieves dropped their sticks and ran in terror. Had they turned around, they would have witnessed the "undead" Washington Reeves stumbling forward—a pint of whiskey clutched in his hands.

Poor Man's Psychologist

Even Black Herman encountered webs that could not be slipped out of. By the 1930s, New York State had enacted a stringent (and still extant) anti-fortune-telling law that prohibited the "claimed or pretended use of occult powers" for commercial purposes. Police spotted a very big target in Harlem's most famous magician.*

While touring, Herman had known brushes with the law and usually understood how to sell his "spiritual products," such as Black Herman's Body Tonic, with standard label disclaimers like

---

* The law was later narrowed to target con artists who tailor predictions to cheat believers out of large sums of money, rather than storefront palm readers or psychics.

alleged and *sold as a curio only.* But he hadn't expected that police would come after him on his home turf for another line of work. In Harlem, Herman offered private services as a mind reader, spiritual adviser, and root doctor. He maintained a formal waiting room and regular office hours at his town house. In a 1927 sting operation, a "lonely wife" visited Herman several times to seek help in winning back her cheating husband.

Consulting with his distressed client, Herman freely prescribed hoodoo formulas and methods—including sachet powders of herbs to be worn on the body, a John the Conqueror root, magical repetitions of the Psalms, and special uses of the husband's foot scrapings to keep him home. It was a traditional hoodoo consultation, with Herman playing the role of "poor man's psychologist," as he often described himself. On June 17, the jilted wife—who turned out to be an undercover policewoman by the name of Nettie Sweatman—arrested him for "fortune-telling" and practicing medicine without a license.

Harlem Healer Given Setback by Woman Cop, announced the nationally read African–American newspaper *Chicago Defender* the next day. It was a bitter slap to the famous magician. Another came in September from his hometown paper, the *New York Amsterdam News: "Black Herman," Magician, Held for Trial in Special Sessions as "Quack."* In October, he received a short sentence at Sing Sing prison. Herman attempted to put up a brave face for his admirers, to whom he boasted of making so many breaks from his jail cell that the authorities could barely hold him. But the humiliated Herman never quite regained his stride. As the Great Depression hit Harlem in the early 1930s, spending money and leisure time for stage shows dried up. He found ways to continue performing, often by playing to segregated audiences in tours of the Deep South. Herman got back a little of the old fire in 1930 when he visited Detroit, the *Defender* reported, and proclaimed "that the depression enveloping the Motor City is chiefly mental, and he being chosen by God, is seeking to lift it."

While he was preparing to open a tour of Kentucky, the forty-two-year-old Herman died on April 17, 1934. There exist two versions of his death—one that Herman probably would have liked the world to remember and another that was more modest. According to the more popular version, Black Herman collapsed onstage in the middle of a performance at the Old Palace Theater in Louisville, Kentucky. The stunned audience refused to leave—they believed it was all part of his act and that the magician would rise again. When the body was sent to a local funeral home, pandemonium broke out, and police had to be called in to control thousands of mourners who wanted one last look at the stage great. Press reports and Herman's death certificate, however, indicate that Benjamin Rucker died more quietly, at the Louisville boardinghouse where he and his touring troupe were staying. He complained of indigestion after dinner, and when several "home remedies" failed to work, a doctor was called. The confusion resulted in friends telling the *Chicago Defender* that Herman had been felled by "acute indigestion." In fact, he was dead of heart failure before he could be taken to the hospital. His body was returned home to New York, where it lies today in Woodlawn Cemetery in an unmarked grave.

Black Moses

Despite the cultural awareness of Henri Gamache and Black Herman, hoodoo was not directly political. Most conjure and root work focused on regaining lost lovers, fixing troublesome neighbors, avoiding trouble with the law, overcoming unfair bosses, gambling on the right numbers—all practical concerns for men and women taking on life day by day. But a voice was rising on the American scene that combined mystical beliefs and political purpose in a wholly new way.

It belonged to the black-nationalist leader Marcus Garvey. Garvey, who had sojourned from Jamaica to America in 1916, envisioned the creation of a pan-African superpower that would take its place among the empires of the world. For a time, he came closer than many would have imagined possible, attracting tens of thousands of cheering followers to rallies and parades in America,

England, and the Caribbean, creating a publishing empire of black newspapers, and assembling the first and largest international black political organization in history. Followers wept openly at Garvey rallies, as the uniformed orator extolled the dignity of black heritage and told of the history and destiny of Africa on the world stage. For many listeners who were old enough to remember slavery, and for others who lived in its shadow, hearing Garvey felt like a spiritual awakening. An FBI report in August 1920 observed of Garvey's movement that "among the followers it is like a religion," its leader "looked upon as a black Moses." In a pillar of Garvey's program often missed by those who scrutinized him, Garvey, like the social radical Wallace D. Wattles, believed that New Thought metaphysics could build the dreams of disenfranchised men and women around the world. Garvey's movement represented the boldest—and least understood—effort in history to combine the magic of mind power with the quest for political gain.

Born in the north Jamaican seaside town of St. Ann's Bay in 1887, Garvey experienced a childhood that verged on brutality. His father was a stonemason and sometime gravedigger who had been born a slave. The elder Marcus, after whom his son was named (Garvey's mother had wanted to call him Moses), passed on to his children a tough-as-nails view of the world and a demand for the strictest respect. The older Garvey determined to teach Marcus about the rigors of life and the need for absolute self-reliance. One night, Garvey took his son with him to dig a grave, for which the mason had fashioned a headstone. The father told the boy to drop into the grave, and he then snatched up the ladder behind him—leaving Marcus to shiver and cry in the hole all night. It was a torment he never forgot.

Under the island's colonial education system, Marcus was forced to leave school at age fourteen. Around the same time, a neighboring white Methodist minister abruptly cut off a childhood friendship his daughter had maintained with Marcus. "It was then," Garvey wrote, "that I found out for the first time that there was some difference in humanity, and that there were different races, each having its own separate and distinct social life."

The heavyset, bulldoglike teen was apprenticed to a printer—and a burgeoning interest in journalism was born. In 1910, Garvey traveled through Central America, where he was appalled to witness the second-class status occupied by black laborers completing the Panama Canal. "Where was the black man's country?" Garvey wondered, watching blacks labor for meager wages on the projects of other nations and colonial powers.

A few years later, he read educator Booker T. Washington's *Up from Slavery*—and the book's philosophy of self-sufficiency hit Garvey with the force of a religious conversion. Garvey took these ideas, merged them with his own form of radical opposition to white authority, and in 1914 transformed them into the platform of his Universal Negro Improvement Association (UNIA). Eventually claiming three-quarters of a million members, UNIA generated a surge of pride among members with its plans to create a shipping empire and a restored pan-African nation—with Marcus Garvey as its uniformed, imperial president.

"Always think yourself a perfect being," Garvey told followers, "and be satisfied with yourself." His philosophy of faith-in-self and perpetual self-improvement formed Garvey's deepest appeal. And, to careful observers, it was firmly rooted in the grand tradition of American metaphysics. "What was deemed a new racial philosophy," wrote historians Robert A. Hill and Barbara Bair in their *Marcus Garvey: Life and Lessons,* "was in fact Garvey's wholesale application of the dynamics of New Thought to the black condition. . . . Metaphysics and politics were explicitly linked in Garvey's mind."

UNIA newspapers and pamphlets abounded with telltale phrases of the New Thought movement, such as the call for a "universal business consciousness" in Garvey's *Negro World* newspaper. Garvey's Negro Factories Corporation advertised shares of stock by declaring, "Enthusiasm Is One of the Big Keys to Success." And a front-page headline in Garvey's *Blackman* newspaper announced: *Let us Give Off Success and It Will Come,* adding the indispensable New Thought maxim: *As Man Thinks So Is He.*

One of the only books that Garvey publicly recommended to

followers was *Elbert Hubbard's Scrap Book,* a collection of life lessons by Hubbard, the social-reform journalist admired by Wallace D. Wattles and hero of motivational thinking within New Thought circles. Garvey's favorite poet was Ella Wheeler Wilcox, the poet laureate of mind power, whose lines he used to conclude a 1915 UNIA rally:

> *Live for something,—Have a purpose*
> *And that purpose keep in view*
> *Drifting like a helmless vessel*
> *Thou cans't ne'er to self be true.*

While figures like Wallace D. Wattles and Marcus Garvey occupied two completely different worlds, they nonetheless shared a critical trait that alternately retreated and surfaced throughout each man's career: Their social radicalism rested on a metaphysical component, shrewdly couched in language to which every American, black or white, could instantly relate.

"A Scientific Understanding of God"

Garvey made little direct reference to the source of his ideas. A degree of secrecy and confidentiality characterized almost all of Garvey's affairs, notes historian Hill, including those of the mind. In a speech he delivered in January 1928 in Kingston, Jamaica, however, Garvey's New Thought ideas were outlined perhaps more clearly than at any other time in his career. "Get you[rself], as the white man has done, a scientific understanding of God and religion," he told his listeners, continuing:

> *What marks the great deal of difference between the Negro and the White man is that the Negro does not understand God and His religion. God places you here in the world on your responsibility as men and women to take out of the world and to make out of the world what you want in keeping with the laws of the spirit. God has*

> *laid down two codes that man cannot afford to disobey:*
> *the code of Nature and the code of the Spirit. The code*
> *of Nature when you violate it makes you angry, makes*
> *you unhappy, makes you miserable, makes you sick,*
> *makes you die prematurely. . . . Every sickness and*
> *every disease, I repeat, is a direct violation of the code of*
> *God in Nature.*

Making a definite spiritual use of the term *science*, Garvey told the audience that whites "live by science. You do everything by emotion. That makes the vast difference between the two races. . . . Get a scientific knowledge of religion, of God, of what you are; and you will create a better world for yourselves. Negroes, the world is to your making." Contemporary readers of Garvey's words could easily miss, or simply wonder at, the political leader's references to religion and science—but the signposts abounded in Garvey's day. The mental healer Phineas P. Quimby had made a direct link between religion and science. Quimby believed that religion was, above all, a lawful phenomenon guaranteed to produce certain results. In his writings, which appeared to the public for the first time a few years before Garvey's address, the metaphysical healer used phrases like *Science of Christ, Science of Health and Happiness,* and, most tellingly, *Christian Science.*

Garvey's spiritual "science" also had roots—occult roots—in his Caribbean boyhood. In the West Indies, the term *science* sometimes connoted magical practices. Writer–activist C. L. R. James, in his 1936 novel of Trinidadian domestic life, *Minty Alley,* showed how "science" and "magic" got tangled up when an older man confronted a younger neighbor:

> *"These books you always reading," he picked up one*
> *and looked at the title. "About science! Ah! you read*
> *about science. Then you have books by de Laurence?"*
>
> *This de Laurence was an American writer on magic*
> *and psychic science, whose books had some vogue in the*
> *islands.*
>
> *"No," said Haynes. "It isn't that sort of science."*

> *"A man with your intelligence, if you read books on science you would do well. See now, about two o'clock, all the spirits of the air passing up and down. And if you know what to do you can compel them and make them do what you like."*

The writer "de Laurence" was a real person, a Chicago-based mail-order retailer of occult supplies who was especially popular among Caribbean, African, and African–American consumers. A handsome, angular man who liked to be photographed wearing a turban over his blondish hair, L. W. de Laurence was not above sometimes affixing his name to occult volumes that others had written. He was not quite a plagiarist—rather, he was a "book pirate," freely pilfering the work of others in an age of flimsy copyrights, much like English occultist Francis Barrett did in 1801 when he swiped large swaths of Agrippa's *Occult Philosophy*. (In a karmic cycle of occult "borrowing," de Laurence lifted Barrett's ghoulish illustrations of "evil spirits" for reuse in his massive *Great Book of Magical Art, Hindoo Magic & Indian Occultism*.)

Though white, de Laurence specifically targeted Afro–Caribbean buyers. His overseas customers—who abounded in Garvey's Jamaica—may have found a kind of magical appeal in the fact that de Laurence peddled his wares from the "Institute of Hypnotism and Occult Philosophy" in the heartland of America, a nation that still had the majestic sheen of promise and progress.

Almost single-handedly, de Laurence introduced the texts and formulas of American hoodoo to the Caribbean Islands. Indeed, de Laurence's "scientific," American-made formulas (with names typical in hoodoo catalogs, like *compelling powder, destruction powder,* and *oil of turn-back*) often displaced indigenous forms of herb magic in Jamaica's cities. Fearing de Laurence's influence as a foreign agent of black magic, the nation's legal authorities banned his books. Even when the populist government of Michael Manley in 1972 slashed away at the list of officially censored publications, the magical works of L. W. de Laurence remained illegal. So suspect was de Laurence that any of his titles "relating to Divination, Magic, Occultism, Supernatural Arts or other esoteric subjects" formed the last vestiges of the Jamaican government's blacklist, alongside a few subversive tracts like Che Guevara's *Guerrilla Warfare*.

Circle 7 Koran

The magical uses of "science" were not limited to the West Indies or Garvey. Indeed, the man who styled himself as Garvey's American successor used a philosophy of mystical science to form the basis for one of the most beguiling and influential inner-city religious movements of the twentieth century, the Moorish Science Temple. Founded in Newark, New Jersey, in 1913 and moved to Chicago in the early 1920s, the movement was led by a mysterious North Carolinian named Timothy Drew, known to followers as Noble Drew Ali. In a handful of grainy photographs, Ali appears as a slender man with a thin mustache, outfitted in an Oriental silk robe and Masonic sash, alternately wearing a turban or tasseled fez, with his right hand crossed to his chest Napoleon-fashion. He told followers that he was born black in 1886 but raised among the Cherokee Indian tribes. His ceremonial title of "Noble" and other aspects of his regalia were very likely taken from Freemasonry's Ancient Arabic Order of the Nobles of the Mystic Shrine, the order better known as the Shriners. In the late nineteenth century the Masonic group had introduced America to the imagery (if not the actual ideas) of Islam.

Some of the New York businessmen who founded the Shriners lodge in 1877 did, in fact, take a serious interest in the philosophies of the East. Members even claimed a spurious connection with the Bektashi Sufi Order, a legendary Turkish brotherhood of mystical Muslims known for wine-drinking and ecstatic worship. But by the early twentieth century, the Shriners operated chiefly as a philanthropic guild, responsible for developing a remarkable network of free children's hospitals. The group's Byzantine symbols—including the fez, star and crescent, and scimitar—were relegated mostly to pageantry and decoration.

While Noble Drew Ali often invoked Allah and Islam (or "Islamism," as he sometimes called it), he had almost no ties or traffic with the actual faith of Muhammad. Rather, Moorish Science was an American inner-city mystery religion built upon New Thought, Masonry, Theosophy, and occultism. Noble Drew Ali's marriage of Garveyite themes to esoteric rites and symbols helped respond to the yearnings for economic, cultural, and political power being felt in the cities to which the descendants of slaves had begun migrating.

Elusive as his background was, the prophet of Moorish Science was rumored to have toured America as a magician in a traveling circus. A remarkable crumbling flyer discovered by writer Prince-A-Cuba and reproduced by Peter Lamborn Wilson in his extraordinary book on apostate Islam, *Sacred Drift,* depicts a Noble Drew Ali close in spirit to the miracle-working Black Herman. *THE PROPHET NOBLE DREW ALI,* announces the 1927 advertising sheet, *WILL BE BOUND WITH SEVERAL YARDS OF ROPE, AS JESUS WAS BOUND IN THE THE [sic] TEMPLE AT JERUSALEM.* The flyer goes on to promise that Noble Drew Ali practices "the same art, after being bound by anyone in the audience, and will escape in a few seconds." Here again was an emancipator in the mold of a Scriptural hero—now Jesus himself.

But the true magical key to Ali's "science" was his ultrasecret *Circle 7 Koran,* which members were sworn to keep hidden from outsiders. So serious was this oath that, even long after Ali's death in 1929, the sociologist Arthur Huff Fauset in his groundbreaking 1944 study, *Black Gods of the Metropolis,* would quote only from its front and back covers:

THE HOLY KORAN
of the
MOORISH SCIENCE TEMPLE
OF AMERICA

KNOW YOURSELF AND YOUR FATHER
GOD ALLAH
THAT YOU MAY LEARN TO LOVE INSTEAD OF HATE
EVERYMAN NEED TO WORSHIP UNDER HIS OWN
VINE AND FIG TREE
THE UNITY OF ASIA

The cover featured the numeral 7, a reflection of Ali's penchant for occult and numerological symbols. The front and back encapsulated Noble Drew Ali's philosophy: that all people mistakenly labeled black, Negro, or colored were, in fact, "Asiatic" or Moorish–Americans whose natural form of worship was found in a monotheistic mystical Eastern faith that he called Islam. To Noble Drew Ali, Islam meant an unspoiled esoteric religion that extolled the holiness of Confucius, Jesus, Buddha, Zoroaster, and Noble Drew Ali himself. Jesus in particular, Fauset noted, "figures prominently" in his secretive text—a fact that may have helped Moorish Science appear reassuringly familiar to Southern migrants raised within the Baptist Church. It was not until many years later that outsiders finally detected the actual contents of the long-concealed holy book.

Its forty-eight chapters—packed into sixty-four tightly set pages—contained a dramatic narrative of the "lost years" of Jesus. It depicted the young carpenter as a great seeker of wisdom, traversing Tibet, India, and Egypt in search of self-knowledge and universal truth. The portrait of Jesus as a master adept or great initiate occurred frequently in occult and mystical literature of the late nineteenth and early twentieth centuries. And in this instance, the depiction was one that Noble Drew Ali lifted nearly word for word from sections of a 1908 work that would go on to become a New Age classic. It was *The Aquarian Gospel of Jesus the Christ* by "Levi," actually Levi H. Dowling of Ohio, a former Civil War chaplain, homeopathic healer, publisher of Sunday-school materials, and progressive Church of Christ pastor. Dowling, "the messenger," psychically received his epic of Jesus's "lost years" through contact with the "Akashic Records," an ethereal hall of records that figured prominently in modern occultism and about which more will be heard. Dowling's *Aquarian Gospel* was, in its way, the most ambitious and endearing of all self-generated literature about the life of Christ. It had a moral heart and message of universality in which all religions were part of a great wide table. In the hands of Noble Drew Ali, it became repurposed—and uncredited—as the prime narrative of the so-called *Circle 7 Koran.*

Portions of the *Circle 7 Koran* not copied from Dowling amounted to lessons in good living—fundamentals of self-sufficiency and moral conduct that later resurfaced in Elijah Muhammad's Nation of Islam and other black-nationalist groups. Many of these passages were borrowed from a peculiar "ancient" wisdom book published in 1925 through the San Jose, California-based Rosicrucian group Ancient and Mystical Order Rosae Crucis, or AMORC. The book was called *Unto Thee I Grant.* AMORC billed it as the "Secret Teachings of Tibet," a land that assumed Oz-like proportions in the minds of early-twentieth-century occultists. The Rosicrucian publishers ultimately credited the work to manuscripts written by Pharaoh Amenhotep IV around 1360 to 1350 B.C., an association that must have attracted their fellow Egyptophile Noble Drew Ali.

In actuality, *Unto Thee I Grant* was copied not from pharaonic manuscripts but from an eighteenth-century English instructional guide to manners and morals. It first appeared in 1750 under the title *The Economy of Human Life.* The book of moral aphorisms had always been intended to provoke intrigue. Attributed by its English publishers to nameless sources, *The Economy of Human Life* was mystical in conceit: *TRANSLATED FROM AN IN-DIAN MANUSCRIPT WRITTEN BY AN ANCIENT BRAHMIN,* read its title page. But it was distinctly bourgeois and Anglican in tone and content. Alternately rumored to be the work of Lord Chesterfield or an English bibliophile named Robert Dodsley, the book appeared in expanded versions over time, including from a Scottish press in 1785, which is one of the earliest editions in general circulation. The question of who wrote *The Economy of Human Life*—and who added to it along the way—provoked a literary debate in nineteenth-century Britain, culminating in an ultimately inconclusive work of sleuthing in 1854 by one "W. Cramp" in the adventurously titled journal *Notes and Queries*.

As with the Levi passages, Noble Drew Ali simply recast the Anglican text with a mystico-Eastern tinge:

> *From the creatures of God let man learn wisdom, and apply to himself the instruction they give.* (The Economy of Human Life, 1785)
> *From the secrets of Allah let man learn wisdom, and apply to himself the instruction they give.* (Circle 7 Koran, 1927)

Never one to be cut out of the action, the redoubtable L. W. de Laurence produced his own version of this "ancient Piece of Eastern Instruction" under the title *Infinite Wisdom*. He advertised it inside the prominent African–American newspaper *Chicago Defender*. Such notices almost certainly would have caught the attention of de Laurence's fellow Chicagoan Noble Drew Ali.

Astoundingly, this pseudo-Eastern British work of the mid-eighteenth century, which later morphed into pseudo-Egyptian versions in the hands of AMORC and de Laurence, became the moral template for Moorish Science and other urban religio-political sects that followed in its steps. Indeed, a veritable who's who of early black-power figures joined or came in close contact with Moorish Science in the 1920s, including the elusive ideological architect of the Nation of Islam, Wallace D. Fard; the Nation of Islam's preeminent early leader, Elijah Muhammad; and the self-declared God incarnate and spiritual teacher called Father Divine.

But before pounding a gavel of judgment on the matter, a pause is in order. It is too easy in the present day to cast terms like *plagiarist* in the direction of figures like L. W. de Laurence or Noble Drew Ali. In fact, many surviving religious texts stretching back to an unfathomable oral tradition have been redacted, recast, rewritten, and co-opted, ever since the great Egyptian god of learning, Thoth, was remade literally millennia later as the wing-footed Mercury of the Romans. The Caesars of Rome routinely adopted the gods and deities of those lands they conquered. Scholars observe that the Hebrews almost certainly drew upon the cultic ideas of the once-powerful desert worshippers of Baal. The early Christians clearly adapted the winter solstice and sun-worshipping festivals of the polytheists they overcame. Religious ideas travel. It is only due to the nature of twenty-first-century record-keeping that we sometimes get to see the trail. Contemporary religious innovators have no more or less innocence than those who went before them; rather, it is only our understanding of how religions get made that has changed. Laws, it has been famously observed, are like sausages: One should never watch their creation. The same could be said of religions.

"Not Even His Publisher Knows His Identity"

Marcus Garvey's influence inspired an unusual depth of emotion in followers—and reached people from vastly different walks of life. In the early 1920s, an erudite mathematician and cosmological philosopher, Robert T. Browne, fell under the Garvey spell. "This same Marcus Garvey," wrote Browne in Garvey's *Negro World* newspaper in June 1922, "divinely inspired, heaven-sent and God-directed, formed the U.N.I.A., which is, with but one exception, the greatest spiritual force that has ever swayed the minds of men since the world began." To Browne, the one and only force greater than Garvey's organization was "the religion of Jesus Christ." But this was no starry-eyed believer in the Garvey gospel. Browne was a figure worthy of an accolade too often given but, in his case, uniquely deserved: a man ahead of his time. He was among the nation's first black esoteric philosophers and a person whose life would touch and change the fortunes of people around him.

Born in Texas in 1882, Browne attended the all-black Samuel Huston College and became a high school teacher. By his early thirties he'd ventured to Harlem, where he befriended the influential bibliophile and Freemason Arthur A. Schomburg. The two collaborated on exhibitions of Afro–American books and cultural artifacts, and Browne became president of the Negro Library Association. For several years, he had been nurturing an interest in the color-blind philosophy of "higher mathematics." Attracted by the Theosophical Society's commitment to universal brotherhood and religious diversity, Browne became a member in 1915.

Regardless of his growing reputation, he felt embarrassingly compelled to conceal his background from publishers E. P. Dutton when they issued his 1919 treatise, *The Mystery of Space*. The writer feared that no critic or editor would take seriously a black metaphysician. Schomburg, in a personal letter marked *confidential*, informed a colleague, "Browne doesn't want to be advertised, not even his publisher knows his identity."

Browne's book—an inquiry into hyperspace, mathematical theory, and unseen dimensions—would today be called "new science" or "quantum theory." In it, Browne posited that matter and space are products of the one truly limitless resource: the human mind. He surveyed ideas from Egyptian geometry to the thought of Kant to argue that mind is the ultimate reality. On March 14, 1920, *New York Times* critic Benjamin De Casseres, in a sometimes irritatingly self-regarding review that probably failed to attract many readers to Browne's book, called it "the greatest of all latter-day books on space," a work by "a mathematician, a mystic and a thinker, one who, endowed with a tremendous metaphysical imagination, never lets go any point of the threads of reality."

The same Robert T. Browne would later earn the loving gratitude of his fellow inmates in a Japanese prisoner-of-war camp during World War II when he used metaphysical visualization techniques, similar to those preached by Garvey, to keep them from starvation in a tropical prison. Browne worked as a purchasing agent for the U.S. Army in the Philippines. After Japan invaded in late 1941, Browne was rounded up with thousands of other Americans living in the islands and thrown into the infamous internment camps, first at Santo Tomas and later at Los

Baños. Unspoken Japanese policy was to allow prisoners to slowly starve to death. While inmates were free to go about their daily business fairly unimpeded, they were given threadbare provisions and left to care for themselves on whatever they could barter, grow, or manage to purchase from the world outside. As the war dragged on, malnutrition and starvation set in. Similar to the withering physical decline of most prisoners, Browne dropped from a robust 212 to 120 pounds.

For everyone, food became an obsession, and Browne sought to help fellow inmates with the one tool he had to offer: training in mind-power techniques and other "Esoteric Christian" methods. "See the orange and taste it," taught Browne. "Feel its nutrients going into your body and making you stronger." He instructed internees to collect recipes wherever they could find them and to concentrate on the individual ingredients, using their mind as a nourishing force.

According to historian Christopher Paul Moore in his remarkable recovery of Browne's history in *Fighting for America: Black Soldiers—the Unsung Heroes of World War II*, the mystic philosopher became the unlikeliest of prison heroes.

> *Of all the courses and lectures taught by the teachers among the internees, none seems to have had more impact on the camp's population than Browne's mind-power techniques. . . . Browne's philosophy spread throughout the camp and may have actually helped defer or at least delay some of the intense psychological pain associated with malnutrition and starvation. The visualization technique became a camp phenomenon.*

In February 1945, Browne and more than two thousand prisoners were liberated from Los Baños in a historic airborne raid. He returned home to the United States and was welcomed by New York's African–American *Amsterdam News* on August 11 as a "famous mathematician, philosopher and author" who had survived Japanese imprisonment for three years until he and his fellow prisoners were "miraculously rescued" by paratroopers. Aside from an allusion to Browne lecturing internees on "Oriental Philosophy" and "the newer physics," no mention was made of those miracles rendered by Browne himself in the jungle camp.

Although Browne had briefly edited one of Garvey's newspapers, he was largely unknown in either the white or black press. But he remained a man on the move. In 1950, he and his wife, Cecilia, founded the Hermetic Society for World Service, a Theosophical-influenced religious order claiming guidance by the same Masters who had taught Blavatsky and Olcott. Browne died in 1978, but his Hermetic Society still has members in the United States and Latin America—it is headquartered in the Dominican Republic, where Browne had established a branch in 1970. Foremost in the order's founding statement, Browne called for "the protection of America, designated as the Grail in which will manifest the Great Cosmic Light which is destined to Illumine the whole world."

"Our beloved America," Browne wrote, is "the Future Holy Land" from which world enlightenment would arise. Until the very end, Robert T. Browne—a man born not twenty years after the end of slavery, a mystic whose cosmological work was quickly celebrated and just as quickly forgotten—was still defending his vision of America, a harsh, magical land filled with limitless hope.

CHAPTER SEVEN

THE RETURN OF THE "SECRET TEACHINGS"

✦ ✦ ✦

In this house I chanced to find a volume of the works of Cornelius Agrippa. I opened it with apathy; the theory which he attempts to demonstrate, and the wonderful facts which he relates, soon changed this feeling into enthusiasm. A new light seemed to dawn upon my mind; and, bounding with joy, I communicated my discovery . . .

—MARY SHELLEY, *FRANKENSTEIN*

Reference librarians had gotten accustomed to the hulking young man with the penetrating eyes and unstylishly long hair. Each day he entered the cavernous reading room of the New York Public Library and requested books that few others did: old works of esoteric lore, Hebrew Kabala, Hellenic mythology, Pythagorean mathematics, papyrus transcriptions, and the like. Day by day he sat silently, combing through curious volumes with clockwork precision.

It was the mid-1920s, the era of big money, bootlegged gin, and the Charleston—pleasures for which the precocious twenty-five-year-old cared little. Rather, the amateur scholar and some-time banking clerk was on a mission: to save the ancient wisdom teachings from obscurity in a world that he believed was going ethically illiterate.

He bore the stately name of Manly P. Hall. And though to many the young man laboring over ancient tomes might have seemed just one more eccentric who passed daily through the library's great doors, the book he was preparing would become one of the most unusual and accomplished studies of esoteric lore and literature in modern history.

The *Real* "Know-How"

In the years following World War I, when Theosophy and New Thought had directed fresh attention to occult philosophy and "secrets of the ages," a bevy of self-styled mystics and turbaned "scholars" produced thick works purporting to unlock hidden doctrines. Many were patchwork affairs, pieced together from Renaissance-era occult works, academic tracts on myth and symbol, and guides to folklore. The Chicago occult dealer L. W. de Laurence produced one of the most popular in 1919 with his *Great Book of Magical Art, Hindoo Magic & Indian Occultism,* an amalgam of pirated prose, clipped-and-pasted images, and muddled if sometimes earnest attempts at distilling Eastern religious practice and myth. Mail-order ads tantalized readers with *The* Real *"Know-How" of OCCULT, SPIRITUAL & MYSTIC FORMULAE,* as went a typical notice for the hoodoo-house author Lewis de Claremont.

Amid these forgotten offerings stands one study that eluded the empty promises of the day—a virtuoso guide to ancient and occult philosophies whose range and depth surpassed the holdings of many respected libraries. It was called by a breathless title: *AN ENCYCLOPEDIC OUTLINE OF MASONIC, HERMETIC, QABBALISTIC AND ROSICRUCIAN SYMBOLICAL PHILOSOPHY—Being an Interpretation of the Secret Teachings Concealed within the Rituals, Allegories and Mysteries of the Ages.* Or, as it became more simply known: *The Secret Teachings of All Ages.* Had it come from a retired classics professor or aged English antiquarian, the book might have been less surprising though still impressive. But it came from no such source. *The Secret Teachings of All Ages* was privately published in 1928 by the self-taught spiritual scholar Manly P. Hall, when he was twenty-seven years old.

From the start, *The Secret Teachings* was almost impossible to classify. Written and compiled on an Alexandrian scale, its hundreds of entries shone a rare light on some of the most fascinating and little-understood aspects of myth, religion, cosmology, and philosophy. Its breadth of subjects could astound: ancient mathematics; alchemical formulas; Hermetic doctrine; pagan rites; Hebrew number mysticism; the geometry of ancient Egypt; Native American myths; the uses of cryptograms; an analysis of the Tarot; the symbols of Masonry and Rosicrucianism; the esotericism of the Shakespearean dramas—these were just a few of Hall's topics. Initially bound in tabletop-sized dimensions, *The Secret Teachings* featured myriad illustrations, charts, tables, and diagrams, with varying rows of text and inset type, making the volume as jarring to the eye as a page of Babylonian Talmud. For students and enthusiasts of the arcane, the book was like an answered prayer. It sold tens of thousands of copies, often for more than $100, all out of sight of mainstream critics and booksellers, making it one of the most popular "underground" works in American history.

Hall's volume seemed the product of a whole lifetime—and a rare one at that—yet his twenty-seven years provided few clues to his virtuosity. He attended no university; his roots in rural Canada and the American West offered him little obvious exposure to higher learning; his youthful letters betrayed no special fluency with the complexities of the ancient world; his family tried to steer him into the more practical career of selling fire insurance; and one of his first forays into professional life was as a banking clerk—the "outstanding event of which," he recalled, "was witnessing a man depressed over investment losses take his life."

Even a generation later, the question reasserts itself on nearly every page of *The Secret Teachings:* How did this large-framed young man with little traditional education produce the last century's most original and masterly book on the esoteric wisdom of antiquity?

A Philosopher's Progress

During his life, Hall refused to discuss more than the most cursory aspects of his background. Although he wrote many thousands of articles, lectures, and pamphlets and dozens of books, his sole published biographical record is a thin volume called *Growing Up with Grandmother,* a tribute to the woman he called "Mrs. Arthur Whitney Palmer." (Her name was Florence Palmer.) Often written in hagiographic singsong anecdotes, the pamphlet-sized work is notable for what it reveals about Hall's reticence to broach virtually any intimacy of his childhood. Born at the close of the Victorian Era, he was a man marked by a period in which the details of private life were closely held.

Hall was born in the rural city of Peterborough, Ontario, on March 18, 1901, to a father who was a dentist and a mother who was a chiropractor. Hall's parents had separated while his mother was still pregnant, and the infant soon came into the care of his maternal grandmother. When the boy was two years old, Florence Palmer brought him to Sioux Falls, South Dakota, where they lived for several years. It could only have been a lonely existence: A sickly child, Hall saw little formal schooling and spent long hours reading voraciously on his own. His contact with other children was limited. But there was a spark of some indefinable brilliance in the youth, which his grandmother nurtured on trips to museums in Chicago and New York.

For a time, the boy and his grandmother lived in a high-end Chicago hotel, Palmer House, which was owned by relatives. There, Hall was mostly in the company of grown-ups, including a traditionally garbed Hindu maître d'hôtel, who taught him adult etiquette. Later on, the bookish adolescent was enrolled—briefly, to his almost certain relief—in a military school.

Tragedy struck early: His grandmother died when he was sixteen. He traveled to California to be with his mother and came under the influence of a self-styled Rosicrucian community in Oceanside, California. He lived at the Rosicrucian Fellowship, where he formed close relationships but also grew suspicious of the order's claims to ancient wisdom. Soon he moved on his own to Los Angeles, where he fell in with metaphysical seekers and discussion groups. In 1920, Hall began a precocious career in public speaking, giving an address on reincarnation in a small room above a Santa Monica bank. Word spread of the boy wonder's mastery of arcane and metaphysical subject matter. He began addressing a liberal evangelical congregation called the Church of the People, and quickly rose to the rank of minister.

In 1923, the *Los Angeles Times* seemed positively smitten with the twenty-two-year-old, covering his lectures and sermons in several articles. "He is tall," the *Times* reported on May 28, "with unusually broad shoulders—football shoulders—but he wears his curly, dark brown hair bobbed like a girl's, and even his face and eyes convey an almost feminine impression." In a practice that he would maintain for the rest of his life, the youth lectured from a wooden mission-style chair, enrapturing his listeners without physical movement or gesticulation. He promoted classical ethics as a balm for the torpor of contemporary life. "Let us remember, also," the young idealist told congregants,

> that our main problem with the criminal is to seek to adjust his motives and mode of thinking so that the same force and persistence which he uses to accomplish evil deeds will be turned to the accomplishment of worthy purposes. . . . Our hard pavements and stool lunch counters have a tendency, by playing havoc with the nervous constitution of man, to produce thieves, libertines, and murderers.

Hall had already begun attracting benefactors and traveling abroad in search of lost knowledge. Yet his early letters from

Japan, Egypt, China, and India were, in many respects, ordinary. They contained little of the eye-opening detail or wonder of discovery that one finds in the writings of other early-twentieth-century seekers encountering the East for the first time, such as legendary British soldier and writer T. E. Lawrence.

Like a bolt from the blue, however, a short work of immense power emerged from the young Hall—a book that seemed to prefigure the greater work that would come. In 1922, Hall produced a brief, luminescent gem on the mystery schools of antiquity, *Initiates of the Flame*. With ease and gracefulness, Hall wrote across a spectrum of subjects, describing Egyptian rites, Arthurian myths, and the practices of alchemy, revealing the psychological underpinnings of arcane methods. "Man has been an alchemist from the time when first he raised himself," Hall wrote. ". . . Experiences are the chemicals of life with which the philosopher experiments."

The book inaugurated Hall's collaboration with illustrator J. Augustus Knapp, whose watercolor plates would later run throughout *The Secret Teachings*. For the rest of Hall's career, his friend Knapp's work elicited cheers and groans among readers. Knapp's paintings were fanciful, Disneyesque, minutely detailed imaginings of ancient events, both playful yet surprisingly subtle, like the work of an occult Norman Rockwell.

A Fitful Idealist

Like many young artists, Hall felt himself a stranger to his times. He fretted over the Jazz Age giddiness and the hunger for money that he saw firsthand in his brief career at a New York brokerage firm before the Great Depression. In addition to witnessing a distraught investor's suicide, he recalled an elderly bookkeeper who was discovered dead at his desk after nearly a half century on the job. During a dangerous flu epidemic, Hall remembered, people trudged into work as though "devotion to the business was the symbol of true character."

The numbing influence Hall detected in high commerce was

not all that disturbed him. He bemoaned the phony "Mahatmas" who had begun hanging out shingles in large American cities—turbaned figures like Chicago's de Laurence who extolled Tibetan wisdom and "Hindoo" magic, often without having ventured beyond American shores. Hall later wrote:

> *Self-appointed teachers arose without adequate backgrounds, knowledge or credentials, and swept through the nation. . . . Glamorous ladies in thousand-dollar evening gowns, waving ostrich-plumed fans, taught "prosperity" to the hungry poor at twenty-five dollars a course. . . . Mysterious swamis, yogis, and the like entranced audiences of from two to four thousand at a meeting . . .*

Nor did he find succor in mainline religious scholarship, which, in his eyes, treated esoteric and primeval religions as museum pieces, not living philosophies with relevance for contemporary people. "With very few exceptions," Hall wrote, "modern authorities downgraded all systems of idealistic philosophy and the deeper aspects of comparative religion. Translations of classical authors could differ greatly, but in most cases the noblest thoughts were eliminated or denigrated . . . and scholarship was based largely upon the acceptance of a sterile materialism." Indeed, one of the period's most influential academic studies of myth and arcana, *The Golden Bough,* disparaged the meaning of its own subject matter: "In short, magic is a spurious system of natural law as well as a fallacious guide of conduct; it is a false science as well as an abortive art."

Barren religious scholarship, fake gurus, worship of mammon—wherever Hall looked, he was dismayed. *The Secret Teachings of All Ages* took shape in his mind as a way to reestablish a vital, living connection to the search for meaning that he believed characterized the academies of the ancient world. To signal how his approach differed from materialist scholarship, Hall quoted his philosophic hero, Francis Bacon, early in the massive work: "A little philosophy inclineth man's mind to atheism; but depth in philosophy bringeth men's minds about to religion."

The "Great Book" Appears

Hall's world travels in the early 1920s gave him some degree of proximity to the monuments and philosophies of antiquity. But the materials that finally made it possible for him to complete his book of wisdom were those he discovered in the great Western libraries just opening to widespread public use. Through the influence of benefactors—including General Sir Francis Younghusband, who led Britain's invasion of Tibet at the turn of the century—the budding scholar gained access to some of the rarest manuscripts at the British Museum. While living in New York in the mid-1920s, Hall found a resource to rival Britain's own: the vast beaux arts reading room of the New York Public Library.

Sitting at one of the huge oak tables that line the cathedral-size space, Hall toiled over books of myth and symbol just steps away from the Times Square razzmatazz that represented everything he chafed against. He amassed a bibliography of nearly one thousand entries. The books he requested were always available—at once a reminder and by-product of the general lack of interest in the topics he loved.

By mid-1928, having presold subscriptions for almost a thousand copies (and printing 1,200 more), Hall published what would become known as the "Great Book"—and it has never gone out of print since. While self-published and self-financed, and invisible to mainstream scholars, the book soared on the wings of enthusiastic reports from readers. Hall received a letter from the Crown Prince of Sweden praising the work. Freemasonic lodges everywhere bought copies, and to this day the book remains a standard in Masonic libraries. Its admirers ranged from General John J. Pershing, the ramrod-straight commander of American forces in World War I, to, a generation later, Elvis Presley, who possessed his own signed copy.

To enthusiasts of the esoteric, *The Secret Teachings* solidified

Hall's reputation as a scholar of mythic proportions. And it gave the young writer new clout in attracting benefactors. Hall collected enough money from his growing list of acolytes—including the wife of an L.A. oil tycoon and highly placed Freemasons (Hall joined Masonry himself in 1954)—to open an art-deco faux-Mayan campus in 1934 in the Griffith Park neighborhood of Los Angeles. Calling it the Philosophical Research Society, or PRS, Hall fancifully spoke of modeling his organization after the ancient mystery school of Pythagoras. More practically, PRS provided a cloistered setting where Hall spent the rest of his life teaching, writing, and assembling a remarkable collection of antique texts and devotional objects. His small campus eventually grew to include a fifty-thousand-volume library with catwalks and floor-to-ceiling shelves; a three-hundred-seat auditorium with a thronelike chair for the master teacher; a bookstore; a warehouse for the many titles he wrote and sold; a wood-paneled office (complete with a walk-in vault for antiquities); and a sunny stucco courtyard. Designed in an unusual pastiche of Mayan, Egyptian, and art-deco motifs, PRS became one of the most popular destinations for L.A.'s spiritually curious, and remains so.

After Hall's death on August 29, 1990, the idyllically self-contained campus barely survived simultaneous legal battles—one with Hall's widow, who claimed it owed her money, and another with an eccentric con artist who, in the estimation of a civil-court judge, had befriended an ailing octogenarian Hall to pilfer his antiques and assets. Hall signed over his estate to this shadowy "trustee" just six days before his passing. As will shortly be seen, the timing and other circumstances rendered Hall's death sufficiently suspicious for Los Angeles police to label the case as "open" for several years after.

The financial damage from these stormy years was irreversible. Following a protracted court battle in which a superior-court judge nullified Hall's will and turned over control of PRS from his dubious beneficiary to a group of longtime supporters, the nonprofit organization faced a crushing $2 million legal debt. To survive, it was forced to sell off some of its most

cherished items—including 234 alchemical, Hermetic, and Rosicrucian manuscripts to the Getty Museum in Los Angeles. Other
valuables, including 214 rare manuscripts that Hall had spent a
lifetime amassing, were delivered as part of a settlement to his
widow, who reportedly earmarked them for sale to a European
collector.

Its holdings permanently diminished, PRS regained fiscal
health beginning in 1993 under a new president, Obadiah
Harris, the man who had once been a protégé to Science of Mind
founder Ernest Holmes. Harris was now a religious scholar and
respected university administrator. He took the job for no salary.
Under Harris, PRS established a state-accredited "distance learning" university, which granted graduate degrees. The school fulfilled a goal that Hall had spoken of toward the end of his life.
Through both good times and bad, PRS kept in print the sump-
tuous, oversize editions of Hall's "Great Book."

Beginning in 2001, PRS partnered with a trade publisher to
create a newly designed "Reader's Edition" of *The Secret Teachings of All Ages,* a compact, textually unabridged version of
Hall's original.* Within a few years, the Reader's Edition had
entered more than sixteen printings, probably reaching more
readers than *The Secret Teachings* had throughout its previous
lifetime. More than a decade after his death, Hall had not only
eluded the obscurity that time held in store for most of his contemporaries but had became one of the few esoteric figures from
the twentieth century whose work grew in reach in the next.

A Private World

Hall wrote scores of other books over the course of his life and
composed literally thousands of pamphlets and articles. He is
estimated to have delivered about eight thousand lectures—

---

* This edition was published by the present author.

typically given without notes, recited with crystalline precision. Yet for all his output, Hall remained a riddle to those around him. Following his Sunday-morning lectures at PRS, he would promptly exit the auditorium from a side door, enter a car, and be driven back to his nearby house.

A first marriage in 1930 ended with his wife's suicide a little more than a decade later. He was into middle age in 1950 when he remarried, to a petite German–American divorcée, Marie Bauer. His second bride harbored a deep interest in the occult and an all-consuming belief that a buried vault in Williamsburg, Virginia, contained the secret mystical manuscripts of her and Hall's hero, the philosopher Francis Bacon. (Marie and her husband also considered Bacon the hidden genius behind the Shakespearean plays—a theory that Hall took considerable efforts to defend in his "Great Book.") Possessed of a mercurial temper and fierce determination, Marie Bauer was, in the eyes of some, a formidable equal to her imposing husband. To others, she raised the question of Hall's choice of companions. Marie was known for sharp mood swings and a dictatorial manner toward friends and guests who would venture near her husband. Two years after Hall's death, two acolytes of Marie's ideas were convicted of trespassing in Virginia's Bruton Parish churchyard, where they conducted an illegal dig for the mythical Bacon vault.

Unlike his histrionic wife and the many spiritual teachers who flocked to Hollywood, Hall showed relatively little interest in attracting publicity or hobnobbing with movie stars. Later in Hall's life, his best-known friend was the folksinger and balladeer Burl Ives, famous for his rendition of "Frosty the Snowman." Ives was also a fellow Freemason. Hall rarely involved himself in the movie business, though in 1938 he did contribute the story to a forgettable murder yarn with an astrological theme: *When Were You Born?* In a segment at the film's opening, a young Hall looks into the camera and explains to the audience the meaning of the zodiac signs.

In those instances when Hall did succumb to Hollywood glitz, the results were more humorous than glamorous. In 1940, an entertainment columnist reported that Hall—"famous Los Angeles student of occult sciences"—hypnotized actor Bela Lugosi for a death scene in a low-budget Lugosi–Boris Karloff vehicle called *Black Friday*. Universal Pictures trumpeted Lugosi's portrayal of a man suffocating to death in a closet as "the first scene ever filmed of a player under the influence of hypnotism." The movie trailer briefly showed an angular, mustached Hall sitting over Lugosi and waving his hands across the actor's face in the style of Mesmeric "passes" found in the books of Andrew Jackson Davis. Entertainment pages reported that Lugosi, hypnotically convinced he was in mortal danger, wrecked the movie set in a desperate fight to escape. The affair gave rise to an urban legend that Hall had hypnotized Lugosi before his legendary performance as Dracula.

Off the movie set, the Hungarian actor and Californian occultist became close friends. The two men bonded over their shared love for classical music, which they listened to together on phonograph records. In 1955, the seventy-three-year-old Lugosi wed his fifth bride at Hall's Hollywood home. Newspaper photos showed an ashen-faced Lugosi—the very image of Martin Landau's portrayal years later in the movie *Ed Wood*—clinking champagne glasses with his thirty-nine-year-old bride, a cutting-room clerk who met the actor while he was being treated for drug addiction. When it came to friendship, celebrity glamour was no requisite for entering Hall's world.

The Mystic in Decline

As an old man, Hall continued to sound much like he did as a young one. A year before his death, he fretted to a reporter that colleges produce "financially and academically successful students, but not good persons. They don't teach honor and integrity." At times he could disappoint New Age–era acolytes with chestnuts like: "Old-fashioned common sense is one of the most uncommon things we have." After Hall's death, the *Los Angeles*

Times offered an austere tribute: "Followers say he believed in reincarnation and in a mixture of the Golden Rule and living in moderation." In this sense, the prodigious scholar had fashioned the study of occult ideas into a search for ethical living.

If the point of all higher knowledge, as Hall saw it, was to refine and improve a person's life, his own existence would have to be judged a failure as often as a success. In his later years, Hall often slipped into a routine of doing that which he simply knew how to do: delivering another lecture, writing another book, and issuing another pamphlet. In an address at PRS in the closing years of his life, Hall sought to put forth a major statement on the social, political, and environmental threats facing America and the world. The physical frame and confident phrasing were still that of Hall, speaking extemporaneously for a long stretch, rarely shifting in his thronelike chair, and never losing a beat. Yet the content was tedium itself, filled with political bromides such as the need for environmental stewardship and the caretaking of democracy—points with which no sensible person could argue or fail to anticipate.

In the late 1980s, Hall appeared to lose his personal judgment and his ethical compass. He turned over all of his household and business affairs, and even his and PRS's financial assets, to a self-professed shamanic healer and reincarnate of Atlantis named Daniel Fritz. More prosaically, Fritz was known as a computer marketer, health-products entrepreneur, and, in the eyes of Hall's friends and colleagues, a grifter. Colleagues say Hall disregarded—and in one case even fired—longtime employees and associates who questioned the relationship. Even a seasoned superior-court judge found Fritz worthy of disdain. "Did Mr. Fritz effectively steal from Mr. Hall?" said Judge Harvey A. Schneider upon invalidating Hall's belatedly amended will. "I think the answer is clearly yes. The evidence is so overwhelming that Mr. Fritz exerted undue influence over Mr. Hall . . . the whole thing just doesn't pass any reasonable person's sniff test."

Ill and dangerously overweight in his final years, Hall had apparently bought in to Fritz's claims as a mystical healer and his

Barnum-like promises to spread the aged scholar's work across the world. One friend observed that Fritz did help Hall drop his weight from three hundred to two hundred pounds through diet and exercise, and relieved his painful constipation with the help of colonics. But in a troubling move, the eighty-nine-year-old Hall signed his estate over to Fritz less than a week before he died. It is tempting to speculate that the aged Hall suffered from senility, yet he delivered a typically well-attended lecture just days before his death. It was a death that Hall's widow, Marie, stoked intense concerns over, telling the *Los Angeles Times* in 1994: "I firmly believe it was murder."

She wasn't the only one. Investigators with the Los Angeles Police Department found the circumstances suspicious: Hall was alone with Fritz and Fritz's son when he died; hours passed before the death was reported; the body appeared to have been moved from the outdoors to inside; and there was the strange timing of the new will. Charges were never pursued, and, after Fritz's death from a rare form of cancer in 2001 and his son's death two years later from an autoimmune disorder linked to AIDS, the file was closed on Hall's death. The cause was listed as heart failure.

Aged, obese, and suffering from a strained heart, Manly P. Hall was probably not the victim of foul play, as friends feared, but his final days were still puzzling. One longtime friend of Hall's wondered how someone like Fritz could so suddenly grow "unduly influential over a man noted for his independence of thought and action." Hall's intimate companions—the shifty Fritz, the erratic Marie, the sometimes sycophantic staffers—all seemed to point to a man who proved a poor judge of where to place trust. The wisdom that Hall had cultivated his whole life appeared to abandon him when its fortification was most needed. As though prophesying his own decline, Hall wrote in the *PRS Journal* in 1986: "Noble thoughts out of context lost most of their protective meanings."

For all his emphasis on the practicality of ancient wisdom, Hall's life, in some respects, was a case in point of a truth not found in his writings: A person can accumulate the "wisdom of the ages"—gleaning knowledge from the greatest books, lectures, and research—with none of it penetrating one's self. That perplexity of human nature, a puzzle at the heart of all ethical philosophies, seems never to have occurred to him.

The Enduring Value of *The Secret Teachings*

"Every writer," literary critic Irving Howe once noted, ". . . must be read and remembered for his best work." So it is with Manly P. Hall. The depth of Hall's early achievement remains undiminished—and throws an observer back to the question: How did a modest young man complete what can be considered a one-of-a-kind codex to the ancient occult and esoteric traditions of the world, all by age twenty-seven, with little traditional education? To read Hall's "Great Book" is to experience a readerly joy rarely associated with ordinary compendiums of intellectual or religious history—its depth, breadth, and detail are, simply put, not ordinary and not easily understood.

In an obscure astrology magazine of the 1940s, an Indian journalist wrote a personal profile of Hall, which held an interesting, if somewhat fanciful, passage:

> The question is constantly asked on all sides as to how Mr. Hall can know and remember so much on so many different and difficult subjects. . . . Perhaps a direct answer to this constant question may be discovered in the following episode in the life of Mr. Hall himself: The first question Mr. Claude Bragdon, American mystic,* asked Mr. Hall after their first meeting in New York in 1937 was:
>
> "Mr. Hall, how do you know so much more about the mathematics of Pythagoras than even the authorities on the subject?"

---

* Bragdon was not a mystic but rather an accomplished architect and publisher, who served as a prod and muse to many twentieth-century metaphysical writers.

> *Standing beside both these dear American friends of mine, I was wondering with trepidation in my heart what reply Mr. Hall would make.*
>
> *"Mr. Bragdon," answered Mr. Hall quickly, unhesitatingly, and with a simultaneous flash of smile in his eyes and on his lips, "you are an occult philosopher. You know that it is easier to know things than to know how one knows those things."*

To the question of how Hall achieved what he did, his most fervent admirers suggest that he was born with knowledge from other lifetimes; others believe he had a photographic memory. In the end, perhaps one can only conclude such a question with still more questions. But the accomplishment of *The Secret Teachings* is finally this: It was the only serious, comprehensive codex of its era that took the world of myth and symbol on its own terms. Hall peered into sources that many historians refused to consider—from Masonic and Rosicrucian tracts to alchemical and astrological works—and recent scholarship has justified some of his historical conclusions. Up through the late twentieth century, most classical scholars would have considered Hall's descriptions of oracular rites at Delphi as near fairy tale, with their portraits of soldiers and statesmen visiting an intoxicated trance medium seated on a tripodlike throne above a smoky crevice in a cave. Yet Hall's portrayal, based on esoteric source literature, has since been validated by early-twenty-first-century geological and archaeological finds at Delphi.

Hall was not a writer who sifted through and repeated accounts that others had written. His chapters on Pythagorean mathematics displayed graceful ease over vast complexities, capturing the essence and splendor the ancient sage had discovered in the geometry of the natural world. Likewise, Hall cataloged and analyzed the complex symbols and ideas of alchemy, the arcane practice that formed the basis for modern chemistry.

While *The Secret Teachings of All Ages* has always been ignored within academia, it influenced some who chose more-traditional scholarly paths than Hall's. The University of Chicago historian of ancient religion Mircea Eliade, whose work brought new respect to the study of Gnostic and esoteric belief systems in the twentieth century, confided to friends that as a young man it was Hall's book that awoke in him the love of myth and symbol.

Hall was able to reach hungry young minds because he never lost his own sense of youthful idealism and wonder over the esoteric cultures he observed. He clarified ancient ideas that could otherwise seem beyond reach, writing not as a distant judge but as a lover of the rites and mysteries embodied in the old ways.

CHAPTER EIGHT

NEW DEAL OF THE AGES

Politics and the Occult

+ + +

*People that are really very weird can get into sensitive
positions and have a tremendous impact on history.*

—VICE PRESIDENT DAN QUAYLE ON THE CAREER
OF RUSSIAN OCCULTIST GRIGORI RASPUTIN

It was a case study in how rumors start. At the beginning of an
anxious summer in 1968, in a nation that had just experienced
the murders of Martin Luther King, Jr., and Bobby Kennedy,
writer and raconteur Truman Capote made strange pronouncements about a link between the killings. Since the 1966 publication of *In Cold Blood*, Capote had become sought after as an
expert on the criminal mind, and on June 21, 1968, he was making one of his first appearances on NBC's *Tonight Show*. From
a live studio in New York City, he told host Johnny Carson of a
chilling hypothesis: The assassination of both leaders was part of
an occult–political conspiracy, the aim of which was to ignite a
violent overthrow of the American government.

Within the writings of Theosophy's Madame Blavatsky,
Capote explained, "was a theory of how you could undermine
the morale of a country and create a vacuum for revolution by
systematically assassinating a series of prominent people." The

murderers themselves, he surmised, may have been brainwashed sleeper agents, of the sort found in *The Manchurian Candidate*. As a tantalizing bit of proof, Capote noted that Kennedy's killer, Sirhan Sirhan, had requested (and received) from his jailers Blavatsky's 1888 tome, *The Secret Doctrine*.

The writer's remarks got picked up in newspapers and magazines, launching stories that the Russian madame had written a "Manual for Revolution," now being used by leftist guerrillas in America. The ultraright-wing John Birch Society, in what must have been its one and only political alignment with the chic New York writer, purchased full-page ads in California newspapers decrying the long-dead Blavatsky as a force for violent revolution.

Capote's theory was almost total imagination. There was no "Manual for Revolution," nor had any such idea ever appeared in Blavatsky's writing. It was correct that Sirhan had requested Blavatsky's exegesis of occult philosophy and lost civilizations, *The Secret Doctrine*. He had also requested a far more obscure 1922 Theosophical text, *Talks On: At the Feet of the Master.* The latter was a series of commentaries by a leading English Theosophist, Charles Webster Leadbeater, on an earlier work, *At the Feet of the Master,* by the young Indian spiritual teacher Jiddu Krishnamurti.* Nothing in any of the books even hinted at political violence or the overthrow of governments. In particular, the Leadbeater and Krishnamurti volumes proffered homily-like messages of self-sacrifice and humble living, no more challenging to worldly powers than the sermons of the Publick Universal Friend had been generations earlier.

The Blavatsky–Sirhan affair was, however, typical of how ready people were to believe in whispers of an occult conspiracy behind world events. And such credulity was not entirely without reason. In modern Europe, seers and men of magic had been known to advise the powerful. In the years leading up to World War I, the Russian imperial court was famously enthralled and

---

* Sirhan's reading habits also included the Rosicrucian literature of California's Ancient and Mystical Order Rosae Crucis, or AMORC. But he was dropped from its membership rolls after neglecting to pay a $2 lesson fee.

repelled by the presence of the Siberian mystic–healer Grigori Rasputin, who wielded enormous personal influence over the czarina. To the magus's enemies, who eventually murdered him, Rasputin was a debauched charlatan with an unnatural hold over royal affairs (though this wasn't so much the case that the czar would heed his most prophetic advice—to keep out of the war).

Arcane influences were not confined to foreign courts alone. America, too, saw a man of veritable occult tendencies at the highest levels of power—yet this figure was as dramatically different from the shadowy Rasputin as his home state of Iowa was from Siberia. He was a corn breeder, an intellectual searcher, and a farmer—a man Jimmy Stewart could have played had his life ever come to film. His career illuminates connections between modern occultism and politics that, in their way, were more remarkable—if less salacious—than anything fantasy could conjure.

"He's Not a Mystic"

By the 1940 Democratic National Convention in Chicago, Franklin Roosevelt had cut ties with his then vice president, John Nance Garner. The tough-talking Texan had opposed Roosevelt's pursuit of an unprecedented third term. Behind the scenes, the president determined that a new running mate had to be a true-blue supporter of the waning New Deal, someone who could rally disparate constituencies from big-city unionists to heartland farmers. He opted for a man who had initially joined his cabinet as a Republican but had since become a hero to liberals: the farm-bred, intellectually driven Secretary of Agriculture Henry A. Wallace. "He's honest," FDR said of the Iowan. "He thinks right. He's a digger."

It couldn't be done, argued Democratic National Committee Chairman Jim Farley. Wallace was just too, well, weird. He had been a Theosophist, for God's sake—and was known for his interest in astrology, reincarnation, Eastern religions, Native American mysticism, and occultism. While professorial in demeanor and possessed of scrubbed Midwestern looks, Wallace could shock Washington dinner-party habitués by describing how he cured his headaches by rubbing a Tibetan amulet on his forehead.

Farley recalled a tense exchange in his memoirs. "The people look on him as a mystic," Farley complained to the president.

"He's not a mystic," Roosevelt snapped. "He's a philosopher. He's got ideas. He thinks right. He'll help the people think."

In fact, Wallace did have ideas—extraordinary ones that helped save American agriculture during the Great Depression. The third-generation editor of a family-run farm journal, *Wallaces' Farmer,* and also the son of the secretary of agriculture in the Republican Warren Harding's administration, Wallace knew how to get things done on a farm. When farmers' incomes plummeted at the start of the Roosevelt presidency, Wallace pushed major innovations, such as high-yield seed, soil conservation, planting rotations, and curbs on overproduction. His reforms were credited with saving thousands of family farms during the Great Depression. To historian Arthur Schlesinger, Jr., Wallace was "the best secretary of agriculture the country has ever had." Wallace was a success in business too. His talents for biogenetics and crop hybridization made the ardent New Dealer a wealthy man through the launch of a seed company familiar to many people who had never set foot on a farm: Pioneer Hi-Bred.

In political and private life, Wallace's success seemed to arise from the unconventional broadness in how he defined himself. He wasn't a farmer or a businessman, a publisher or a politician, a Republican or a Democrat. He was, above all, a seeker. "Fundamentally," he told a friend, "I am . . . a searcher for methods of bringing the 'inner light' to outward manifestation and raising outward manifestation to the inner light." He freely connected his metaphysical interests to his public work: "Religion is a method whereby a man reaches out toward God in an effort to find the spiritual power to express here on earth in a practical way the divine potentialities in himself and his fellow beings."

FDR got his man. The farmer–seeker–statesman won the convention's approval, even as some grumbled that Wallace was too liberal and too strange. After FDR's reelection, Wallace seemed to have greatness in reach. He developed a reputation as the New Deal's Renaissance man and the administration's philosopher-in-residence. He maintained a frenetic speaking schedule and, through his public appearances and personal popularity, held together critical elements of the New Deal coalition, ranging from Southern blacks to Midwestern farmers to Northeastern intellectuals. He was even discussed as a potential successor to FDR.

But it was Roosevelt's final vice president and the man who replaced Wallace—Harry Truman—who instead became a household name, while few today remember Henry A. Wallace. And in this turn of events, Jim Farley's initial misgivings about the farmbelt mystic may have been correct.

A Searcher for the Infinite

Wallace freely called himself a "practical mystic." His interest in esoteric philosophy came as the result of a long and considered journey, and he often seemed baffled that others could not respect the seriousness of his search.

As a young man growing up in Des Moines, Iowa, he left the Presbyterianism of his youth to journey through the various occult and metaphysical systems, from Theosophy to Native American shamanism. In high school in the early 1900s, he hungrily took in William James's classic of comparative religion, *The Varieties of Religious Experience*—a volume marked by the deep interest with which the philosopher viewed New Thought, mental healing, and other metaphysical strains. Wallace read Ralph Waldo Emerson and took a particular interest in the work of the twentieth-century metaphysician named for him: Ralph Waldo Trine, author of the inspirational best seller *In Tune with the Infinite*. Trine's idea of the mind as a material, creative force deeply touched the young Wallace. But it was Theosophy that placed the deepest mark on his expanding worldview.

Around 1919, when Wallace was entering his thirties, he attended a meeting of the Des Moines Theosophical lodge. And by 1925 he had become active in the Liberal Catholic Church, a movement closely linked with Theosophy and founded by one of its most colorful and controversial leaders, the English author Charles Webster Leadbeater. The Liberal Catholic Church was designed as an alternative to the Anglican and Catholic Churches: It practiced traditional Christian liturgy and the Mass but permitted worshippers the freedom—very much in the vein of Theosophy—to acknowledge and pursue truths in all the world's religions. The church's doctrine noted: "There is a 'communion of Saints' or Holy Ones, who help mankind, also a ministry of Angels." This cracked open the door for belief in the hidden Masters spoken of in Theosophy. For several years, the Liberal Catholic Church was Wallace's spiritual home—he performed elements of the service, wore vestments, and helped organize its Des Moines branch. He left by 1930, after the reemergence of one of many scandals over Leadbeater's intimacies with underage boys.

Following in the footsteps of his father, Wallace also joined Freemasonry, in which he attained all but the order's highest rank. In the early 1930s, he entered a serious study of astrology, trying to determine if heavenly phenomena could predict the weather for farmers. In a way, his inquiry wasn't terribly foreign to the world of farmer's almanacs in which he was raised. Many planting almanacs in the nineteenth and early twentieth centuries featured lore on how the moon and planets affected weather patterns and included zodiacal information on the earth's position amid the constellations. In some respects, Wallace's inquiry into the occult—as into new farming methods—represented a deepened study into all that existed around him while he was growing up.

Indian rituals were another subject of fascination. In 1931 he grew close with a "medicine man"—a white Minnesotan poet and composer named Charles Roos. Roos studied Indian mysticism, of which he considered himself a master. Through Roos, Wallace began to believe that he might have had a past life as an Indian brave, a theory he determined to explore. In 1932, Franklin Roosevelt, then governor of New York, invited the respected agriculturalist to his Hyde Park home for a getting-to-know-you session. Wallace was thrilled to accept. "There was, however, another reason the invitation delighted him," wrote Wallace biographers John C. Culver and John Hyde, "and Roosevelt would have been flabbergasted by it. He saw the trip as an opportunity to explore American Indian religion and search for a past life in which he and Charles Roos roamed together as warriors." And, indeed, Wallace did spend some time with elders of the Onondaga tribe in the environs of New York's Burned-Over District, northwest of Hyde Park. The tribal elders apparently confirmed his past-life recollections and initiated him into their mysteries, including in the use of "true Indian tobacco," wrote Culver and Hyde.

But all of this was a prelude to Wallace's brief, though intense, involvement with the Russian émigré, artist, and mystical philosopher Nicholas Roerich. It began in full in 1933, the year that marked Wallace's ascendancy to Roosevelt's cabinet. It was a relationship that produced bracingly original political ideas—and that would later haunt and damage Wallace's political career beyond recovery.

"Dear Guru"

Nicholas Roerich was many things: a spiritual writer and philosopher, a Theosophist, a distinguished set designer who collaborated with composer Igor Stravinsky, and a modernist painter whose work captured Russian churches and Buddhist monasteries in a way that revealed stark similarities between the composition of Western and Eastern holy sites. He was also a self-styled cultural ambassador who appeared on the New York scene in the 1920s, where he attracted a great deal of attention and patronage, including from Governor Franklin D. Roosevelt, who met with him in 1929. Roerich had an intriguing idea for establishing a worldwide treaty to protect cultural sites and artifacts during war. He designed a three-ringed flag intended to fly above great monuments to signal their being off-limits to bombers and invaders, in the fashion of the Red Cross insignia.

Most historians and journalists scornfully recall Roerich

as a makeshift mystic and con artist who managed to get Roosevelt, Wallace, and others to bankroll his schemes. But the Banner of Peace flags and the Roerich Pact, as the proposed treaty was known, attracted widespread attention among serious people, like Wallace, and represented a prescient, even pioneering, effort at international law. For Wallace, the treaty took a mystical principle—unity among the world's religions and artistic expressions—and sought to apply it on the political stage. At the high-water mark of Roerich's influence, FDR commissioned Wallace to sign the Roerich Pact on behalf of the United States, which Wallace proudly did at a White House ceremony on April 15, 1935, with FDR and signatories from several Latin American nations looking on. While other nations followed suit, the treaty was acted on only spottily.

Wallace's relationship with Roerich brought out a less attractive side of the agriculturalist, however. As though in rebellion against his straightforward Midwest persona, Wallace displayed a weakness for the kinds of secrecy and spiritual theatrics found within the European occult—traits that Roerich reveled in. The pale Russian often scowled before cameras in Oriental robes and a Fu Manchu–style beard, resembling the Hollywood image of a mystic. (In fact, Roerich's tales of his faraway Asian travels are often rumored to have influenced the popular novel and Frank Capra film *Lost Horizon,* which depicted a mythical land of Shangri-La tucked deep in the Himalayas.) In the early 1930s, Roerich bestowed on his friend Wallace an initiate name, "Galahad"—after the Arthurian knight—and Wallace then used his *nom de mystique* to sign dramatic, imagery-laden letters to Roerich.

"Dear Guru," began one of the most oft-quoted and enigmatic, in 1933, "I have been thinking of you holding the casket—the sacred most precious casket. And I have thought of the New Country going forth to meet the seven stars under the sign of the three stars. And I have thought of the admonition 'Await the Stone.'" Imbued with the insider jargon of the Roerich circle, Wallace's letters could sound like scenarios from the fantasy role-playing game Dungeons & Dragons. Wallace's love for mythical terms and code words spilled over into White House correspondence to FDR. This 1935 note from Wallace to Roosevelt probably ranks as one of the oddest interoffice memos in White House history:

> *I feel for a short time yet that we must deal with the "strong ones," the "turbulent ones," the "fervent ones," and perhaps even with a temporary resurgence, with the "flameless ones," who with the last dying gasp will strive to reanimate their dying giant "Capitalism." Mr. President, you can be the "flaming one," the one with an ever-upsurging spirit to lead into the time when the children of men can sing again.*

On one such occasion, FDR was reported to remark, "By God! What's the matter with Wallace?" An undersecretary joked, "I don't dare let a Theosophist in to see Henry—he'd give him a job right away." Wallace cooled suspicions by breaking with Roerich in the fall of 1935, just months after the signing of the Roerich Pact. The mystic and his son had turned a White House–funded agricultural expedition to Mongolia into an international charade in which Roerich proved more interested in political skulduggery than gathering strains of drought-resistant grass. For inscrutable reasons of his own, Roerich managed to pick up an armed band of White Russian Cossacks on the Mongolian frontier, whom he led on a traverse of Russo–Asian borderlands, alarming Soviet, Chinese, and Japanese authorities. The ill-defined detour got Roerich branded as everything from a White Russian spy to a general pest meddling in Eurasian hot spots. White House colleagues were relieved when Wallace finally ordered the mission to an end and cut all ties with Roerich.

The Eye and the Pyramid

The last thing Wallace wanted was for his spiritual interests to cast a shadow over his cabinet duties. But slowly that shadow began to fall, even while his political influence continued to rise.

In his own oral histories of the White House years, Wallace proudly took credit for calling to Roosevelt's attention the little-known image of the eye and pyramid on the back of the Great Seal of the United States and suggesting that it be used on currency. From America's founding up through the New Deal era, the Great Seal had been used mostly for treaties and other official government business and was an unfamiliar ceremonial insignia when it first caught Wallace's attention in 1934. He considered its Latin maxim, *Novus Ordo Seclorum*—New Order of the Ages—as translatable to *New Deal of the Ages*. At the signing of the Roerich Pact, Wallace spoke of the need for a "spiritual New Deal," one that "places that which is fine in humanity above that which is low and sordid and mean and hateful and grabbing." Roosevelt, himself a Freemason, was not uncomfortable with portentous symbols and grand imagery. Wallace recalled that when he raised the issue of using the image, Roosevelt

> *was first struck with the representation of the "All-Seeing Eye," a Masonic representation of The Great Architect of the Universe. Next he was impressed with the idea that the foundation for the new order of the ages had been laid in 1776 but that it would be completed only under the eye of the Great Architect.*

According to surviving records, FDR personally supervised the placement of the heraldic imagery on the back of the dollar bill in 1935, handwriting instructions to reposition the "pyramid" side (the seal's reverse) in front of the "eagle" side (the seal's obverse) so that the eye and pyramid would appear first when reading the bill from left to right. Thus most Americans, intentionally or not, were left with the impression that the mysterious pyramid and its heralding of a "new order" were the foremost symbols of the American republic, rather than the more ordinary eagle and shield.

Treasury Secretary Henry M. Morgenthau was displeased with the whole affair. He suspected Wallace's "strange mystical drives," as he recalled in his memoirs, and questioned his motives. "It was not till later," an unhappy Morgenthau recalled in *Collier's* magazine in 1947, "that I learned that the pyramid . . . had some cabalistic significance for members of a small religious sect," by which he meant the Roerich circle. Morgenthau was actually mistaken in connecting the eye and pyramid to Roerich. But it was the kind of judgment that was taking hold and falsely cementing the belief that Wallace was a propagandist for esoteric causes.

After Wallace's nomination for the vice presidency, rumors arose about the "Dear Guru" letters, and members of the Roerich circle may have been responsible for several that were leaked to the press. But the White House managed to keep the matter quiet, suggesting behind the scenes that no such correspondence was trustworthy—especially coming from Roerich, who at that point was under investigation by the Internal Revenue Service. The matter died and Wallace avoided embarrassment. He was a popular vice president, but by 1943 he began to face political losses. As head of the Board of Economic Warfare, Wallace wanted guarantees of fair wages and working conditions for foreign workers producing the raw materials for America's munitions industry. It was another early attempt at international lawmaking, this time pertaining to global labor standards. But foes in the administration and Congress fought the measures, and Wallace's initiative floundered when Roosevelt failed to back him. Sensing a more conservative national mood in 1944, Roosevelt was willing to let his vice president twist in the wind. Conservatives and political bosses wanted Wallace off the next presidential ticket, and Roosevelt issued only the most tepid of defenses. While Wallace was greeted with thunderous cheers at the 1944 nominating convention in Chicago, political insiders maneuvered against him. The Missourian Harry Truman was nominated in Wallace's place. When a somewhat bewildered Truman approached Wallace to ask whether the two men could still be considered friends, Wallace smiled and replied, "Harry, we are both Masons."

The years that followed were punishing ones for Wallace. Although he was awarded the enticing consolation of becoming secretary of commerce in the final Roosevelt administration, Wallace first saw the job's power reduced and then he lost it after FDR's death, when Truman removed him. Embittered by the experience and alarmed at the decline of New Deal influence in the White House, Wallace determined to mount a progressive challenge to Truman's reelection. In 1948, he ran for president under the ticket of the leftist Progressive Party. Democrats feared that Wallace could rally the New Deal faithful and steer the election away from Truman, perhaps introducing a real third-party force into national politics. But for Wallace the whole episode amounted to one last political loss when his "Dear Guru" letters finally came to light.

"Am I in America?"

The jaunty right-wing columnist Westbrook Pegler—widely read in newspapers through the Hearst syndicate—had managed to obtain a cache of Wallace's letters, probably from the hands of the jilted Roerich's followers. Pegler used them over a period of months in 1948 to steadily bury the liberal icon, routinely goading the former vice president with names like "Old Bubblehead" and "drooling mystic." Wallace unintentionally assisted Pegler's efforts by refusing to confirm whether he had penned the letters to Roerich, which served only to deepen suspicions that Wallace had something to hide.

To worsen matters, Wallace's upstart Progressive Party was heavily staffed by members of the Communist Party U.S.A., an open secret that seemed lost on no one but the candidate himself. When Wallace spoke around the nation, he sometimes attracted hostile crowds, especially in the South, where members of his integrated campaign staff were harassed, beaten, and in one case even stabbed. To admirers, Wallace remained a liberal lion: He refused to address segregated crowds, openly violated Jim Crow laws, and often slept in the homes of black supporters. He stood up to audiences that jeered him or pelted him with tomatoes and eggs and sometimes needed an armed guard to walk up to rostrums amid shoves and boos. "Am I in America?" he once challenged a riotous crowd in 1948. For all the physical bravery of his campaign, however, his candidacy fizzled.

Afterward, Wallace continued to travel internationally and maintained correspondence with world leaders. But mostly he retired from public life at his experimental farm, called Farvue, in Westchester County, New York. Some may have imagined it to be the place where Wallace was most comfortable, amid his plants and books. For Wallace, though, esoteric philosophy and intellectual searching were never retreats from life but ways to see justice carried into the world. Looking back on his spiritual explorations, he said, "Karma means that while things may not balance out in a given lifetime, they balance out in the long run in terms of justice between individuals, between man and the whole. It seems to me one of the most profound of all religious concepts. To that extent, I'm everlastingly grateful to the Theosophists."

Seven Minutes in Eternity

It would be comforting to conclude that the intellect and integrity of Henry A. Wallace represented the occult's chief expression in American politics. But at the same time as Wallace made his political rise, his career was paralleled by that of another man of mystical leanings—but one with far darker intent. He was one of the nation's most notorious hate leaders: an avid admirer of Hitler, the organizer of America's prototype neo-Nazi order, a literary influence on the anti-Semitism of poet Ezra Pound, and a popular writer who reported receiving "hyperdimensional instruction" from "Spiritual Mentors." He met them during an out-of-body experience in 1928, which he wrote about for a large and enthusiastic audience. In fact, if this man hadn't become a neo-Nazi, he might have been remembered as one of the liveliest metaphysical authors of the twentieth century. Instead, his name—William Dudley Pelley—is remembered today only on the grimmest fringes of white supremacy, a movement that he helped style.

Pelley was the rarest of political animals: a hatemonger with actual talent. Before his turn to fringe politics in the 1930s, he was a prolific journalist and successful short-story writer. First in 1920 and again in 1930, he won the O. Henry Award for short fiction. For this largely self-taught son of a minister, sent early to work during a hard-knock childhood in Lynn, Massachusetts, it was a remarkable achievement.

Most of Pelley's short fiction centered on the struggles and quiet nobility of life in his mythical hamlet of Paris, Vermont—an idealized, pathos-free version of William Faulkner's Yoknapatawpha County. His later turn to anti-Semitism and racialist politics was visible in his writing only in flippant asides or oddly couched phrases—the kind of soft bigotry or ill humor that was sufficiently common at the time to be overlooked, if not for what was to follow later. His 1930 O. Henry Award–winning short story, "The Continental Angle," which appeared in August 1929 in the *Chicago Tribune,* described the ordeal of a Germanic bakery owner facing bigotry and "cheap patriotism" during a tide of anti-German attitudes at the start of World War I. Portraying a Prussian shopkeeper as the victim of hate in 1929, when the nationalist tide had begun to rise in Europe, suggested an unusual sympathy.

Pelley's career went beyond the printed page. He spent the 1920s as a successful Hollywood screenwriter, penning a string of studio vehicles at the height of the silent-film era. In Pelley's high mark as a screenwriter, two of his films featured horror pioneer Lon Chaney. In 1922's *The Light in the Dark,* the changeling actor played a heart-of-gold hoodlum who steals the Holy Grail in order to heal an injured girl. Better remembered is *The Shock* from 1923, for Chaney's performance as a crippled hit man compelled to reevaluate his life. The screenwriter and actor became good friends for the rest of the decade.

Pelley's public profile took an immense leap in March 1929 with the publication of a hugely popular article on the cover of

The American Magazine: "Seven Minutes in Eternity—the Amazing Experience that Made Me Over." Pelley depicted a quiet spring night in 1928 in which a near-death experience transported him to the regions of the spirit world. As he described it, the evening began ordinarily enough—that is, if your idea of ordinary includes falling asleep over a book on "ethnology" in an isolated California bungalow with only the company of a massive police dog. Between three and four A.M., the dozing Pelley let loose a "ghastly inner shriek": *I'm dying! I'm dying!,* as he plunged through "cool, blue space." The fall was followed by a frantic whirling, similar, he recalled, to when he had been in an airplane over San Francisco that went into a tailspin and almost crashed into the Golden Gate. Just as suddenly, "someone reached out, caught me, stopped me." It was two people—"two strong-bodied, kindly-faced young men in white uniforms not unlike those worn by internees in hospitals." They laid him naked on a "beautiful marble-slab pallet" and began to massage and talk reassuringly to him.

This was Pelley's first encounter with the "Spiritual Mentors" who tutored him, as they would many times in the years ahead, on karma, reincarnation, and the realities of the afterlife. Only later would their ideas turn political. Revived by the "cool, steadying pressure of my friends' hands," the nude Pelley was gently directed to bathe in a soothing marble pool. The magical waters seemed to remove his sense of nakedness, and he then strolled through the illuminated Roman porticos of the Higher Realm, where he encountered "saintly, attractive, magnetic folk . . . no misfits, no tense countenances, no sour leers, no preoccupied brusqueness or physical handicap." *How happy everybody seems!* he inwardly exclaimed. Suddenly he was surrounded by a "swirl of bluish vapor" and he floated up, once more launched through space. He then heard a mechanical *click* in his body—"the best analogy is the sound my repeating deer-rifle makes when I work the ejector mechanism"—which signaled his return to his physical form. The writer shot up in bed and yelled: "That wasn't a dream!"

Pelley told readers that the experience had remade him into

a more peaceful, loving person whose sharper edges had been smoothed by his contact with his spirit brothers. In the months ahead, he said, his nerves calmed, he stopped smoking (until the higher Mentors told him that tobacco helped free his subconscious), he was kinder to editors, business associates, and neighbors. Weirdly enough, all of them—and even total strangers—seemed mysteriously to want to *help* him.

If not quite the first, "Seven Minutes in Eternity" was certainly the nation's most influential tale of near-death experience. Given that *The American Magazine* reached over 2.2 million subscribers, Pelley's article, surmised historian Scott Beekman, "became one of the most widely read accounts of paranormal activity in American history." In effect, it introduced the near-death narrative into mass culture, where it later became a mainstay of daytime television and best-seller lists.* The article generated tens of thousands of letters from readers anxious to learn more. And no wonder: As a piece of writing, Pelley's account towered above the day's typically hackneyed narratives of metaphysical journeying. With its heavenly Mentors in a Romanesque portico reassuring a stunned earthman, the story of "Seven Minutes in Eternity" seemed to prefigure the reassuringly familiar aliens and life-affirming metaphysics of a *Star Trek* episode. Would only it had the same happy ending.

Somewhere between Pelley's out-of-body experience and the triumph of the fascist ideologies of the 1930s, something in the writer's outlook became terribly, tragically twisted. His gifts for crafting a memorable phrase were abruptly refocused on producing some of the darkest anti-Semitic tracts in American history. The vehicle for his hatred was a mystico-political magazine he founded, *Liberation*. And he did more than just write: By 1933, acting under "clairaudient" instructions from his cosmic Mentors, Pelley started the Silver Shirts, a paramilitary neo-Nazi order that served as a template for some of the worst hate groups of the twentieth century.

---

* The term *near-death experience* entered the popular lexicon in 1975, when physician Raymond A. Moody, Jr., used it in his book *Life After Life*.

What had happened to the man who spent "Seven Minutes in Eternity"?

"Something Clicked in My Brain!"

To behold the large photograph of Pelley's face as it appeared with his *American Magazine* piece, one would never imagine the career in front of him. The writer of "Seven Minutes" looked trusting, mild, relaxed, with gentle features and softly graying hair—so much the image of a small-town druggist from one of his Paris, Vermont, stories. Within a few years, however, Pelley appeared transformed: Photographs showed his goateed face squinting and scowling and his diminutive five-foot-seven-inch frame decked out in a paramilitary uniform of pantaloons, a silver shirt, and a leather band strapped across his chest. By 1939, his icy visage on a sheriff's *WANTED* poster in North Carolina—where he was convicted of securities fraud—reveals a contrast that is so dramatic, so Jekyll-and-Hyde in nature, that it would have intrigued the master of disguise himself, Lon Chaney.

A few hints to the Pelley mystery appear in material that had been cut from the article-length version of his astral adventure and that Pelley later restored in his "unabridged" (though actually carefully and selectively edited) book-length version. In the longer version, Pelley professed fascination with "racial urges" and how they shaped history. He groused, even in the published article, over "unfriendly bankers" and "the swarming millions of Asia." Pelley later disclosed—though it is difficult to tell when he is revealing his past attitudes versus projecting his later ones backward—that during his trip to the higher realms the Spiritual Mentors explained the true nature of human races: "They're great classifications of humanity epitomizing gradations of spiritual development, starting with the black man and proceeding upwards in cycles to the white."

As the 1930s began, Pelley led something of a double life. Best known as the author of "Seven Minutes in Eternity," he became

a kind of Spiritual Mentor himself, publishing mystical magazines and newsletters and running Galahad College, a small
metaphysical school in Asheville, North Carolina. But, as directed by the Mentors, he explained, he was also studying
the career of Adolf Hitler—with fascination and awe. In 1932,
Pelley reported a clairaudient message from his Higher Mentors:
"We are presenting through you and your fellows of Our Order
the complete delineation of a New World Society, politically, so-
ciologically, and religiously . . ." When Hitler secured the German chancellery on January 30, 1933, Pelley recorded in his
memoirs, "Something clicked in my brain!" On January 31, he
sprang into action. Pelley transformed the large mailing lists of
his magazines and his correspondence courses into a radically
different enterprise: the Silver Legion of America, a paramilitary
order that would weigh in on "the ultimate contest between
Aryan mankind and Jewry." Some of his spiritual students fled,
others remained, and many newcomers joined for the new line
that Pelley, or the "beloved Chief," was now peddling: hatred of
Jewry and support for Hitler.

The Silver Shirt Legion's popularity was centered mainly on
the West Coast. It engaged only sporadically in armed training—
though notably so in its San Diego chapter. More typically, the
Silver Shirts served as a vehicle for pro-Hitler rallies and Pelley's fringe campaign for the White House. The group also developed into a clearinghouse for Pelley's string of propaganda
publications—professionally produced hate sheets that blamed
all the world's ills, from the Lincoln assassination to Pearl Harbor, on the wiles of international Jewry. The most shocking
element of Pelley's magazine *Liberation* was the sheer relent-
lessness of its hatred. Its "humor" is best summed up in one of
Pelley's proposed Christmas cards in 1937:

> *Dear Shylock, in this season*
> *When we're all bereft of reason,*
> *As upon my rent you gloat,*
> *I would like to cut your throat.*

In 1934, *Liberation* had attracted its most famous subscriber: the modernist poet Ezra Pound. The long, tortuous path of Pound's own anti-Semitism and his support of fascist ideology appear to have taken a leaf directly from Pelley. Apparently in an effort to dissuade Pound from his growing attachment to racialist conspiracies, one of Pound's literary friends and interlocutors, the Jewish modernist poet Louis Zukofsky, sent him a Pelley article alleging that a cabal of Jewish bankers had instigated the American Civil War. The effect, however, was the opposite of what Zukofsky had intended. Instead of seeing the absurdity of it, Pound delighted in the article, praising Pelley in letters back to Zukofsky as a "stout felly" and rhetorically asking if "all bankers is jooz?" For Pound, it was a turning point: "With two exceptions," wrote historian Leon Surette in his masterly study *Pound in Purgatory,* "this is the earliest occurrence of overtly anti-Semitic remarks I have found in Pound's correspondence or publications." A further reference to Pelley's Civil War theory emerged in one of Pound's famed *Cantos.* "It seems reasonable to conclude," Surette wrote, "that Zukofsky unwittingly set Pound on the course of anti-Semitism and conspiracy theory by sending him *Liberation* in early 1934."

Prophet of Hate

By the mid-1930s, the Silver Shirts reached a peak membership of about fifteen thousand. Pelley had become sufficiently infamous to serve as the model for novelist Sinclair Lewis's American dictator, Buzz Windrip, in *It Can't Happen Here.* In the pages of *Liberation*—whose subscriber list may have run as high as fifty thousand—Pelley repeatedly hammered the Roosevelt administration for its support of England, declaring that the president was a puppet of the "house of Judah" and calling him a scheming, Dutch-descended Jew. Pelley finally pushed a button that Roosevelt would not ignore. In a 1939 pamphlet, "Cripple's Money," Pelley wrote that the polio-stricken president was personally pocketing money raised through his Warm Springs Foundation for Crippled Children (and, of course, sharing it with his Jewish puppeteers). Roosevelt asked Attorney General Frank Murphy and FBI Director J. Edgar Hoover about prosecuting Pelley for libel. But the plans were dropped for fear that Roosevelt would be subpoenaed to testify.

At the dawn of World War II, however, with the nation reeling from Pearl Harbor and Pelley praising Hitler as "the outstanding statesman–leader of the world," the federal government was ready to strike. "Now that we are in a war," Roosevelt wrote Hoover in January of 1942, "it looks like a good chance to clean up a number of these vile publications." In April the FBI raided Pelley's offices, and by August a circuit court in Indianapolis sentenced him to fifteen years in federal prison on eleven counts of sedition.

The government had made Pelley an example in a general mop-up of racist cults and paramilitary movements at the start of the war. He was likely seen as an easier target than better-known Axis sympathizers such as the "radio priest" Father Charles Coughlin, who had far more followers and political connections. The Pelley prosecution was a warning shot—and it seemed to work. Coughlin was soon silenced, the Ku Klux Klan continued a precipitous decline, and several other religio-political organizations, such as Arthur Bell's conspiracy cult Mankind United, faced federal prosecution or fell under intense scrutiny.

The cult leader Bell narrowly escaped prosecution for sedition after telling followers that U.S. planes disguised as Japanese Zeros had bombed Pearl Harbor under orders from the "Hidden Rulers of the World." In a 1999 paper, historian and religious scholar Philip Jenkins keenly surmised that some of the very visible support for the war effort coming from Psychiana's Frank B. Robinson may actually have been a political calculation designed to keep his own controversial organization off the FBI's watch list.

As the war wound down and America faced a new foe in Communism, the controversy around Pelley ebbed. In early 1950, friends and supporters—recasting their jailed chief as a pioneering foe of Bolshevism—secured his release on parole. He had served about seven and a half years. Legally barred from political activity, Pelley spent the rest of the decade creating a massive output of channeled writings from his higher messengers, which he called the Soulcraft teachings. Moving with the times, Pelley saw the burgeoning phenomenon of UFOs as evidence of divine intelligences—or "Star Guests." For the remaining years of his life, the "beloved Chief" crafted an astral–Spiritualist religion based on cosmic messages from interstellar guides.

In 1965, at age seventy-five, Pelley died quietly of heart failure in Noblesville, Indiana. His passing was marked by an anonymous cross-burning on the lawn of the funeral home where he lay. It would appear that the prophet of hate went to his grave a largely forgotten man.

But Pelley's brand of paranoid pseudopatriotism touched the imaginations of other mystical sects that also attempted to "save" America under the guidance of hidden powers. The largest was the Chicago-based "Mighty I AM" movement, which offered a mélange of teachings from "Ascended Masters" who extolled prosperity, ultrapatriotism, and mystical awakening. As will be seen, the group gained and quickly lost wide popularity during the 1930s under the leadership of a husband–wife team, Guy and Edna Ballard. The Ballards' efforts, in turn, served to influence the Church Universal and Triumphant (CUT). Under its guru, Elizabeth Clare Prophet, CUT gained notoriety in the late 1980s, when church members dug an elaborate network of underground chambers near Yellowstone National Park, stockpiled weapons and provisions, and awaited American–Soviet nuclear Armageddon.

By far the grimmest legacy of the career of William Dudley Pelley was the influence he left among America's emerging hate groups. The Silver Shirts were an identifiable starting point for the careers of at least two figures whose names became synonymous with violence and bigotry later in the twentieth century. Henry L. Beach, a former Silver Shirt chapter leader, cofounded the white hate group Posse Comitatus, known for a series of 1983 shootouts that killed two federal marshals in North Dakota and a sheriff in Arkansas. Another ex–Silver Shirt, Richard Butler, founded the violent Aryan Nations, which he directed from Idaho until his death in 2004, going to his grave as the most visible leader of white hate. Pelley's writings and theories, and the Silver Shirts' uniforms and paramilitary posturing, gave post-Klan hate groups a style, a language, and an aesthetic.

Those were the most lasting bequests of a man who, while still in the initial glow of his out-of-body episode, enthused in 1929: "I know that the experience has metamorphosed the cantankerous Vermont Yankee that was once Bill Pelley and launched him into a wholly different universe that seems filled with naught but love, harmony, health, good humor, and prosperity."

Fascism and the Occult

The career of William Dudley Pelley raises a complex question: Is there a natural affinity between fascism and the occult? Today, commentators and historians increasingly speak of occultist and pagan influences on Hitler. The subject is a favorite of cable-television documentaries. It has even spawned a subgenre of historical literature, ranging from speculative to serious, that casts the Third Reich as an occult empire. To consider this contentious issue requires taking a road that briefly leads us away from America before returning to it.

Europe in the early twentieth century was a hothouse of ideologies and doctrines—spiritual, scientific, and political—and these ideas often crisscrossed among themselves. Occult ideas sometimes spilled into social movements, both fascistic and democratic. On the democratic end of the continuum was the Austrian occultist–educator Rudolf Steiner, an early scourge of the Nazis. Steiner pioneered influential methods in humanistic education. His theories of human development—based on explorations into reincarnation, clairvoyance, and lost civilizations—produced Waldorf Schools for grade-school children, one of today's most respected forms of alternative education, and Camphill Villages, extraordinary living–learning communities for mentally challenged adults. Both are found throughout America and Europe today.

The darker uses of occult ideas on the European continent are better known. Fascist movements discovered intriguing symbols within the occult lexicon, such as the all-seeing sun, the serpent, and the skull. Such images are magnetic, as are pseudoevolutionary concepts of primordial superraces and myths of a final showdown between forces of light and dark. The Nazis made sinister reuse of the ancient Vedic symbol of eternal recurrence—the swastika. The curved spokes of the swastika entered Europe through the influence of Theosophy. The Theosophical Society combined the symbol with other religious images—including the Egyptian ankh, the star of David, and the Sanskrit character *om*—to design its organizational insignia. For Theosophy, the swastika represented karma and rebirth; its inclusion among the other symbols was intended to express the unity of all faiths. Around the insignia revolved the Vedic maxim: *There Is no Religion Higher than Truth*. Yet for a handful of racial mystagogues—particularly the pan-German theorist Guido von List—the swastika became falsely conflated with images found in Germanic runes, which had been experiencing an early-twentieth-century revival. Ripped from its moorings, the swastika began appearing in Austrian occult journals as early as 1903.

Likewise, in the years preceding World War I, a handful of German pamphleteers and racial–mystical demagogues—List chief among them—seized upon the concept of the "Aryan" race, probably from Madame Blavatsky's massive work *The Secret Doctrine*. The term *Aryan*, as used by Blavatsky, derived from Vedic literature, where it described some of the earliest Indian peoples.* She adapted it to include the present epoch of human beings, which she classified as the fifth of seven "root races." These races stretched from the ancient past into the faraway future, eventually to be surpassed by a new branch of humanity, possibly exhibiting greater psychical or physical development. (On this, Blavatsky was vague.)

The notion of a primordial race emergent from Asia had long

---

* Competing notions of "Aryanism" began to appear in the late eighteenth century, but Blavatsky's was among those that German occultists would most likely have heard of in the early twentieth century.

been attractive to German racialists: "If the Germans could link their origins to India," wrote historian Joscelyn Godwin, "then they would be forever free from their Semitic and Mediterranean bondage"—that is, from Abrahamic or Hebrew lineage. How exactly Germany's racial theorists came to conflate these patently Asian "Aryans" with their blond, blue-eyed ideal is the very essence of muddled thinking. Especially since Blavatsky wrote that the Aryan race would reach its zenith in centuries ahead in America—a nation whose good character she unambiguously, if oddly, praised as, "owing to a strong admixture of various nationalities and inter-marriage."

So it was that the swastika and the concept of an Aryan race, reprocessed through the paranoia of racialist magazines and lodges, were imbibed by Hitler when defining his early political program. But the following cannot be stated clearly enough: Hitler was not an occultist. He contemptuously dismissed the work of fascist theorists who dwelled upon mythology and mystico-racial theories. In *Mein Kampf,* he specifically condemned "*völkisch* wandering scholars"—that is, second-tier mythically and mystically inclined intellects who might have belonged to occult–nationalist groups, such as the Thule Society, with which the Nazis shared symbols. From the earliest stirrings of Hitler's career in the tiny German Workers' Party and its street-rabble rallies, he was consumed with brutal political and military organization, not theology or myth. He employed a symbol as a party vehicle when necessary and immediately discarded the flotsam around it, whether people or ideas. He castigated those members of his inner circle who showed excessive devotion to Nordic mythology, dismissing the theology of Nazi theorist Alfred Rosenberg as "stuff that nobody can understand" and a "relapse into medieval notions!"

Historian Nicholas Goodrick-Clarke, who has done more than any other scholar to clarify these issues, noted that:

> *Hitler was certainly interested in Germanic legends and*
> *mythology, but he never wished to pursue their survival*
> *in folklore, customs, or place-names. He was interested*

in neither heraldry nor genealogy. Hitler's interest in mythology was related primarily to the ideals and deeds of heroes and their musical interpretation in the operas of Richard Wagner. Before 1913 Hitler's utopia was mother Germany across the border rather than a prehistoric golden age indicated by the occult interpretation of myths and traditions in Austria.

Under the Nazi regime, Theosophical chapters, Masonic lodges, and even sects that had produced some of the occult pamphlets that a young Hitler may have encountered as a Vienna knockabout were shunted or savagely oppressed, their members murdered or harassed. Despite astrology's well-publicized appeal to a few of Hitler's cadre, the ancient practice was effectively outlawed under Nazism, and many of its practitioners were jailed or killed. The man sometimes mislabeled "Hitler's astrologer," Karl Ernst Krafft, had no contact with Hitler but briefly reached the attention of mid-level Reich officials for predicting the 1939 assassination attempt on him. Krafft later died en route to Buchenwald. Nazi authorities sentenced Karl Germer, the German protégé of British occultist Aleister Crowley, to a concentration camp on charges of recruiting students for Crowley, whom they branded a "high-grade Freemason." History has recorded a few self-styled magi or occult impresarios who, often from the safety of distant borders, venerated Hitler as a dark knight of myth. Those same figures would have suffered the fate of Krafft and Germer had they lived within the Reich's reach. However tantalizing some may find it to conceive of Hitler as a practitioner of black magic, it is fantasy.

"Hinduism at Its Best"

Fascination with the Third Reich has blurred the most decisive connection between the occult and politics in the past century, one with far-reaching consequences in the present world. The connection appears in the career of one of the twentieth century's leading humanitarians, a man whose career produced the largest democracy in the postwar era and influenced the American civil rights movement. He spoke freely and openly of his debt to the founders of Theosophy, those denizens of Midtown Manhattan's magical mystery street, West 47th. It is a connection by no means hidden, just typically overlooked.

Growing up in Western India under English rule, the sensitive young Mohandas K. Gandhi had little interest in religion. His ambitions were to be a lawyer—and to leave behind the esoteric Hindu philosophies and ideologies of his parents' generation. When Gandhi turned nineteen in 1888, he ventured to London to study law. He was overjoyed to be in the grimy, bustling metropolis, the world's largest city and the beating heart of the British Empire. Gandhi tried to fit the very picture of an English barrister, with neatly parted hair and crisply starched collars. But something got in the way of his mind's eye image of where he was headed.

In 1889, following a difficult school year in which Gandhi struggled with his studies at London University (and later failed his matriculation exams), he met two friendly Englishmen who called themselves Theosophists. The law student recognized Theosophy as the pro-Hindu, anticolonial movement that had been spreading about his homeland through the American Colonel Henry Steel Olcott and his mysterious partner, Madame Blavatsky. These two Theosophical "brothers" asked the young Indian if he could help them read the original Sanskrit of the central holy text of Hinduism, the *Bhagavad Gita* ("Song of God"). "I felt ashamed," Gandhi wrote in his memoirs, "as I had read the divine poem neither in Sanskrit nor in Gujarati. I was constrained to tell them that I had not read the *Gita*, but that I would gladly read it with them."

The three began meeting together, and Gandhi became unexpectedly enchanted: "The *Gita* became an infallible guide of conduct. It became my dictionary of daily reference." As for his new friends, they were not just any Theosophists but a wealthy nephew and uncle who had recently opened their Notting Hill home to Blavatsky, who was fleeing charges of fraud and scandals in India. They made Gandhi an offer that filled him with intrigue and dread: Would he like to personally meet the high priestess of the occult—along with her most recent "convert," the esteemed British orator and social reformer Annie Besant? "I was a mere Bombay matriculate," he recalled. "I could not understand the British accent. I felt quite unworthy of going to Mrs. Besant."

But Gandhi did go. And while no records survive of the meeting between Blavatsky, Besant, and Gandhi, he later credited Theosophy for instilling in him the principle of equality among the world's religions, a revolutionary idea to a student from a caste-based society. In this sense, he explained in 1946 to biographer Louis Fischer, "Theosophy . . . is Hinduism at its best. Theosophy is the brotherhood of man." The organization's motto—*No Religion Higher than Truth*—appeared to move Gandhi toward one of his central principles: that "all religions are true," to which he carefully added, "all have some error in them." A generation later, Gandhi's ideal of universal brotherhood and his ethic of nonviolence touched the heart of an American social reformer and seminary student named Martin Luther King, Jr.

Gandhi partnered with the Theosophical Society during India's independence movement, crediting it with easing relations between Hindu and Moslem delegates to the Indian National Congress, the movement's policy-making body. So prominent was Theosophy in India's political life that even the Congress's founding in 1885 had been instigated by an early Theosophist, A. O. Hume, a retired Anglo–Indian government secretary who said that he was acting under "advice and guidance of advanced initiates." In 1917, Blavatsky's successor, Annie Besant, was elected president of the Congress, making the Theosophist the first woman and last European to hold the position. Besant herself bestowed upon Gandhi the title by which he became world famous: *Mahatma,* a Hindu term for "Great Soul" and the same name by which Theosophy called its own Masters.

For all that Gandhi discovered within Theosophy, however, he was suspicious of the organization's secrecy, including its communiqués from hidden Masters. He declined to become a member. (Lodge records from London show that he did briefly join in 1891, his last year there.) Unlike Henry A. Wallace, who grew temporarily consumed and then politically disgraced by his attachments to an arcane teacher, Gandhi was shrewder, carefully stepping around his occult allies and knowing when to keep them at a distance. In a letter he published in the newspaper *Young India* in 1926, Gandhi drew a line that forever divided his fealty to Theosophy's ideals from Theosophy as an organization. It could have served as a guide to Wallace, or to any leader who dwelled in the worlds of politics and the arcane. "Whatever critics may say against Madame Blavatsky or Col. Olcott or Dr. Besant," Gandhi wrote, "their contribution to humanity will always rank high. What has been a bar to my joining the society . . . is its secret side—its occultism. It has never appealed to me. I long to belong to the masses. Any secrecy hinders the real spirit of democracy."

CHAPTER NINE

THE MASTERS AMONG US

+ + +

Whatever is published and made known to everyone concerning our Fraternity . . . let no man take it lightly, nor consider it an idle or invented thing, much less dismiss it as a mere personal conceit of ours.

—THE CONFESSION OF THE LAUDABLE FRATERNITY OF THE MOST HONORABLE ORDER OF THE ROSY CROSS, 1615

For months it was the talk of the Unity Metaphysical Center of Helena, Montana—this strange book that told of wonderful miracles performed by centuries-old teachers living in farthest India. Many hungered to learn more about the holy beings venerated in its title: *Life and Teaching of the Masters of the Far East.* Their curiosity extended to the book's mysterious author, the bald, professorial-looking Baird T. Spalding, who had carried out a "metaphysical research" expedition for an Ivy League university at the distant corners of the earth.

"So many Helena men and women have been reading a book, the subject of so much speculation and hot controversy," reported the *Helena Daily Independent* in March 1931, that Ruth E. Chew, a Smith College–educated teacher of positive thinking and the town's doyen of the metaphysical, had selected it for a series of "five Lenten lectures." A New Yorker by birth who gained brief national note for her "diet of joy" teachings, Chew had received

Spalding's personal blessing to lecture about his journeys. Her audience was no cluster of starry-eyed Californians or avant-garde New Yorkers. They were spiritually curious heartland folk enthralled with Spalding's claim that wise immortals dwelled in the Himalayas, preaching a gospel of love, self-realization, and human potential. The lecture series was so popular that within a few years Spalding himself came to town to speak. For two evenings the crowd so overflowed the Unity Center that the auditorium of a nearby Baptist church had to host the messenger of the Masters.

Since a private printing of one thousand copies, financed by the wife of a California railroad magnate in 1924, Spalding's book had run into many tens of thousands of copies. It would sell more than a million in years ahead—popularizing early themes of New Age spirituality. The Masters taught that all religions are one, there is no hell outside "man's mortal thought," and the seeds of "Christ Consciousness" exist within all people. Spalding produced a popular second volume three years after the first, recounting dialogues with Jesus Christ himself, who, Spalding wrote, had studied as an adept in India, where he now lived among his fellow Masters in the form of an ordinary man but for "a peculiar translucent quality about the flesh."

For those believers who had grown up on hellfire Christianity or within the cold formality of Anglican faiths, and for whom faraway places like India or Tibet could seem as magical as never-never land, Spalding's books came as a liberating uplift. They passed among the hands of thousands of people who had heard little of Theosophy or the other mystical and occult sources upon which Spalding drew, and to whom they arrived with the impact of a new testament.

Invisible College

Spalding was vastly more readable, and more likely to be read, than the voluminous literature to emerge from Theosophy or the metaphysical writings of Emanuel Swedenborg. His works were the result of two underground channels that converged and burst to the surface in America: The first was the Theosophical notion of hidden adepts sent to aid humanity, and the second was a modern mythos that Christ had spent his "lost years"— roughly from the ages of thirteen to thirty—as a Far Eastern initiate of wisdom.

The idea of hidden masters had long circulated in the modern West. The Rosicrucian manuscripts of the early seventeenth century told of an "invisible college" behind the scenes of ordinary life. In 1842, a popular novel titled *Zanoni*, by the British nobleman Edward Bulwer-Lytton, ignited the occult imagination with tales of immortal superinitiates walking the earth. Possibly taking inspiration from *Zanoni*, Madame Blavatsky later wrote that she made her very first contact with an Indian Master at the international exhibition at Hyde Park's Crystal Palace in 1851; he was said to have been a hugely tall man who arrived with the royal Nepal delegation. World's fairs seemed to be a magical bridge for bringing the influence of the East across the oceans. The 1893 world's fair in Chicago featured the first World Parliament of Religions, which attracted religious leaders from around the globe, including a large number of robed swamis, yogis, and gurus who heightened the perception that there were, indeed, mysterious teachers of whom the West knew little.

One of the most beguiling and charismatic visitors who reached America through the Chicago World's Fair was Swami Vivekananda, a Hindu teacher who remained in America for two years, teaching and traveling around the nation. At once friendly and exotic-looking in his turban and robes, Vivekananda—a serious purveyor of Hindu ideas—seemed to enjoy his contact with the refreshingly unpretentious, caste-free Americans. He discussed reincarnation with cowboys, chided Americans for their materialism, and teased Spiritualists for showing more interest in conjuring up "creepy things" than the higher goal of self-knowledge. In good humor, the swami repeated the story of a husband–wife team of spirit mediums with whom he shared a kitchen at a New York rooming house. The couple performed a stage show together and would often get into domestic spats. Vivekananda recalled that after one of their arguments the wife turned to the Eastern master and complained: "Is it fair of him to treat me like this, when I make all the ghosts?"

If wise men had always existed in the ancient cultures of India and Tibet, some Western observers began to wonder—with greater or lesser levels of discrimination—whether the wisest man in history had traversed east from Nazareth during his long stretch of "silent years" in Scripture. *The Unknown Life of Jesus Christ*, a "rediscovered" Tibetan narrative published in 1894 by Russian journalist–impresario Nicolas Notovitch, had done much to popularize this notion, as had the 1908 *Aquarian Gospel* of Ohio's Levi H. Dowling. In the early twentieth century, Theosophy's Annie Besant went further, describing "The Master Jesus" as an immortal adept living "mostly in the mountains of Lebanon." (This was ascertained, presumably, through clairvoyant perception or a higher-dimensional visit. Besant rarely claimed such abilities herself, but they were frequent methods of her closest deputy, Charles Webster Leadbeater.)

Spalding's point of view, however, reached a wider public than had any of his predecessors'. He possessed what few of them did: a sprightly writing style and the ability, found so completely in perhaps no American scribe since Joseph Smith, to convey the drama and portent of a new gospel. Spalding's Master Jesus spoke in a distinctly twentieth-century early Atomic Age idiom that seemed, in the mind of his readers, to reveal a confluence between science and spirit. In a third volume of his Masters series, published in 1935, Spalding had a modern Christ turning back a group of bandits set to raid a holy temple:

> As I stand alone in Your great silence, God my Father, in the midst of me there blazes a pure light and it fills every atom of my whole being with its great radiance. Life, Love, Strength, Purity, Beauty, Perfection, stand forth in all dominion within me. As I gaze into the very heart of this light, I see another light,—liquid, soft, golden-white and radiantly luminous,—absorbing, mothering and giving forth the caressing fire of the Greater Light.

> *Now I know that I am God and one with God's*
> *whole universe. I whisper to God my Father and I am*
> *undisturbed.*

Looking back, it can seem puzzling that many thousands of readers could accept Spalding's tales of a Christ extant in India, living among other Masters who performed acts of teleportation, clairvoyance, and levitation. But time and again Americans had flocked to fantastic visions or stories of occult prowess that, regardless of the believability of their outer details, touched people's innermost religious emotions or hopes: the Fox sisters summoning the spirit world, Andrew Jackson Davis's dispatches from the Summer Land, Joseph Smith's record of America as a land of biblical patriarchs, Phineas Quimby's mental healing, William Dudley Pelley's reports from the afterlife, and Frank B. Robinson's claims to have "talked with God." Each tore the lid off a yearning that existed just beneath the surface of popular religious culture.

Like Miss Chew's congregants in Helena, Montana, Spalding's readers felt a particular hunger to know more about the Masters and the "world traveler" who recorded their metaphysical testament. The scribe of the Masters was, however, someone about whom almost nothing could be said with certainty: not his age, his background, his vocation, or whether he had really visited the Far East or even set foot outside the United States.

The Book of Gold

Spalding was, in fact, a Western mining prospector with an uncanny knack for reciting dead-to-rights details about people and places that all reasonable deduction precluded his having ever encountered. He likewise possessed the ability to speak movingly on spiritual systems—Hinduism, Buddhism, and ancient forms of mysticism—with which he had little direct contact. Spalding spent most of his time laboring as a solitary claims prospector. And while his mining ventures left him broke, his first Far East narrative—which the miner initially called *The Book of Gold*—attracted and thrilled readers, as did the enigma of the man himself, from the time when his manuscripts began privately circulating in the early 1920s to the day of his lonely death on the morning of March 18, 1953, at a Tempe, Arizona, motor inn.

The motel owner discovered Spalding's body half draped over a bed that he had just managed to reach before collapsing. The best-selling author had $15.98 in his pockets, wore bedraggled miner's clothes, and drove a '47 pickup. Though once married, he had spent much of his final year living alone in New Mexico in an old mining shack with no modern conveniences. From the conflicting reports he had given friends—further confused by the two different driver's licenses found on his body—Spalding could have been anywhere from middle age to ninety-five years old. Later investigations showed that he was probably eighty.

A smallish man whose nose had become misshapen—he said from atomic radiation exposure—Spalding had died of a heart attack while stopping en route to Reno, Nevada, to visit one of his mining claims. Even in his aged years, however, Spalding was reported to be capable of remarkable feats of physical stamina, including sleepless nights behind the wheel and the physically grueling routine of solitary drilling—in one case, an observer said, for twenty-four hours straight.

Spalding was by nature a wanderer. Acolytes believed him when he said he had traveled to the most exotic places on earth. Beginning in the year 1894, so went his story, he set off with a party of eleven to probe hidden truths in the still-mythical regions of Tibet, India, China, and Persia. He was, he initially said, working as a researcher in the employ of Columbia University (a claim to which Columbia authorities quickly put an end). Closer to the truth was that, aside from an ill-conceived tour of India that his publisher sent him on with a handful of credulous pilgrims in 1935, Spalding may never have traveled farther than the upstate New York town where he was born and the Western and Pacific states where his mining activities took him.

At least one member of the 1935 India tour wrote back home that, strangely, faculty members at Calcutta University fondly remembered Spalding from his student days there. But most other eyewitnesses described the whole excursion as a disaster of comedic proportions. During the trip, Spalding was supposed to conduct his party of California pilgrims to the locales where he'd encountered the "Elder Brothers"—maybe even snagging a meeting with one in the process. The composite of stories from returning participants had Spalding disappearing for days at a time, tossing off a few tall tales, spuriously reporting that washed-out roads and earthquakes precluded their visiting sites from his books, and then finally ditching the tour group altogether, cashing in his ticket, and returning home aboard a freighter.

The few authentic Hindu worshippers who did cross paths with the Spalding party regarded its leader as a curious, likable, though off-balance man. The British mystical scholar and writer Paul Brunton, at the time a student of Hindu teacher Ramana Maharshi, encountered Spalding knocking about with his fourteen pilgrims in southern India and spent a little time with them. Brunton wrote in his notebooks that Spalding "finally admitted" to him that his Far East travelogues "dealt with visits made in his astral body, not in his physical body as readers were led to believe." Another disciple of Ramana Maharshi, a British army major named A. W. Chadwick, spent more time with Spalding and his travelers. In his memoirs, Chadwick recalled a "showdown" in which members of the party "turned on Spaulding [sic] and accused him of having swindled them, that the story about the Masters was nothing but an invention and that he had never been in India before. However, he seemed quite equal to the occasion and held his own in spite of the odds."

Chadwick discovered some "very nice and sincere people" among the Spalding party. While he agreed they had been snookered, he took a more philosophical tack on the whole affair, noting that it did bring some of these hapless tourists into contact with at least one genuine Hindu swami, Ramana Maharshi. One woman in the group, a Mrs. Taylor—who traveled with her husband, a retired postmaster—came into Ramana Maharshi's presence. In the bombastic style once infamous among traveling

Americans, Mrs. Taylor insisted to the Hindu ascetic that she wanted "self-realization"—and wanted the swami to be quick about it. "Wait," replied the teacher, "it will come in due time." Mrs. Taylor wasn't budging. "No," she replied, "that's no good. I want it here and now." After Mrs. Taylor repeatedly refused the teacher's entreaties for patience, Chadwick recalled, the Hindu master stopped speaking, "but gazed steadily in her eyes for some five minutes or so. She suddenly burst into tears and rushed out of the room, but would never tell anybody what had happened."

As for Spalding himself, Chadwick recalled him as "a decent sort of person who obviously suffered from delusions. He told me some fantastic tales which he certainly believed himself. . . . For, surely, he would never have had the courage to lead such an expedition which could only end in fiasco if he had not been slightly mad." On this point, Chadwick may have been right, and in the strictest sense. According to U.S. census records from April 21, 1930, a "Baird Spalding" was an inmate at Patton State Hospital, a mental institution in San Bernardino, California, for patients committed by the courts. Amid the Spalding résumé of birth dates and background stories—the census identifies him as sixty-nine years old, married, unemployed, and a native of England (another background Spalding was known to give)—it stands as one more odd entry.

Spalding also had frequent run-ins with the law. According to California newspaper reports, he was arrested no fewer than three times between 1928 and 1935. The incidents ranged from mine fraud in Los Angeles, to forgery in New York, to charges stemming from a paternity claim in San Francisco. He was cleared on the paternity claim, but by 1937, his wife, Stella, had had enough and obtained a divorce.

The Camera of Past Events

Despite the chaos that ran through Spalding's personal life, even his critics marveled at the million-selling author's gifts. His biographer, David Bruton, a West Coast metaphysical writer and lecturer who argued with Spalding as much as he agreed with him, decided to test the mystic chronicler's reputed talent for relating vivid details about nearly any person or idea put to him. Bruton mentioned to Spalding his father-in-law, a man of no note whom he was sure the miner had never known, only to hear Spalding expound on his old pal "Charlie" in accurate and eerie detail. "I was soon convinced," Bruton wrote, "that there was no end to Spalding's ready knowledge. I heard him repeatedly come up with the right answers on almost any topic, any place or any time. . . . The manner in which Spalding talked of people, places and events made the whole world seem about the size of a golf ball."

Indeed, Spalding's tales would have gotten a less gifted speaker hooted off podiums—especially when he told audiences of inventions like his "Time Camera," which he said could capture images of the past by tuning to the proper "band of vibratory frequency." He told of inventing the marvel with no less a luminary than electrical-engineering pioneer Charles Steinmetz (who conveniently died the year before Spalding's first book appeared). Spalding explained to audiences that he could film historic events, soundtrack included, such as the signing of the Declaration of Independence, George Washington's inaugural address, and (never one to stop before reaching the top) the Sermon on the Mount, each of which he recounted in pleasingly quirky detail. But for Spalding's apparent seriousness, it could have been Mark Twain putting on a satire.

But when Spalding would push his lecture audiences too far, just as people might cast glances around them, wondering, *Is anyone buying this?*, he would change course and offer a moving homily on universal spiritual values. And at such times, Spalding was no cipher. When a questioner at a 1935 lecture asked him whether the Jews had killed Christ, the author turned the question back on him:

> *We do not put that at the door of any nationality at all.*
> *Had He not wished to present a condition through*

*which all men could go, they could not have crucified
Him. It was a definite method to show His people that
they could go through these conditions without the least
effect upon themselves. Had it not been for that purpose, He could have taken His body and gone on with it
as He showed many times. It was not a thing imposed
upon Him except that He allowed the imposition for a
purpose.*

Spalding exemplified the one facet found fairly consistently in
the work of popularizers and fabulists who refashioned Theosophy's theme of hidden Masters: a complete absence of religious
chauvinism or bigotry. And this is no mere happenstance. As seen
in the testament of Gandhi, the vision opened by the Theosophical Society placed all historic faiths and nationalities on equal
footing. Theosophy, possibly more than any other nineteenth-
century organization, crafted a modern reaction to religious
chauvinism, the tone of which carried into most tagalong movements. It was an unrecognized channel (though far from the only
one) through which ecumenism became a basic part of the American liberal outlook.

Darkness Falls

Seen from one angle, Spalding pulled off a massive metaphysical
caper on thousands of unsuspecting believers. But if money were
all he was after, he would have operated along different lines.
While held in thrall by a legion of readers, Spalding had no organization, offered no products beyond his books, and created no
money-raising apparatus. Biographer Bruton, who on several occasions made clear that he put little stock in Spalding's tall tales,
recounted seeing him, impromptu, give $400 to a distant ac-
quaintance who had lost her home. And while Spalding's various
editions of *Life and Teaching of the Masters of the Far East* series
sold hundreds of thousands of copies during his lifetime (and

appeared in several translations), he seems to have reaped limited benefit. According to Bruton, who administered Spalding's estate after his death, the writer had a dubious system of recompense with his Los Angeles publisher and business manager, Douglas DeVorss. DeVorss, who founded one of the premier metaphysical imprints and book distributors of the dawning New Age, kept Spalding on a monthly stipend that Bruton estimated at $150. By the night Spalding died in Tempe, Arizona, the scribe of the Far East had all of $110.74 in savings. And, in a most unusual arrangement, DeVorss retained total control of Spalding's copyrights, which he owned flat out by the time of the writer's death. To all appearances, Spalding had been fleeced.

In a tragic twist of events, the financial advantage of this arrangement would prove of little benefit to DeVorss. The year 1953 hung darkly over the lives of the Spalding circle. After Spalding's death in Arizona in March of that year, DeVorss suffered the terrible loss of his young wife, Dorothy, in complications following childbirth in June. The couple had just moved into a twelve-room home on a landscaped property in Pasadena; after his wife's death DeVorss was seen alone in the gardens, sobbing. Their newborn daughter was sent to Lincoln, Nebraska, to be raised by a maternal aunt. And the clouds darkened still. The following September, a gunman burst into DeVorss's offices in downtown Los Angeles and fired four times, shooting the fifty-two-year-old publisher to death at his desk. After turning himself over to police eight hours later, the shooter, a former Minneapolis mail carrier, was revealed to be an enraged husband who suspected the metaphysical publisher of carrying on an affair with his estranged wife.

And that was not the end of the fog that surrounded Spalding and his friends. Spalding's executor and biographer Bruton completed his thoughtful, meticulous memoir of the writer in fall 1954—and he then died, a relatively young man, the following March, almost two years from the death of Spalding himself. With these events, the mysteries of Baird T. Spalding were largely sealed.

A *Real* Phony

In the final years of Spalding's life, a woman approached him after a lecture and said: "Mr. Spalding, I think you are the biggest liar I ever heard." But for those who would demand a reckoning of the New Age pioneer, none will be found by branding him a charlatan. He was something else altogether. In the novel *Breakfast at Tiffany's,* Truman Capote's heroine Holly Golightly—the hillbilly girl who transformed herself into a party-going sophisticate in New York City—was deemed no ordinary phony, but "a *real* phony." Holly wasn't trying to con anyone but to embody her ideal that life should always be beautiful. In this sense, Spalding, too, was "a *real* phony." From within a cloak of absurdities he proffered sincere religious principles and a discernible set of ideals.

His was a sensitive theology, emphasizing a message of universal hope for self-realization. "The path is right within," Spalding would repeat, in what became a mainstay of New Age metaphysics. "Search ever deeper within yourself. *Know* that this great light belongs to you." All religions, in the Spalding view, were part of a revolutionary world gospel in which the Great Teacher would once again burst into the temple, ridding it not of money-changers but of religious sectarianism. "The Masters," Spalding wrote in his first volume, "accept that Buddha represents the Way to Enlightenment, but they clearly set forth that Christ IS Enlightenment, or a state of consciousness for which we are all seeking—the Christ light of every individual; therefore, the light of every child that is born into the world."

Spalding's gospel was strongly suggestive of the New Age Christianity that gained popularity more than a generation later through such writers as Matthew Fox and Andrew Harvey. It prefigured the cross-pollination of Jewish, Christian, Sufi, Buddhist, and Hindu ideas, today derided by critics as "cafeteria religion" but indelibly stamped on the spiritual experience of countless Americans. For a generation of readers and religious experimenters, the tales of this Western mining prospector became a source of encouragement that spiritual understanding is possible through many doors, open to any who seek.

Black Magicians

Although Spalding was nearly broke when he died, the commercial success of his books was not lost on the canniest observers. One of the oddest strains of mystical religion in America appeared in a 1930s movement heavily influenced by Spalding: the "Mighty I AM"* teachings of Guy and Edna Ballard. The Ballards were a charismatic Chicago couple who briefly built a huge prosperity cult based on hyperpatriotism and the teachings of their own "Ascended Masters."

Guy and Edna Ballard were catholic, in the occult sense of the word. In the 1920s and '30s, the couple maintained an occult bookshop and absorbed a wide range of metaphysical ideas: Frank B. Robinson's Psychiana, New Thought, Christian Science, the Rosicrucian-styled teachings of the Ancient and Mystical Order Rosae Crucis (AMORC), and a variety of books and novels on "hidden masters," including the works of Silver Shirt leader William Dudley Pelley, whose members they actively recruited. They seem to have been fairly forthright about wanting to start their own for-profit, membership-based mystical movement. According to Frank B. Robinson, Guy sought out the prophet of Moscow, Idaho, and told Robinson of his ambitions. Robinson said it was okay with him—as long as Guy knew where they stood. "I told him I didn't mind," he recalled to columnist Westbrook Pegler in 1939, ". . . I just warned him to keep off my stuff."

The itinerant Spalding had stayed as a houseguest at the Ballards' Chicago home. Like Spalding, Guy Ballard was a professional prospector with a passion for speculative digging. And on a mountain, Ballard found his gold. As Ballard described it,

---

* *I Am* is a mystically rooted term for God that attracted considerable use in twentieth-century occult teachings.

his first encounter with an "Ascended Master" came in 1932 during a day hike on Northern California's snow-peaked Mount Shasta. Shasta was a kind of Mount of Olives for the West Coast occult, steeped in local legend as a place of hidden tunnels, mythical races, UFO landings, and remnants of lost civilizations from Atlantis or Lemuria. During his leisure hike, Guy met the ethereal being that would ever after serve as his heavenly teacher, Saint Germain: "a Magnificent Godlike figure in a white jeweled robe, a Light and Love sparkling in his eyes that revealed and proved the Dominion and Majesty that are his."

The personage called Saint Germain had considerable pedigree in occult tradition. His legend began with an altogether real Count of Saint Germain, an eighteenth-century European courtier, diplomat, musician, and purveyor of mystical ideas. His life and career later took on wondrous dimensions among early Theosophists who conceived of him as an ageless, beneficent messenger of the Great White Brotherhood. In the twentieth century, his reputation traveled in many directions: from the pages of Manly P. Hall's *Secret Teachings of All Ages* to the theology of Elizabeth Clare Prophet, who cited Master Saint Germain as a sage and guide behind her apocalyptic-minded Church Universal and Triumphant.

In the hands of the Ballards, Saint Germain's teachings came across a lot like the prosperity gospel of New Thought, though couched in a mind-numbing dirge of cosmic language that could make its message seem foggy compared to the to-the-point writings of a Wallace D. Wattles or Ernest Holmes. For many readers, the over-the-top tone of the I AM "decrees"—*Mighty Sacred Fire! Come forth and do your Perfect Work Now!*—seemed to romanticize the appeal of old-fashioned New Thought. By the early 1930s, the Ballards embarked on an ambitious program of books, classes, and speaking appearances. In short order, they filled large auditoriums with pageants and services, often peopled with well-dressed and apparently well-to-do men and women.

Yet it soon became clear that the Ascended Masters of I AM and their messengers, Guy and Edna Ballard, had a different outlook from the beneficent brothers recounted by Blavatsky and

Spalding. Following on from William Dudley Pelley and his Silver Shirt Legion, the Ballards combined their mysticism with a heavy dose of ultrapatriotism, vowing to eradicate "vicious forces" threatening America. And the organization went further still. Although I AM's activities could be closely guarded, a religious scholar, David Stupple, undertook a field study of the I AM movement and found that it maintained racially segregated temples, even as late as 1975. Stupple discovered one Midwestern temple that actually relegated black congregants to an auxiliary hall to listen to live services via an audio hookup from the main white temple. He witnessed one I AM meeting descend into an argument over whether to include "Luther King and the Communist Conspiracy" on the organization's list of "Black Magicians" whom the Ascended Masters would "blast and annihilate."

Even though I AM was never anything like the hate machine of Pelley's Silver Shirts, federal investigators began keeping an eye on it in the years leading up to World War II. The government was deeply suspicious of any sects with far-right ideology, fearful that such organizations might act as fifth-column sympathizers if Axis forces invaded the West Coast, where many of the nation's mystical movements were grounded. The turn of the decade ended on a dismal note for I AM: Guy died in late December 1939, and the organization, caught in the same right-wing mop-up that imprisoned Pelley, faced federal charges of mail fraud in mid-1940. *Time* magazine responded almost gleefully with an August 5, 1940, headline, *I AM in a Jam,* reporting that the Ballards had pocketed more than $3 million from "deluded followers."

From the start, the trial was tangled up in First Amendment issues, specifically when the judge instructed jurors to consider whether the Ballards held their religious beliefs sincerely. A flurry of appeals followed and in 1944 the case landed in the U.S. Supreme Court, which overturned the convictions but remanded the case to a lower court for retrial. In a historic dissent, Supreme Court Justice Robert H. Jackson argued that the high court should have dismissed the case outright and "have done with this business of judicially examining other people's faiths."

Any attempt to explore the Ballards' theology or how sincerely they held it, Jackson wrote, "is precisely the thing the Constitution put beyond the reach of the prosecutor, for the price of freedom of religion or of speech or of the press is that we must put up with, and even pay for, a good deal of rubbish."

It was a decisive stroke for religious freedom, though not an all-out victory for I AM. The Ninth Circuit Court in San Francisco once more convicted the Ballards, and in 1946 the Supreme Court heard the case for the last time—ultimately throwing out the indictments upon determining that women had been excluded from the grand jury selection. As the legal fires subsided, I AM quietly resumed its activity as a smaller, more suspicious organization, with a lower profile and an arm's-length attitude toward outsiders. The group that wanted to save America from dark forces achieved a bruising victory that it never sought: Justice Jackson's dissent came to be seen as a rallying defense of the rights of new or controversial religions to be left alone.

CHAPTER TEN

SECRETS FOR SALE

✦ ✦ ✦

I do a better business when things are bad. I think the churches find the same thing is true.

—ZOLAR FROM "DEAN OF ASTROLOGERS,"
THE NEW YORKER, 1959

The European occult lodges of the late nineteenth and early twentieth centuries could seem to cling to secrecy almost as an end in itself. Theosophy's Annie Besant never tired of creating elite offshoots of the organization: orders within orders and inner lodges, each with its own badges, seals, and ceremonies. The Hermetic Order of the Golden Dawn, the preeminent organization of Europe's occult revival, required that initiates pass through a grueling series of degrees before being allowed in on its inner doctrine and ceremonial rites.

Starting in the 1920s in America, however, that approach to the occult was blown to pieces. A generation of teachers and impresarios, who arose from ordinary backgrounds in cities and farming communities, wrestled occult ideas away from secretive lodges and exposed them to so broad an audience that, by midcentury, practices like astrology and numerology became as widespread as bridge games and crossword puzzles.

Occult Rebel

The revolution began around 1900, when a pole-thin, intellectu-ally curious teenager named Paul Foster Case was struggling to make a living on the American vaudeville circuit. Born in 1884 out-side Rochester, New York, he began his stage career at sixteen. Case's mother, Ella, had died three years earlier, probably of ty-phoid. His father, Charles, planned to remarry and move away, and told the boy that it was time to prepare for life on his own. Case vis-ited a Rochester talent agency and found work as a performer of card tricks and as a piano player. He had learned the organ at his community church and otherwise pulled together his own educa-tion—and probably his early stage act—from the books he found at the local free library, where his parents had been custodians.

A chance encounter soon altered the course of his life. In 1901, as Case recalled it, he was performing at an area charity benefit when backstage he met a publisher and architect, a man who had designed several prominent buildings in Rochester: Claude Bragdon. Bragdon was an American patron of mysticism who befriended Manly P. Hall and helped translate work by the influ-ential Russian mathematician and philosopher P. D. Ouspensky. The older man asked Case a simple but pivotal question: Where did he suppose ordinary playing cards came from, the kind he used in his magic act? For a bookish teen whose education had been cut off, the question presented an enticing challenge. Case began an intensive study of playing cards, a move that led him to learn about the Tarot, a seventy-eight-card deck of mysterious images—such as Death, the Juggler, and the Tower—that ap-peared, without obvious precedent, in early-fifteenth-century Italy. European occultists later extolled Tarot as everything from an oracle to a record of hidden wisdom.

For several years, Case balanced between the study of oc-cultism and his stage act—until another fateful encounter, far more dramatic than the first. In a scene now recognizable from the mythos of American occultism, Case described meeting an imposing stranger who called himself a messenger from a "Mas-ter of Wisdom." The man approached him on a Chicago city street in 1909 and declared that the vaudevillian was now at a "crossroad" and had to choose between a life devoted to the stage or the serious pursuit of occult knowledge. A stage career would be easy, the stranger said, while an occult career would be filled with difficulty and require "dedicating yourself to fully serve humanity and play a vital part in its evolution for this coming Aquarian Age." It was a reference to an era of spiritual growth that some astrologers forecast for the late twentieth century, when the mystical constellation of Aquarius appeared at the spring equinox.* Case chose the hard path.

He remained in Chicago, a great city for a budding occultist in the early twentieth century. Chicago had been home to the influential New Thought teacher Emma Curtis Hopkins and had bustling subcultures in "mental science" and metaphysical publishing. A Chicago lawyer named William Walker Atkinson produced an imaginative array of occult books from his Yogi Publication Society based in the twenty-two-story Masonic Temple Building, once a jewel of the city's skyline and later demolished. Atkinson himself wrote many books, under the pseudonyms Yogi Ramacharaka, Magus Incognito, and, most famously, Three Initiates. The Chicagoan used the last of these aliases in 1908 to publish his most successful book, one of the occult classics of the twentieth century: *The Kybalion*. This compendium of "lost" Egyptian–Hermetic wisdom read a lot like New Thought principles recast in antique language but nonetheless enthralled readers, partly due to the secrecy of its authorship. A long-standing rumor, which now abounds online, named Case as one of the Three Initiates. But *The Kybalion* reads to the letter like Atkinson, and it was published before the two men would have been likely to meet.†

---

* Astrologers strenuously disagreed among themselves about the timing of the zodiacal phenomenon.

† *The Kybalion* is often misdated to 1912. But the copyright and first edition were actually from 1908. The error arose from a 1940 edition in which the publisher listed the initial registration as 1912, almost certainly in an attempt to reassert control over a copyright that had fallen into public domain after failing to be renewed at the required 28-year interval.

Back in New York in 1920, Case found his way to a remnant of the storied Hermetic Order of the Golden Dawn. In earlier decades, the Golden Dawn had attracted a remarkable range of artists and intellectuals: Aleister Crowley was a member; so were W. B. Yeats and Constance Wilde (the wife of Oscar); and there were many others, less known but highly influential, such as the writer–occultist Arthur Edward Waite. The Brooklyn-born and British-bred Waite codesigned the twentieth century's most recognizable Tarot pack, the Rider–Waite–Smith Deck.

By the time Case joined the Golden Dawn in 1920, the order was on its last breaths. Its prime mover, British occultist S. L. MacGregor Mathers, had died of flu in Paris two years earlier. His widow, Moina, the sister of philosopher Henri Bergson, possessed a suspicious and emotionally delicate nature and often found herself struggling to control the factional fighting that followed her husband's passing. When Case arrived, American initiates were in open revolt, complaining that they were not receiving the proper manuscripts for their training and advancement in the order's coveted ranks and degrees. Worsening matters, Moina Mathers—who advocated celibacy as a tool for spiritual growth—became incensed over a love affair between Case and another American recruit, Lillian Geise. In a 1921 letter, Case diplomatically (if peculiarly) acknowledged the relationship: "The Hierophantria and I were observed to exchange significant glances over the altar during the Mystic Repast."

And there were still other sources of Mathers's discomfort. Case was rapidly developing into a respected teacher of the occult arts, attracting a small following of his own and further threatening her hold on the American branch. Rather than viewing Tarot strictly as a book of coded symbolism, Case tended toward a more psychological interpretation of the cards. He taught that by meditating on a certain image, you could embody its virtues, such as the gentle power of the mistress on the Strength card or the self-control of the angel on the Temperance card. "We become what we contemplate," he later wrote. "Contemplate these pictures in spare moments, and they will alter your whole life in no time." Case's approach appealed to the practical, do-for-self style of American acolytes. And it typified the New Thought influence on American occultism and the later spiritual ideas of the New Age: that the mind is an instrument of Divine power, through which outer circumstance can be shaped.

Tempers fraying and jealousies growing, Mathers expelled Case and Geise from the Golden Dawn in January 1922. To many, it was a fatal misstep. Case was the kind of attractive American teacher whose leadership the order desperately needed. "*When you got rid of Mr. Case*," a Philadelphia member wrote to Mathers, "*you 'killed the goose that laid the golden egg.'*"

For Case and Geise, however, their expulsion was like the unlocking of a door. They had grown tired of the Golden Dawn's oaths of secrecy and Old World hierarchy. The couple wanted to teach magic their own way—and offer it to all comers. "I am convinced," Geise wrote Mathers in a mood of revolutionary zeal, "that no Order can claim the 'private ownership' of ways to perform magic. Apparent disappointments have turned out to be blessings in disguise and now our freedom from an old alliance is another step towards realizing what we now consider our life's work." It was very nearly the end of the Golden Dawn in America—and the coming of a newer, freer form of American occultism.

Joined as newlyweds, Case and Geise laid plans in 1922 for an organization of their own. They produced a series of carbon-copied correspondence lessons offered by the School of Ageless Wisdom. Their simple, hand-typed lessons in Tarot interpretation and number symbolism reached students through ads in occult journals and by word of mouth. It was a bare-bones operation: The carbon copies had to be retyped each time they ran out. But the couple had found their freedom. It ended too suddenly. In 1924, Geise died of causes that are unclear. Once more, Case was on his own.

The taste of producing his own lessons, however, spurred him to more ambitious plans. Although struggling for money and living in the late 1920s in a Boston rooming house, Case launched a new "school of wisdom." He called it Builders of the Adytum

(Greek for "inner temple"), or B.O.T.A. One of his first public references to B.O.T.A. appeared in 1927 as a brief, understated notice at the back of one of his Tarot pamphlets inviting readers to contact him at his Boston address. B.O.T.A. was Case's breakthrough. His well-organized and broad-ranging correspondence lessons—encompassing Tarot, astrology, number mysticism, and Qabalah (as he spelled it)—gained a reputation as the most in-depth mail-order materials of their kind. They circulated through the hands of thousands of ordinary people, from students to homemakers to laborers—anyone willing to pay a modest monthly fee. He became the Charles Atlas of home-study occultism, and his B.O.T.A. lessons commanded a following that has continued to the present day.

Although he had chosen the occult path, the esoteric scholar never fully left behind his career as a stage magician. In the early 1930s, Case relocated to Los Angeles—a town large enough and sufficiently hospitable to magic as a spiritual pursuit and as stagecraft for him to cultivate both careers at once. Case joined the International Brotherhood of Magicians and occasionally performed with his B.O.T.A. protégée and successor, Ann Davies. Notes from a 1946 brotherhood meeting recall the pair in "a well worked out mindreading routine." *The Linking Ring,* a professional magician's magazine, complimented Case's "outstanding" cards-up-the-sleeve routines.

Case was a rarity among professional magicians. He meticulously separated his career as a stage performer from his role as an occult teacher. Offstage, Case never used mentalist tricks or hoodwinked his followers for money. In fact, his finances were so precarious during the 1940s that friends were asked to bring meals to the bungalow-style home Case shared with his last wife, Harriet, in a working-class section of Central L.A. Though he pursued his occult studies with integrity, Case probably felt constrained to keep that side of himself quiet around his stage friends. Ever since Houdini began exposing fraudulent mediums in the 1920s, magicians tended to consider themselves sworn foes of any who claimed traffic with the supernatural or esoteric.

Case's colleagues in the world of professional magic appeared to have had an inkling that he was involved in occultism but were otherwise little aware of his double life. In a December 1972 column in *Genii*, another magazine for stage professionals, Los Angeles magician Charlie Miller recalled:

> Years ago I was very friendly with Paul Case. Paul Case
> was an expert on Tarots, although at the time I never
> paid much attention to this. Paul was a modest man and
> seldom mentioned it. . . . Paul was a very good magician.
> He used to give lectures or talks on psychology. I never
> did quite know the name of the lecture that he gave.

A Magician's Legacy

Every artist dreams of a magnum opus, and in 1947 Case completed his. Building on his lessons and pamphlets, he published a book with a Freemasonic press in Virginia, called simply *The Tarot*. The sum of his life's work, *The Tarot* rendered public many of the Golden Dawn's most closely held ideas, along with Case's own psychological insights and mapping of correspondences among mythical symbols.* The book explored Tarot's theoretical connections to Hebrew letters, natural elements, musical tones, astrological aspects, Scriptural passages, ancient myths, numbers, colors, and even ethical philosophies. While its ideas are sometimes speculative and self-referencing, Case's opus is notable for the concision with which it attempts a complete cross-collating of world religious concepts. It shows a consistent internal theology and probably stands as the single highest expression of the various philosophies that emerged from the European occult revival. The

---

* Case was not alone in airing Golden Dawn philosophy. Israel Regardie, a former secretary to British occultist Aleister Crowley and an accomplished intellect in his own right, published a four-part series of Golden Dawn documents from 1937 to 1940. Regardie's volumes are broader, though less accessible, than Case's.

book has never fallen out of print, and in the early twenty-first century it appeared for the first time in paperback with a trade publisher.*

In 1954, seven years from *The Tarot*'s appearance (a portentous number in occult terms), Case died while on vacation with his wife Harriet in Mexico. In the end, he was an accomplished magician in two worlds. The man who began his career as a teenage performer from small-town America had successfully torn down the curtain of secrecy from Europe's leading occult order. The inner doctrine of the Old World was now available to anyone who knocked on the temple door.

Try!

Case's correspondence lessons were part of a growing phenomenon. In the early decades of the twentieth century, the U.S. Postal Service was handling a huge flow of mystical and self-improvement literature. In addition to B.O.T.A.'s program, some of the most popular correspondence lessons emerged from the self-styled Rosicrucian Order, or AMORC. The organization even developed its own impressive, Egyptian-styled campus occupying a whole city block in San Jose, California. But AMORC could place the same kind of premium on organizational rank and claims to ancient lineage that marred the European occult. The order spent too much time arguing with rivals over who represented the "real" Rosicrucians, when history has left open the question of whether there were any Rosicrucians to begin with. But a contemporary of Case, and someone who shared his democratic ideals, devised a mail-order school that saw occultism as a new kind of progressive faith for the broadest possible public.

Born in 1882 in Adel, Iowa, Benjamin Williams was two

---

* The edition was published by the present author.

years Case's senior and his physical opposite. A tall, powerfully built athlete and outdoors enthusiast, Williams had an unlikely affinity for the arcane. As a voraciously curious adolescent, he witnessed the work of a traveling Mesmerist—or hypnotist, as the term was increasingly known—and discovered his own talent for entrancing neighbors. His next challenge was the study of astrology. Ordering pamphlets and books by mail, he learned enough to cast horoscopes for his Adel neighbors. After reviewing the birth charts of friends and relatives, Williams concluded that astrology offered authentic insight into human character. He was enthralled to find an ancient art that really seemed to work in the present.

To avoid embarrassing his religiously conservative parents—his father was a physician and a deacon at a Disciples of Christ church—Williams began corresponding under the alias Elbert Benjamine (probably adopting the first name from the motivational hero Elbert Hubbard). Anxiously searching for a school or organization to advance his metaphysical studies, he traveled to Denver in 1909 to meet fellow Westerners who claimed to be the surviving remnant of a highly secretive European occult order called the H.B. of L., or the Hermetic Brotherhood of Luxor.

In the 1880s, the Hermetic Brotherhood of Luxor was locked in a kind of rivalry with its contemporary organization, Theosophy. The H.B. of L. founders—who ranged from serious scholars of mysticism to one mail-fraud felon—believed that Theosophy had failed to train its members in "practical occultism," such as the uses of oracles and clairvoyance. The H.B. of L. seized upon this educational mission as its aim. One of its early sources of inspiration came from an American of mixed African and Caucasian ancestry named Paschal Beverly Randolph. In his books and pamphlets, Randolph promulgated the motto *Try!* as an injunction to occult experimentation. Randolph, along with his admirers in the Hermetic Brotherhood of Luxor, believed that magic had to be a hands-on, visceral affair. He advocated the use of "sex magic"—the harnessing of sexual energy as an ethereal force to further one's will—a method later adopted by Britain's

Aleister Crowley. Randolph's practices included invoking prayer for a specific wish before reaching orgasm. Randolph died in 1875, just before the Theosophical tide hit America, but his personal slogan *Try!* reappeared in the letters of Theosophy's Mahatmas, as an injunction to Henry Steel Olcott and others.

An intriguing "secret history" is theorized about the dawn of the American occult and organizations like the H.B. of L.—one that found its way into the work of the respected French religious philosopher René Guénon in the early twentieth century and was later written about by Joscelyn Godwin, a noted musicologist and historian at Colgate University. Like Theosophy, the H.B. of L. claimed to receive guidance from secret adepts. These superinitiates were said to have induced the early phenomena of Spiritualism in order to interject mystical ideas into a culture choking on intellectual materialism. This, says the "hidden hand" theory, ignited a new era of learning and discovery. Or, depending on various versions of the theory, it led to a disastrous wrong turn in which the bump-in-the-night spectacles of Spiritualism turned into an out-of-control Frankenstein monster, which Madame Blavatsky was sent to America to correct. Such was the mythos that connected Spiritualism to the occult flowering of later decades.

The Religion of the Stars

In Denver, the remaining American hangers-on of the Hermetic Brotherhood of Luxor, probably acting in isolation, told Benjamine that their "inner lodge" had a special task for him: The young man was to write a series of metaphysical lessons that would bring occultism to the lives of everyday people. He was at first reluctant, but in 1910 he accepted the challenge upon receiving his own private communiqué from the Masters. Once more shedding his name, he adopted the alias C. C. Zain (the surname is Hebrew for "sword"). The Iowan moved to Los Angeles to begin writing a program of twenty-one correspondence lessons and formed his own organization, the Brotherhood of Light.*

Although Benjamine proved gifted at the mathematics required of an astrologer in an age before computer programs, he tended toward excessive credulity. In his first lesson plan, "Laws of Occultism," he enthused over the "authentic photographs of fairies" that had appeared in Arthur Conan Doyle's 1922 book, *The Coming of the Fairies*. Doyle, the creator of Sherlock Holmes, was a committed though sometimes less-than-meticulous advocate of Spiritualism. After World War I, the storyteller had grown enthralled with a series of photographic plates taken by two English schoolgirls that showed winged fairies frolicking in the Yorkshire countryside. Seen through contemporary eyes, the black-and-white prints hauntingly mirror the hopes of Doyle, Benjamine, and others of the World War I generation for a mythical, childlike world where hidden beings abound and the dead are never really gone. But the images were also appallingly fake: Some of the angelic fairies sported stylish Parisian hairdos (they were cutouts from fashion magazines) and, on close scrutiny, one figure could be seen with a hat pin protruding from its middle.

In another of Benjamine's lesson plans, "The Sacred Tarot," he uncritically stated that the twenty-two major trumps of the Tarot deck were reproductions of images that lined the walls of an Egyptian mystery temple. He seems to have adopted the concept from nineteenth-century French occultist Paul Christian, who fatuously attributed it to Neoplatonic philosopher Iamblichus. The Church of Light advertised Benjamine's Tarot deck as "painstakingly designed from description of the figures seen on the walls of the Ancient Egyptian Initiation Chamber." Many of the images were actually painstakingly copied from those published in 1896 by still another Frenchman, René Falconnier. An actor by profession, Falconnier had enticingly reconstituted the

---

* In 1932, the brotherhood reorganized itself as the Church of Light, seeking legal protection when Los Angeles County passed anti-"fortune-telling" ordinances, similar to those in New York, which curtailed the commercial practice of astrology.

medieval-era figures of Tarot into Egyptian-style characters that resembled early costume designs for a Cecil B. DeMille movie. In fairness to Benjamine, he probably considered the Falconnier images authentic replicas of the "Egyptian" originals and was not trying to copycat another's work.

What Benjamine's writings lacked in scholarly rigor, they made up for in a surprising tone of civic-minded ethics. In his 1934 volume, *Predicting Events,* Benjamine emphasized the "Responsibility of the Astrologer to His Client." He inveighed against manipulation and fatalism, and insisted that the soothsayer should "ever bear in mind the power of suggestion" and always "point out the path of constructive endeavor" so that each reading would urge recipients to "CONTRIBUTE THEIR UTMOST TO UNIVERSAL WELFARE."

In the midst of the Great Depression, Benjamine conceived of a universalist belief system he called the Religion of the Stars. He saw it as an occult religion that could unite humanity under a peaceable, nonsectarian creed based in the study of ancient astrology and the pursuit of social welfare. Benjamine reasoned, quite cannily, that the festivals and cycles of most historic religions—from solstice celebrations to Christmas—coincided with astrological phenomena. Hence, he believed the ancient art could form the basis of a primeval, ecumenical faith. His 1930s print ads for the Religion of the Stars reflected the social values of Henry A. Wallace's "New Deal of the Ages." One showed a torch-bearing horseman riding a winged steed labeled *The New Civilization* and holding a flag that echoed Benjamine's motto: *CONTRIBUTE YOUR UTMOST TO UNIVERAL WELFARE.* The horse and rider leaped over the words *WANT, FEAR, CENSORSHIP, ATHEISM.* It was a stark counterpoint to contemporaneous ads by fellow occultist and neo-Nazi William Dudley Pelley, who advertised his "Silver Rangers" with another flag-bearing horseman, this one encircled by ominous slogans like: *Take Back the Nation from the Alien* and *Liberty Under Law.*

In the late 1940s, Benjamine traveled on lecture tours up and down both American coasts, attempting to recruit converts to his cosmic religion and its ideals of astrology, social welfare, and self-awareness. Shortly before his death in 1951, Benjamine wrote: "It seems inevitable that The Religion of the Stars shall become the world religion of the future because it includes all significant demonstrated facts of both the outer plane and the inner plane." If Benjamine never attracted quite the membership for which he hoped (his newsletters reached a peak of sixteen thousand people), he succeeded in imparting his style of liberal values to the American occult. Paul Foster Case's B.O.T.A. came to voice similar aims to those of the Religion of the Stars, defining itself as a "religious organization whose major objective is the promotion of the welfare of humanity through the realization of the potential inherent in each and every human being, utilizing the methods of the Western Mystery Tradition." It was as though the reformist and occult ideals of the Burned-Over District had migrated west, resulting in a progressive tone that marked the metaphysical culture for the rest of the century.

Go West, Young Magician

A prophet, Christ observed, is never honored in his homeland. So it was that America's occult prophets often traveled, and more than anywhere else they sought (and frequently found) popularity on the West Coast. Ever since the days of the California Gold Rush, the coast had attracted a steady stream of soothsayers, seers, mediums, and dowsers, the first of whom arrived to assist miners hunting after claims. Historian Fawn Brodie observed that Westerners traditionally "demanded personality rather than diplomas from the men who called them to God." Metaphysical teachers journeying from the east in the twentieth century found that they faced little scrutiny concerning educational credentials. Science of Mind's Ernest Holmes was a playground instructor and purchasing agent for Venice, California. The scribe of the Masters of the Far East, Baird T. Spalding, was a gold prospector. William Dudley Pelley, who spent "seven minutes in eternity," was a screenwriter. Psychiana's Frank B. Robinson was a druggist. Levi Dowling, author of *The Aquarian Gospel of Jesus the Christ,* was a homeopathic healer. Spencer Lewis, founder of the Ancient and Mystical Order Rosae Crucis (AMORC), was a commercial illustrator. These were entirely self-made religious leaders. But this is not to say that they were less than able. The occult denizens of the twentieth century, particularly those who found audiences on the West Coast, were extremely capable and often displayed an admirable fluidity to shatter the bonds of social position that might have held back earlier generations.

Occultists had influence in every stratum of California society. In the 1950s and 1960s, the political power couple Ronald and Nancy Reagan openly consulted astrologer Carroll Righter and psychic Jeane Dixon. Dixon, the wife of a wealthy real-estate dealer and a favorite among conservative politicians, had built her reputation on predicting the Kennedy assassination. In an article about Dixon on May 13, 1956, *Parade* magazine reported: "As for the 1960 election, Mrs. Dixon thinks it will be dominated by labor and won by a Democrat. But he will be assassinated or die in office 'though not necessarily in the first term.' " Dixon also made a vast catalog of spurious political and social predictions, some involving communist conspiracies and Israel converting en masse to Christianity.

As governor-elect, Reagan raised eyebrows in 1967 when he scheduled his first inauguration at the otherwise inexplicable hour of 12:10 A.M., prompting persistent questions—which continued throughout his presidency—over the extent of the couple's devotion to astrology. Reagan would admit only that "Nancy and I enjoy glancing at the daily astrology charts in our morning paper." But testimony from friends and political allies and even passages in Reagan's own memoirs attest to the seriousness with which the couple took the occult art and the degree to which they sought the advice of California stargazer Righter, who decided on the midnight inaugural.

While largely forgotten, Righter was once the undisputed dean of American astrology. Born to a prominent Philadelphia family, he began his career as an attorney in the 1930s at a large

Pennsylvania law firm. It was a respectable if colorless role in which he probably would have remained, were it not for the influence of New York astrologer Evangeline Adams. A family friend and famous stargazer who briefly hosted her own radio show until her death in 1932, Adams had encouraged Righter in the art since he was a teen. Bored with his legal career, Righter spent much of the Great Depression casting horoscopes to help the unemployed find work. Looking at his own stars, he determined that the West Coast would improve his fragile health, and he set out for Los Angeles in 1937. Once out west, he dropped his legal career and made his hobby of stargazing into a full-time profession. With his society manners and natty style of dress, Righter quickly attracted an upper-crust clientele in Hollywood, including Marlene Dietrich, Lana Turner, and Princess Grace. On March 21, 1969, he became the only astrologer to appear on the cover of *Time* magazine, staring out pale and gray, as though never touched by California sunshine.

If Righter was the stargazer to the rich and famous, he had a rival in another California arrival, Sydney Omarr, who in the 1950s and '60s was considered the thinking man's astrologer. With his gaunt frame, pencil-thin mustache, horn-rimmed eyeglasses, and intense gaze, the younger man could have been taken for a comic-book villain—the kind of mad scientist who vows, *Those fools at the university will never laugh at me again!* To Omarr, the future of astrology belonged to "ethical astrologers," as fluent in psychology as in the stars. The same issue of *Time* that anointed Righter the high priest of American astrology called Omarr a less flamboyant, "highly intelligent younger astrologer who has given up most of his private practice to devote himself to writing and promoting the cause." While Omarr actually maintained his private practice and, like Righter, published a popular newspaper horoscope column, the bookish forecaster did commit a fair amount of time to debating scientists and critics. He also made inroads with people not often associated with astrology. In 1960, Omarr wrote a short, intriguing book on the theme of astrology in the life and work of writer Henry Miller, titled *Henry Miller: His World of Urania*. Miller, who considered himself a practicing skeptic of astrology, took the book seriously enough to contribute a substantial foreword, calling astrological analysis "of inestimable aid to those who are tormented by the question of their proper role in life."

The Magic Boardwalk

Like Righter, Sydney Omarr was a native of Philadelphia, though possessed of a more modest background: He was born in 1926 to a clan of Jewish grocers with the family name Kimmelman. Sidney (as his name was then spelled) hung around local magic shops during the school year and spent summer vacations with his mother and sisters in Atlantic City, New Jersey, an urban beach town with a similar pedigree to Coney Island. Wandering the boardwalks at age fourteen, he discovered the same Professor A. F. Seward who had inspired the astrologer Zolar. Sidney loved watching the "scholarly-looking" Professor Seward sell dollar horoscopes to vacationers. And those dollars added up: Damon Runyon reported in a 1937 column that Seward owned a hotel and several apartment buildings in Miami Beach.

Seward attracted attention wherever he went, in a specially customized thirty-two-foot "land cruiser" sporting astrological symbols, brocade draperies, wooden griffins, and seven Magnavox loudspeakers. Behind the wheel, Sidney saw the image of the man he wanted to be. At fifteen, Sidney Kimmelman changed his name to Sydney Omarr, adopting the surname from Doctor Omar, a fez-wearing rogue (and "Doctor of Nothing") portrayed by movie idol Victor Mature in a 1941 caper, *The Shanghai Gesture*. The teenage occultist hit upon the unconventional spelling—adding an extra *y* to his first name and *r* to his last— through the magic of numerology, a hugely popular occult practice whereby names were converted to numerals (which had their own mystic interpretation) and sometimes altered to effect a desired outcome. Sydney probably never realized that the "ancient" art behind his new name also originated from his family's New Jersey vacation spot.

Number mysticism had its earliest roots in the Hebrew and Greek cultures, where numerals and letters shared common symbols and were sometimes seen to harbor hidden meaning. The dilemma for curious Americans was that English letters had no numeric equivalents. But an Atlantic City metaphysician remedied that. The first record of modern numerology (though it was not yet called that) appeared in the early 1900s in the writings of Sarah Joanna Dennis Balliett. Married to a local homeopathic physician, she was better known for her byline, Mrs. L. Dow Balliett. A woman of angular beauty, with high cheekbones and intelligent eyes, Balliett was widely respected in Atlantic City for her civic activities, such as the founding of a Women's Research Club, and for her impressive range of books on music, mysticism, and movement therapies. A self-professed student of "Pythagorean number mysticism," Balliett was the first intellect to assign numerals to the letters of the English alphabet. Based on the occult system of multiple digits reducing to single numerals (i.e., 10, as 1 + 0, equals 1), Balliett numbered the alphabet in a repeat pattern of 1 to 9, creating a formula to reveal and interpret the inner meaning of names, dates, and places in the manner of the ancient Greeks and Kabalists (or sort of).

The "Balliett System of Number-Vibration" achieved tremendous popularity under its more memorable name: numerology. The term seems to have been coined in 1871—with no occult connotation at all—by an American anarchist and cosmological philosopher, Stephen Pearl Andrews. He used it to refer to a universal philosophy of numbers. (Andrews also made the first use of the term *scientology*, again to define an all-compassing theory of life.) By the 1920s the term, which had appeared in several other contexts, was finally, and fatefully, attached to Balliett's system by one of her most industrious students, Julia Seton, a dentist and New Thought lecturer. The name stuck, and the practice inspired thousands of books and a widespread industry in modern number mysticism—all of it emanating from the sands of Atlantic City, the Alexandria of pop occultism.

Have You a Problem???

Back home in Philadelphia, the newly anointed Sydney Omarr flummoxed his parents, a couple with the unexotic names of Harry and Rose. But Omarr saw the future in more ways than one. He produced mimeographed editions of "Sydney Omarr's Private Course on Numerology," which sold for $2 at Philadelphia's famous book mart, Leary's. He began writing for astrology magazines, trading articles for classified ad space announcing: *Have You a Problem??? . . . Let Sydney Omarr Help You Solve It.* He charged $2 for a personal astrological and numerological profile. "My father, Harry, a grocer, and mother, Rose, a housewife, stopped worrying about me when the checks started coming in," Omarr recalled.

At seventeen, he joined the Army during World War II and attained the only official military post in astrology, though as an entertainer rather than a stargazing strategist. During the war, Omarr hosted a popular program on Okinawa Armed Forces Radio, where he predicted the results of horse races, boxing matches, and sporting events. His Army career coincided perfectly with the period when astrology was translating into mass entertainment, especially in the form of newspaper columns.

The horoscope column appears to have been born in England on August 24, 1930, when prognosticator R. H. Naylor cast a star chart for the infant Princess Margaret in the *Sunday Express.* Naylor's article included "a few hints on the happenings of this week" and general forecasts for upcoming birthdays. Readers loved it and wrote in for more, leading to a widely read weekly feature. America's newspaper empires took notice. The now ubiquitous "sun sign" columns, in which twelve short daily predictions are pegged to zodiacal birth symbols, probably got started in 1936 in the *New York Post,* which began running a feature by Edward A. Wagner, a reporter-turned-stargazer. By 1945, about 150 newspapers—still fewer than ten percent of all U.S. dailies—ran astrology columns. In the decades ahead, the trend exploded to the point where, by 1968, about 1,250 out of

1,750 daily papers included sun-sign columns. Reaching millions, the columns were dominated by the cohort of Omarr, Righter, and psychic Jeane Dixon (who Omarr complained to *The New York Times* wasn't "running a legitimate astrology column").

For Omarr, the 1960s and '70s were a time flush with regular appearances as the "house astrologer" on *The Merv Griffin Show,* high-flying parties, Santa Monica sunshine, and his own stable of movie-star clients. But, as he aged, the astrologer faced deep difficulties, physically and perhaps in other respects. By the early twenty-first century, in his seventies, he had been blinded and paralyzed by multiple sclerosis, diagnosed three decades earlier. His tone coarsened, as he bragged to biographers of once victimizing a weaker schoolmate. Toward the end of his life—possibly in need of funds or just entertaining a late-career thrill—the thinking-man's astrologer licensed *Sydney Omarr's Horoscope Slot Machine* to Las Vegas casinos. "Other business proposals riding on Omarr's name recognition are in the works," reported the *Los Angeles Times*—proposals that included the postmortem production of his books and columns by ghostwriters. It was not the legacy foreseen for the stargazer that *Time* had once called astrology's "most skillful and sober public protagonist." With success came a new temptation to the American occult, or at least to its biggest names: selling out.

CHAPTER ELEVEN

"THE GREATEST MYSTIC WHO EVER LIVED IN AMERICA"

✦ ✦ ✦

And though I have the gift of prophecy, and understand all mysteries, and all knowledge; and though I have all faith, so that I could remove mountains, and have not Love, I am nothing.

—1 CORINTHIANS 13:2

He came to Edgar Cayce a broken man—with an ugly past. He had been the business manager for the mystico-fascist order the Silver Shirts, and, though he withheld as much from the psychic, he had also been a Pennsylvania organizer for the Ku Klux Klan. Most recently, he helped build the Mighty I AM movement of Guy and Edna Ballard, the mystical sect marked by prosperity teachings and ultrapatriotism. All seemed to be going his way until the early hours of January 13, 1935, when he stepped from the Ballards' car while driving from Washington, D.C., to Baltimore and was struck by an oncoming vehicle.

Suffering from a broken skull and a shattered left leg, he could no longer work, and the Ballards dropped him. The couple spread the story, he told another ex-follower, "that my accident happened because I wasn't in the circle of Light with which they had surrounded the car."

Still in pain and searching for work six years later, the man wrote to Cayce, a reputed miracle worker living in Virginia Beach, Virginia. Cayce was said to be able to go into a sleeplike trance and diagnose and prescribe cures for the illnesses of people he never met; he also gave psychic counsel and advice. Between the opening years of the twentieth century and his death on January 3, 1945, Cayce (pronounced *casey*) delivered more than fourteen thousand documented trance readings. Literally thousands of correspondents, many of whom were diagnosed from long distances away and were known to Cayce only by their names, swore to the effectiveness of the treatments prescribed by a man with no medical training and little schooling. Cayce also performed "life readings" in which he was said to peer into a person's past—including past lives—and help the subject find his proper calling and direction in the present. This was why his new correspondent got in touch. He was having trouble caring for his family and was in desperate need of guidance. He could not even afford the $20 Cayce typically charged for a reading. Could the psychic, he wondered, see a way to help him?

"A reading," Cayce replied on January 9, 1941, "would possibly help and you can arrange to take care of the fee at some future date—no one is ever refused here because of lack of money." The following month, Cayce, in his usual preparation, loosened his tie, belt, cuffs, and shoelaces, and reclined on a lumpy gray-green sofa in the study of his Virginia Beach home. With observers and a stenographer looking on, Cayce uttered a silent prayer and drifted into a sleeplike state from which he transmitted the words of an ethereal intelligence called "the Source." While he claimed to have no recollection of what occurred during his trances, he made detailed responses to questions, often speaking in the vernacular of the King James Bible. His statements could be stilted and difficult to follow, with none of the lucidity of the later "channeled" literature that Cayce inspired. But on scrutiny, the intent could usually be found.

Cayce counseled the man to "[keep] self unspotted from condemnation of others." Condemnation must be "eliminated from the expressions," for "as ye condemn, so ARE ye condemned," he told the former Klansman. "Know," Cayce concluded, "as the choice is made, that it must be only 'The Way.' For, as given, he that climbs up some other way is a thief and a robber."

The recipient was unsatisfied. "Frankly," he wrote Cayce, the reading at first "did not make a very favorable impression on me." Oblivious to the reading's ethical dimension, the man felt he had been misunderstood and wrote back: "I have no desire to make money for money's sake." Cayce twice wrote him to urge that he discuss the reading with one of the clairvoyant's longtime friends and supporters, a New York furniture manufacturer named David Kahn. Like Cayce, Kahn had grown up as something of a misfit—a Jewish grocer's son raised in Lexington, Kentucky, where the pair met in 1907. Cayce came from a small farming town and was still unsure what to make of his psychic "gift." In a clairvoyant reading for one of Kahn's neighbors, he prescribed little-known osteopathic treatments that restored the health of a woman who had been severely hurt in an automobile accident. Kahn became a source of encouragement and a tireless promoter of Cayce, telling journalists he was "the greatest mystic who ever lived in America." It could not have been lost on Cayce that he was now sending a former organizer for the anti-Semitic Silver Shirts to ponder his "life reading" with a Jewish man.

But Cayce was not always so deft or so wise. While in a trance state, Cayce was on rare occasions himself heard to utter racist nostrums. Contrary to his waking behavior, such remarks seemed to bubble from the recesses of his rural childhood under a notoriously bigoted father. He suggested from a trance state on June 18, 1923, that people of African descent had no soul. During another reading, on November 4, 1933, he heralded Hitler as a man "psychically led." Other times, Cayce could make prophecies that were just wrong—predictions of earthquakes and environmental cataclysms, social upheavals and political swings, which never occurred.

Then there was the more familiar Cayce: the man who people of all backgrounds said was marked by unusual personal decency and warmth, who often gave psychical readings for free, at times leaving himself and his family in a state of near poverty.

More typical of Cayce's trance statements was this one from June 16, 1939, when he was asked about black Americans: "He is thy brother! . . . For He hath made of one blood the nations of the earth." This Cayce had an influence so vast that the accumulated record of his readings ultimately altered the American vocabulary, making words like *reincarnation, clairvoyance, meditation, channeling, past lives,* and *psychic* into household terms. The cures he prescribed—involving herbs, whole foods, and mind–body therapies—laid the bedrock for the revolution in alternative medicine that swept the country years after his death. Cayce's readings formed the sourcebook for a generation of spiritual writers and seekers. More than anyone else, this contradictory figure, whose childhood was marked by the traditions of deep-woods Kentucky, became the chief catalyst in opening the nation—and in some ways the world—to the religious–therapeutic ideas of the New Age.

"Help the Sick"

Cayce was born on March 18, 1877, in a town called Beverly in Western Kentucky. It was a place that didn't see its first paved road until 1932. Tobacco was the major crop, and nearly everyone owned farmland or worked for someone who did. Memories of the Civil War ran deep, and the line between blacks and whites was like a razor fence. Although Cayce's childhood could be harsh—his father was known to drink and sometimes mete out beatings—there was unmistakable closeness and trust in the family. Even when Cayce was well into middle age, his father, Leslie, would address him in letters as "My Dear Sweet Precious Boy." Outside of home, school, and church, there were few activities or distractions. Even visiting the larger neighboring town of Hopkinsville required a buggy ride of more than twelve miles.

In this insular world, Cayce grew up as a sensitive, awkward child. Thin and tall for his age, he liked playing and spending time alone and was given to wandering through the meadows and woodlands that surrounded his home. Adults found him distracted and distant. He reported visitations from fairylike "friends" and communications with deceased relatives. At nine, when other boys became obsessed with fishing or sports, Cayce grew enthralled with Scripture and begged his father—a man never quite possessed of steady work—to buy a Bible for their home. He began reading through the entire book each year. One night at age thirteen, this boy who talked with hidden friends and consumed Scripture knelt by his bed and prayed for the ability to be of help to others. Just before going to sleep, he recalled in his memoirs, a glorious light filled the room and a feminine apparition appeared at the foot of his bed, telling him: *Thy prayers are heard. You will have your wish. Remain faithful. Be true to yourself. Help the sick, the afflicted.*

Cayce first discovered his power for trance readings in 1901 when, stricken by chronic laryngitis, he entered a hypnotic state and successfully diagnosed his own illness. In the years ahead, he worked on the fringes of mainstream medicine—with hypnotists, osteopaths, and homeopaths—going into trance states and prescribing folk cures, natural remedies, and more-conventional treatments for hundreds of ill people. Again and again, stories and testimonies held that his readings and remedies worked. Newspapers and medical investigators began paying attention, and, in what represented Cayce's debut on the national stage, *The New York Times* ran a long article on October 9, 1910: *Illiterate Man Becomes a Doctor When Hypnotized.*

Cayce was not illiterate, but neither was he well educated. He never made it beyond the eighth grade of a rural schoolhouse. Though he taught Sunday school at his Disciples of Christ church, he read little outside of Scripture. Aside from a few on-and-off years wildcatting in Texas oil fields in the early 1920s— where he tried, and failed, to raise money for a hospital based on his clairvoyant cures—Cayce rarely ventured beyond the Bible Belt environs of his childhood. Since the tale of Jonah fleeing from the word of God, prophets have been characterized as reluctant, ordinary folk plucked from reasonably satisfying lives to embark on missions they never sought. In this sense, if the impending Aquarian Age or New Age—the sprawling marketplace of Eastern, esoteric, and therapeutic spirituality that exploded on the national scene in the late 1960s and 1970s—was seeking a prophet, Cayce was hardly an unusual choice, but, historically, he was a perfect one.

The Occult Philosophy

If the New Age could be said to possess a starting point, it might be traced to the early autumn of 1923 in Selma, Alabama. After his failed oil ventures, Cayce resettled his family there to resume an intermittent career as a commercial photographer and enroll his sixteen-year-old son, Hugh Lynn, in Selma High. Cayce's readings had reportedly cured Hugh Lynn of blindness at age six, following a flash-powder accident, and the boy was devoted to his father's mission. Cayce's wife, Gertrude, was less certain. She had suffered Cayce's absences while struggling with a new baby son, Edgar Evans, and ached for the family to assume a normal life.

In September, a wealthy printer from Dayton, Ohio, Arthur Lammers, came to visit Cayce at his photography studio. Lammers had learned about Cayce during the psychic's oil-prospecting days. The Ohioan was an unlikely combination of hard-driving businessman—stocky and tough, with sharp eyes and powerful limbs—and an avid seeker in Theosophy, ancient religions, and the occult. He and his wife maintained a Victorian mansion in Dayton with stained-glass windows, a pipe organ, and book-shelves lined with what Poe would have called "many a quaint and curious volume of forgotten lore." The businessman–occultist insisted that the seer could use his powers for more than medical diagnosis. He wanted Cayce to probe the secrets of the ages: What happens after death? Is there a soul? Why are we here? Moreover, Lammers wanted to understand the mysteries of the pyramids, astrology, alchemy, the "Etheric World," reincarnation, and the esoteric religions of ancient Egypt and Greece.

Cayce had been willing to put up with the stares and whispers from churchgoing friends and neighbors regarding his trance readings, but astrology and other occult topics seemed vaguely heretical to him. For all his outer humility, however, Cayce was a man of ambitions. The psychical researcher Martin Ebon noted that Cayce showed "the weakness . . . to give in to the demanding questions of the True Believers, to those who wanted to see him as all-knowing." And after years of stalled progress in his outer life, Cayce was enticed by the new sense of mission. Lammers urged Cayce to move with him to Dayton, assuring the psychic that he and his family would be well cared for there. Lammers offered Cayce not only a way up in the world but possibly funds for the alternative-healing hospital Cayce dreamed of.

Cayce returned with Lammers to Dayton and soon uprooted Gertrude and Edgar Evans to join him in a two-room efficiency apartment Lammers had rented for them. The older boy, Hugh Lynn, remained behind with friends in Selma to finish out the school term. Cayce also brought to Dayton a new intimate of the family: his attractive, meticulous eighteen-year-old stenographer, Gladys Davis, whom he had recently hired to transcribe his readings. Gertrude could only have looked askance at the younger woman living in close quarters with her family. But Davis's devotions seemed limited to the Cayce readings alone, which she spent the rest of her life organizing. For Gertrude, Dayton meant another period of uncertainty. There is little record of the loneliness she must have felt or her difficulty in making new friends when the inevitable question that a homemaker would have been asked was: "What does your husband do?" But for Lammers and Cayce, the move marked the launch of an extraordinary inner journey.

Cayce and Lammers began their explorations at a downtown Dayton hotel on October 11, 1923. In the presence of several onlookers, Lammers arranged for Cayce to enter a trance and give him an astrological reading. Whatever hesitancies the waking Cayce felt over arcane subjects vanished while he was in his psychical state. Cayce expounded deeply on astrological questions, affirming the art's basic value, even as "the Source" alluded to misconceptions in the Western model. Near the end of the reading, Cayce almost casually tossed off that it was

Lammers's "third appearance on this [earthly] plane. He was once a monk." There was a stunned silence in the room. Here was an unmistakable reference to reincarnation. It was exactly what Lammers had been looking for.

For the following month, the men continued their readings, probing further into Hermetic and esoteric spirituality. From a trance state on October 18, Cayce laid out for Lammers, the reincarnated monk, what appeared to be an entire philosophy of life, dealing with reincarnation, man's role in the cosmic order, and the hidden purpose of existence:

> In this we see the plan of development of those individuals set upon this plane, meaning the ability (as would be manifested from the physical) to enter again into the presence of the Creator and become a full part of that creation.
>
> Insofar as this entity is concerned, this is the third appearance on this plane, and before this one, as the monk. We see glimpses in the life of the entity now as were shown in the monk, in his mode of living.
>
> The body is only the vehicle ever of that spirit and soul that waft through all times and ever remain the same.

These phrases were, for Lammers, the golden key to the mysteries: a theory of eternal recurrence that identified man's purpose on earth as perfectibility through karma and repeat cycles of birth, then reintegration with the source of Creation. This, the printer believed, was the hidden truth behind the Scriptural injunction to be "born again" so as to "enter the kingdom of Heaven."

"It opens up the door," Lammers enthused. "It's like finding the secret chamber of the Great Pyramid." He told Cayce that the doctrine that had come through the readings seemed to synchronize the wisdom traditions of the world: "It's Hermetic, it's Pythagorean, it's Jewish, it's Christian!" Cayce wasn't sure what to believe. "The important thing," Lammers reassured him, "is that the basic system which runs through all the mystery traditions, whether they come from Tibet or the Pyramids of Egypt, is backed up by you. It's actually the right system. . . . It not only agrees with the best ethics of religion and society, it is actually the source of them."

Lammers's enthusiasms aside, the religious ideas that emerged from Cayce's trances did articulate a compelling theology. They sought to marry a Christian moral outlook with the cycles of karma and reincarnation central to Hindu and Buddhist ways of thought and with the Hermetic concept of man as an extension of the Divine. If there was an inner, or occult, philosophy behind the world's historic faiths, Cayce had come as close as any modern person to defining it.

The Power of Past Lives

Dayton marked a period in which Cayce went beyond medical clairvoyance (though he never abandoned it as the mainstay of his work), engaging more and more in readings on "past lives." The past lives he found were rarely ordinary. Subjects were often reported to be ancient priests or priestesses, denizens of lost civilizations, historic kings and warriors. Indeed, the figures that populated Cayce's past-life catalog took forms and personas similar to those who peopled a vast project initiated several years earlier by the English Theosophist Charles Webster Leadbeater. Both Cayce and Leadbeater attributed their insights to the same source. Cayce said he was able to access cosmic records imprinted on the *akasha*, or universal ether. These "akashic records" were a concept derived from sacred Hindu writings and popularized in the late nineteenth century by Madame Blavatsky. Cayce, in his Christian worldview, equated *akasha* with the Book of Life.

Leadbeater and Cayce were probably the two most influential occult thinkers in the years between the world wars—yet the men were stark opposites. Leadbeater was the kind of square-jawed Englishman who made others step out of his way: He was built like a mountain, his angular face was softened only slightly by a bushy beard and wavy white hair, and his glinting eyes were sometimes malevolent, his smile unkind. Leadbeater was a bull-dozer, physically and intellectually—world-traveled, well read, witty to a razor's edge, and ruthless toward adversaries. His libertine lifestyle was dogged by charges of pederasty. Cayce, on the other hand, looked and sounded every bit the small-town photographer and Sunday-school teacher, with his gentle bespectacled eyes, jowly face, receding gray hair, stooped shoulders, and potbelly. He was as mild a man as you could hope to meet. Yet the two contemporaries, a world apart geographically and ethically, embarked on a remarkably similar journey.

Leadbeater's venture into the past began in 1909 when he discovered an unusual, sensitive boy, Jiddu Krishnamurti, playing on the beach near Theosophy's headquarters in Adyar, India. He and Annie Besant saw the boy as the incarnation of a new "World Teacher." (Krishnamurti did, after breaking with Theosophy, become a deeply respected and unclassifiable spiritual teacher.) Leadbeater began to construct an epic, encyclopedic timeline of the past lives of Krishnamurti and his companions. Calling him by the esoteric name *Alcyone* (for the entity repeatedly reborn through him), Leadbeater in 1910 began serializing his *Lives of Alcyone*. Alcyone/Krishnamurti and his historical companions made up the temple hierarchies of mythical Atlantis and ancient Egypt and left their marks as statesmen, alchemists, warriors, and philosophers of the ancient world. In a sense, Leadbeater had created a grand prehistory for the lives of his fellow Theosophists.

Cayce's readings favored similar historical settings and characters to Leadbeater's: Atlantis and the cities of Hellenic and pre-Columbian empires. Past lives were not without tragedy: Amid the Egyptian princes and princesses, Hellenic conquerors, and Atlantean priests were also victims of war, rape, and other brutalities—sufferings that, in the philosophy of the Cayce readings, explained present-day neuroses in the lives of their subjects. Indeed, Cayce's subjects often reported feeling relieved at being able to understand current pathologies or obsessions as the result of violence or tragedy in a previous incarnation.

The Cayce family (in its twentieth-century version) provided a case in point. In his biography by journalist A. Robert Smith, Cayce's elder son, Hugh Lynn, made the startlingly frank admission that throughout his teenage years he experienced profound sexual longings for his mother. All this came to a head in 1923 when the high-schooler traveled to Dayton to rejoin his family for a troubling Christmas. When his father came to pick him up at the train station, Hugh Lynn hugged him and felt the crinkle of paper: Edgar had stuffed newspaper into his thin overcoat to protect him from the cold of the Midwest winter. Lammers, it seemed, had experienced a series of sudden business setbacks and had left the Cayce family destitute. While embroiled in out-of-town lawsuits, the great searcher into the unknown had not even bothered to send the Cayces a few dollars for groceries. Their Christmas dinner consisted of a chicken that could be cupped in the hands. In another unsettling discovery for the teen who had stood so solidly behind his father, Hugh Lynn was told by Edgar about his new psychical experiments into past lives. And as a Christmas gift, Edgar explained, he had secretly performed one for Hugh Lynn, discovering that the lad had once been a great ruler in ancient Egypt. Even by Cayce standards, the family seemed to have slid off the edge.

But as Hugh Lynn listened to his reading, things began to change. The reading took on the eerily familiar tones of the boy's innermost conflicts: his agonizing attraction toward his mother and his jealousy and resentment of his father. Hugh Lynn, Edgar revealed, had been an Egyptian monarch who coveted a beautiful dancer named Isis. But Isis's affections were for the kingdom's high priest, Ra Ta, with whom she had a daughter. Infuriated, the ruler exiled them both. The high priest, Edgar explained, was an earlier incarnation of Hugh Lynn's father, and the dancer Isis was the past life of his mother. Hugh Lynn was stunned. He had taken every measure to conceal his feelings, but here was this karmic psychodrama that reframed his neurosis in mythical or archetypal terms.

In its way, Hugh Lynn said, the story helped him find a kind of peace. "The reading explained very clearly that what I felt for my father and for my mother was memory," he told his biographer. "And I was responsible for what kind of memory I had. I was imposing on my father a whole set of ideas that didn't exist. I was jealous of him, but I had no right to be jealous in the present-day situation. . . . You see, I was putting on him my own weaknesses, my own problems—and we all do it."

It was similar to the experience of others who sought out Cayce for past-life readings. Whatever their source, Cayce's hundreds of past-life readings did provide a sense of context and meaning that helped resolve feelings of helplessness and anguish in the lives of their recipients, many of whom returned for multiple sessions. The past-life readings prefigured some of the key themes that later ran through Jungian and transpersonal therapies and the work of widely read mythologists such as Joseph Campbell and Robert Bly. Stripped of occult methodology, the insights of the Cayce readings also echoed Freud's theories of repression and the development of neuroses.

The Esoteric Healer

After escaping the poverty of Dayton through the help of a new donor in 1925, Cayce relocated his activities to Virginia Beach, a town selected by the readings. Cayce enjoyed the ocean climate and nearby fishing. In Virginia, he at last raised enough money to start his "Hospital of Enlightenment." In 1929, Cayce and his supporters opened a thirty-bed facility on a small hill overlooking the Atlantic. It provided a comforting, homey setting that more resembled a shingled seaside inn than a medical facility. But it was a real clinic. Amid the sunshine, shuffleboard, and tennis, the Cayce Hospital had a staff of MDs, nurses, osteopaths, and chiropractors. Patients could receive clairvoyant diagnoses and alternative therapies such as massage and colonics, along with modern X rays, urinalyses, and blood work. Cayce delivered a metaphysical lecture each Sunday. He made some of the first prescriptions of meditation as an emotional and physical aid. But, in one of the deepest tragedies of Cayce's life, the onslaught of the Great Depression closed the hospital within two years. Attempts to open a metaphysical college, Atlantic University, met with similar results. Crestfallen and withdrawn, Cayce sought solace in the activities he knew as a boy: Bible-reading, gardening, fishing, and chopping wood. While his frame sagged under his disappointment, he carried on his clairvoyant readings at an intensive pace.

Readings carried a fee of $20, which included membership in Cayce's nascent organization, the Association for Research and Enlightenment (A.R.E.). Records show that he often reduced or waived payments altogether, particularly during the Depression, when he might give a reading for a dollar or two sent by an injured laborer, an ailing homemaker, or the parent of a sick child. Here is Cayce on March 29, 1940, writing to a blind man employed as a chair re-caner, who asked about paying in installments: "You may take care of the membership any way convenient to your self—please know one is not prohibited from having a reading if they really desire same because they haven't money. If this information is of a divine source it can't be sold, if it isn't then it isn't worth any thing."

In the kind of medical encounter that typified Cayce's career, a respected New York publisher, William Sloane, had an unforgettable brush with the readings. In 1940, Sloane agreed to consider a manuscript on the seer's life, *There Is a River*, by Thomas Sugrue. It was a highly sympathetic biography assembled by a journalist who had been Hugh Lynn's college roommate and who believed a Cayce reading had saved his life. Sloane was initially wary but changed his mind when Cayce's clairvoyant diagnosis helped one of his own children. Novelist and screenwriter Nora Ephron recounted the episode in a 1968 article she wrote for *The New York Times*. "I read it," said Sloane, then an editor at Holt, Rinehart & Winston. "Now there isn't any way to test a manuscript like this. So I did the only thing I could do." He went on:

> *A member of my family, one of my children, had been in*
> *great and continuing pain. We'd been to all the doctors*
> *and dentists in the area and all the tests were negative*
> *and the pain was still there. I wrote Cayce, told him my*

child was in pain and would be at a certain place at such-and-such a time, and enclosed a check for $25. He wrote back that there was an infection in the jaw behind a particular tooth. So I took the child to the dentist and told him to pull the tooth. The dentist refused—he said his professional ethics prevented him from pulling sound teeth. Finally, I told him he would have to pull it. One tooth more or less didn't matter, I said—I couldn't live with the child in such pain. So he pulled the tooth and the infection was there and the pain went away. I was a little shook. I'm the kind of man who believes in X-rays. About this time, a member of my staff who thought I was nuts to get involved with this took even more precautions in writing to Cayce than I did, and he sent her back facts about her own body only she could have known. So I published Sugrue's book.

Come as You Were

There Is a River appeared in 1942, less than three years before Cayce's death, and brought him the kind of national attention his admirers had long wanted. In its review pages, *The Christian Century,* a journal not typically given to occult enthusiasms, called Cayce "a genuine psychic and . . . also a simple, direct and religious personality." The reviewer, Margueritte Harmon Bro, followed up with a widely circulated article, "Miracle Man of Virginia Beach," which appeared in the newsstand digest *Coronet.** The wave of publicity brought equal attention to the spiritual and psychical concepts in the Cayce readings, including astrology, reincarnation, karma, mind–body healing, and trance cognition. Such material was now making inroads into mainstream publishing houses. Another book that began its publish-

---

* Bro was one of the first serious journalists to look into Cayce. Her son, Harmon, later worked with Cayce and in 1955 completed a University of Chicago Divinity School doctoral dissertation on Cayce as a religious seer/healer.

ing life with Sloane went one step further in establishing Cayce and his ideas.

The year 1956 saw the publication of a sensationally popular best seller, *The Search for Bridey Murphy,* by Morey Bernstein, an amateur hypnotist and Ivy League–educated dealer in scrap metal and heavy machinery. (He jokingly referred to his family business as "Ulcers, Incorporated.") Inspired by Cayce's career, Bernstein conducted a series of experiments with a Pueblo, Colorado, housewife who, under a hypnotic trance, regressed into a past-life persona: an early-nineteenth-century Irish country girl named Bridey Murphy. The entranced homemaker spoke in an Irish brogue and recounted comprehensive details of her life more than a century earlier. On paper and in person, Bernstein exuded a likability and genuineness that made him a hugely convincing figure, nothing like the Poe-styled version of a creepy Mesmerist that was making the rounds in Hammer horror films. In fact, when Bernstein's story came to the screen, actor Louis Hayward captured his dry, straight-talking style impeccably in a much-hyped movie version of *The Search for Bridey Murphy,* which was rushed into production later that year.

Suddenly, reincarnation—an ancient Hindu concept about which Americans had heard little before World War II—was the latest craze. In 1956, *Life* magazine wrote of past-life costume soirees called *Come as You Were* parties. A popular joke made the rounds: *Did you hear the one about the man who read* Bridey Murphy *and changed his will? He left everything to himself.* Books on occultism, hypnosis, and reincarnation were suddenly mainstream hits. "It's the hottest thing since Norman Vincent Peale," reported a Houston bookseller. Melvin Powers, a pioneering New Age publisher in Los Angeles, saw sales on some of his titles multiply twenty-five times.

Not everyone was amused. Mainstream medical authorities had long been seeking a proper place for hypnosis, which had made considerable strides since the days of Mesmerism and Andrew Jackson Davis (a seer whose rustic childhood, some noted, closely resembled Cayce's own). A century before *The Search for Bridey Murphy,* a Scottish medical practitioner named James Braid had begun using the term *hypnotism* to demarcate the medically provable applications of trance therapy from its occult associations. Sigmund Freud used hypnosis to begin his researches into the unconscious mind. A more sober view of hypnotism began to reach even the mail-order audience. In 1899, an amateur Chicago hypnotist named Arthur L. Webb published a how-to pamphlet, "Somnambulism," which set about banishing the ghosts of Mesmerism. "I must . . . take issue with those who claim the hypnotist is a person of supernatural power," Webb wrote, calling for the practice to be placed "in the hands of physicians" in order to ensure its fullest potential.

Just prior to the publication of *The Search for Bridey Murphy,* the British Medical Society cautiously affirmed the medical benefits of hypnotism but condemned its use for probing psychical powers. The American Medical Association concurred, noting—in a statement that could sober up a bottle of liquor—that the practice showed particular promise for "a trained and qualified dentist" who "might use hypnosis for hypnoanesthesia, hypnoanalgesia, or for the allaying of anxiety in relation to dental work." A tug-of-war developed between those medical authorities who, like the AMA, saw hypnotism as little more than a method of anesthetizing and others who believed it held potential for the exploration of clairvoyance or higher forms of cognition. Philosophers and scientists including Harvard's William James, British researcher F. W. H. Myers, and Duke University's J. B. Rhine wanted to strip away a carnival atmosphere without imperiling reasoned inquiries into the potentials of the human mind.

Indeed, within the work of Cayce himself there existed something far more than fodder for reincarnation parties, paperback books, and hobby hypnotists. Cayce was often critical of spiritual trends and shortcuts. When followers who were forming a study group asked him about using mental visualizations or affirmations—precisely the kinds of practices favored in most New Thought circles—he said in a trance reading: "To visualize by picturizing [sic] is to BECOME idol worshippers. Is this pleasing, with thy conception of thy God that has given, 'Have no other gods before me?' . . . Then, let rather thy service ever be, 'Not my will, O God, but Thine be done in me, through me.'"

Those who closely looked into Cayce's work discovered that it conveyed a consistent set of values. Cayce returned inquirers, again and again, to the principle that the esoteric core of religions, the search for inner knowing, the mystical teachings of the Bible, or any communication received through some kind of metaphysical faculty was worthless unless applied in the pursuit of higher aims, which he conceived in specifically Christian terms. Here, for example, is Cayce during a trance reading in January of 1935, responding to a question on what is required for spiritual growth: "Faith, hope and—MOST of all—PATIENCE! 'In patience possess ye your souls.' Be patient even in those periods of exaltation, joy, sorrow, woe. For in this do all become aware of the CONTINUITY of life itself; the more and more that this is made aware in the experience of the soul, more and more may the hope and the faith grow. Be patient."

"If You Can't Help Me, No Person on Earth Can"

Cayce's maturation as an ethicist was often unappreciated during his lifetime. The reach of his empathy may be the truest source of his greatness. During the Christmas season of 1935, Cayce received an urgent letter from a young cousin, a Kentucky college student, who confided, "I am a homosexual." The twenty-one-year-old had been seeing a psychologist but was obviously receiving nothing of value. "As far as I can explain for a reason for my condition," he wrote Cayce, "I think masturbation has played a role in it. Of course I realize that environment and other things have also helped to bring about my state of mind. But still I am determined to carry out and believe anything that you say or suggest if it is different from what the psychologist [says] because he never helped me and I have my doubts as to his knowledge of me."

Having nowhere else to turn—and fearful that his strict Catholic family should ever learn the truth—the boy implored

Cayce for advice on how to go on living: "I honestly feel down in my heart that if you can't help me, no person on earth can."

The psychic was now well into middle age—a man raised in a backwoods town, who never finished grade school, was called an "illiterate" in the press, read little beyond Scripture, and taught at religiously conservative Sunday schools. In virtually every respect, Cayce might seem a miscast confidant. But he replied with a letter of unusual depth and sensitivity. Cayce told the young man:

> Sex, of course, is a great factor in everyone's life; it is the line between the great and the vagabond, the good and the bad; it is the expression of reactive forces in our very nature; allowed to run wild, to self-indulgence, becomes physical and mental derangement; turned into the real influence it should be in one's life, connects man closer with his God, and this is the use you should put it to. . . . That your experience has brought you manifestations that have at times, or often, expressed themselves in sex is not to be wondered at, when we realize that that is the expression of creative life on earth.

Those around the youth, Cayce advised, held no control, no key to the meaning of his existence; he said that the young man's purpose in life was to discover who he really was and to follow that, always with the aim of Christian love. Within Cayce's tone and counsel appear the stirrings of the drive toward "self-realization" that marked the alternative spiritual movements and transpersonal therapies of later decades. Yet nothing in Cayce's background would suggest his ability to write with such insight and depth. Leaving aside whatever debate may be had about the question of his psychical abilities or whether such things exist, Cayce appeared to tap in to something that was knowing, humane, and capable of taking a higher measure of situations—and it all seemed to come from somewhere *else*, somewhere other than the obvious cultural touchstones of his life.

"Knowledge not lived is sin," read the masthead of a newsletter Cayce published in the months before his death in January 1945. In both deed and word, Cayce embodied the principle that inner teachings must be—if they are to be anything—methods of service. Cayce would have understood the Talmudic precepts that whoever makes a worldly crown of religion will waste away and that saving a single life is as saving the whole world. As practiced by Cayce, esoteric teachings existed to bring respite, to create a "channel" (as he put it) for good into the world. This prophet of the New Age introduced hope and dignity into lives and places where conventional messages and messengers had failed to reach. And this, in the end, was the highest legacy of occult America.

AQUARIUS RISING
The New Age Dawns

✦ ✦ ✦

*It is in America that the transformation will take place,
and has already silently commenced.*

—H. P. BLAVATSKY, *THE SECRET DOCTRINE*, 1888

As the 1950s ushered in the development of jet propulsion and space flight, Americans became less interested in other-dimensional worlds than in those that lay beyond the stars. For spiritual journeyers, however, the stars and the inner realms could seem intimately related. Space was thought to hold mysteries and possibly unknown intelligences as fantastic as any Masters of Wisdom.

Tantalizing possibilities emerged during the final months of World War II, when Allied fighter pilots—people whose clear-headedness and abilities no one could question—brought home strange reports of flying objects they called "foo fighters." Foo fighters were silvery or fiery spheres that appeared from out of nowhere and flew alongside the pilots' planes. The balls or disks had no obvious means of propulsion but seemed under some kind of intelligent command. "If it was not a hoax or an optical illusion," *Time* magazine wrote on January 15, 1945, "it was certainly the most puzzling secret weapon that Allied fighters have yet encountered." But Allied scientists could detect no last-ditch "superweapon" or anything that explained the weird flying objects.

As returning Crusaders had brought home tales of myth and wonder, so American warriors returned with a new riddle. One can only guess how an idea or observation becomes viral, but starting in 1947, American civilians—most notably a Washington state pilot named Kenneth Arnold—began to report a spate of "flying saucer" sightings. The flying objects appeared over Los Angeles, Washington, D.C., and, most famously, at the Air Force base near Roswell, New Mexico. The U.S. military and the militaries of other nations took the matter seriously enough to launch official investigations, and a new term entered the American lexicon: *Unidentified Flying Object*. But the military investigations, rather than reaching conclusive explanations or framing meaningful questions, became a round-robin of contradictory statements and fodder for theories of a government cover-up.

For pulp fans, a similarly infectious but more sinister narrative was unfolding. In the 1940s, a bounding subculture of readers grew enthralled with reports of "inner earth" and its alien inhabitants. Hollow-earth theories had a long and tangled history, and the legend resurfaced in a series of "true" stories that began running in January 1944 in the pulp monthly *Amazing Stories*. Richard Sharpe Shaver, a Pennsylvanian writer–artist, philosopher, factory worker, and sometime mental patient, promulgated the mythology of an underground race that most definitely did not wish humanity well. His tales were defended and embellished by the magazine's energetic editor, Ray Palmer. Many thrilled to the stories and—as with William Dudley Pelley's "Seven Minutes in Eternity"—wrote in to report their own encounters with evil figures "in the caves."

The larger body of science-fiction fans revolted. Pulp readers wanted tales of rocket ships, laser guns, and Buck Rogers–type heroes, not "strange-but-true" paranormal dramas. In New York, the Queens Science Fiction League (a group you apparently didn't want to get on the wrong side of) passed a resolution condemning Shaver's "inner-earth" tales as a danger to readers' mental health. In 1948, Ziff–Davis, the corporate owner of *Amazing Stories,* got tired of the complaints and cut off the mike: The Shaver mystery was thereafter banned from its pages.

The disappointed editor, Palmer, resigned in protest. Part true-believer and part opportunist, Palmer took a maverick stand to continue on with the Shaver narrative and a range of other occult tales in a series of poorly edited, digest-size monthlies, including *Mystic* and *Search.* The Palmer magazines committed the most oft-repeated sin among occult journals: Their sloppily written pieces actually made the bizarre and unknown seem *boring.* The only endearing factor was Palmer's brand of unfathomable logic: "When you read this story," he told readers of *Mystic* in 1953, "you will tell yourself that it is fiction; the editors assure you that it is. But what if it isn't?" And only Palmer, in the history of American letters, could seriously run this *Notice to Contributors:* "It is not the policy of MYSTIC Magazine to pay for the material it publishes. Its purpose is to present the truth, and the truth cannot be bought." But apparently it could be sold, as the magazine's liveliest content came from its bazaar of advertisements from occult schools proffering Rosicrucian, Mayan, and Yogic mysteries or de Laurence–style pitches for talking boards, magic crystals, and Tarot cards. In what must have been the only UFO-celebrity endorsement for a dandruff shampoo, flying-saucer witness Kenneth Arnold lent his name to the masculine TURN-ER'S: "Because Ken's no sissy, and he doesn't put perfume on his hair."

Readers abandoned *Mystic* and its spin-offs to limp into obscurity through the '60s. The sole occult digest to survive the Palmer era was a magazine that he cofounded and then quickly left in the hands of his partner, Curtis Fuller: *Fate,* a monthly that endures to the present day. With its "true reports" of UFOs, magical powers, monsters, and strange worlds (and a standard of writing that aimed a little higher than what appeared in the Palmer journals), *Fate* ignited the childhood imagination of many sci-fi writers, filmmakers, and special-effects maestros of the next generation.

In the Cards

As the 1950s wore on, the occult could seem like something of a spent force in American life. Foes of Spiritualism had exposed one mediumistic fraud after another; Theosophy, with an aging membership and no more communiqués from the Masters, had begun to seem like a frumpy lecture society; the Reverend Norman Vincent Peale had retooled the Mesmeric and New Thought–based practices of "positive thinking" into mild motivational fare; and the most vibrant personalities of the American occult, from Baird T. Spalding to Edgar Cayce, had passed on to Summer Land. By the end of the decade, the occult could appear to be little more than an amalgam of eccentrics and loners who sat "vain, nervous, inept, neurotic, and fearful in their chintz-curtained apartments," philosopher Jacob Needleman wrote, "complacently treasuring The Hidden Knowledge."

A new voice was needed. And it arrived just as the cusp of the 1960s—or what some considered the opening of the Aquarian Age foreseen in astrology—came into sight. The voice belonged to a New York–based actress, bookshop owner, and student of metaphysical ideas named Eden Gray. As thought movements tend to blend one into the other, so did American occultism give way to the New Age in Gray's immensely readable, sprightly guides to Tarot cards. In her work, one can see the American occult evolving into the larger New Age culture of the second half of the twentieth century.

Born in Chicago in 1901, Gray changed her name from Priscilla Pardridge for the stage. As an aspiring actress in the 1920s, she moved to New York. Gray was cast in a variety of stage roles, playing opposite Edward G. Robinson and Helen Hayes. Over the course of marriage and divorce, travel, and World War II—in which she served stateside as an Army lab technician—her acting career got waylaid. In the 1950s, she attempted to reignite her career using the visualization principles of Religious Science, the mind-power philosophy espoused by Ernest Holmes. Almost immediately, Gray landed an unlikely role in a London stage play.

Gray later returned to New York and became active with the First Church of Religious Science on Manhattan's East 48th Street (another Midtown anomaly, just a few blocks from Blavatsky and Olcott's old Lamasery). Deeply affected by her spiritual experiences, and with encouragement from her Religious Science minister, Gray decided to pursue a new career in the occult—but from her own fresh, energetic perspective. In 1954 she opened a metaphysical bookstore, Inspiration House, on Manhattan's East Side and began giving Tarot readings. Patrons complained to her that no really practical Tarot guide existed. The actress-turned-occultist responded with a book of her own.

Gray's 1960 volume, *The Tarot Revealed*—a beautiful oblong hardcover designed by her artist son, Peter Gray Cohen—arrived like a ray of sunshine to a generation of readers. Occult acolytes of the postwar era had grown wearily accustomed to colorless works like Englishman Arthur E. Waite's 1911 *Pictorial Key to the Tarot,* one of the few "popular" guides available. Waite's manner was hesitant and withholding, as though writing under duress for a general readership. While Paul Foster Case's *The Tarot* had been available since 1947, he committed little space to divination, the area that most interested Tarot enthusiasts. With Gray's work, readers no longer had to pine for a useful "how-to." She combined simple instructions, enticing (if sometimes fanciful) occult history, and a New Thought–inspired tone: "Give those for whom you read encouragement to strive for their highest ideals. The seeds you plant can blossom into lovely flowers of accomplishment."

Gray's writing was friendly, informal, and practical. It would not please everyone. Manly P. Hall, born the same year as Gray, believed the New Age generation cheapened esoteric ideas, proffering quick fixes rather than demanding a lifetime of study. Regardless, the new era belonged to Gray. And, in her own shorthand style, she offered many of the same ideas as Hall and the more "serious" esotericists. New York publishers began to reprint her work and look for more. By the early 1970s, Tarot and occult how-to guides numbered in the hundreds.

The Spiritual Invasion

The dawn of the '60s also opened American society to a new range of foreign religious movements and innovations. Largely through the work of iconic writer Gerald Gardner, a revival, or reinvention, of witchcraft emerged in England in the years following World War II. Only in 1951 did Britain lift its last law against witches. The Witchcraft Act, dating to the mid-sixteenth century, was finally repealed due to the efforts of English Spiritualists who occasionally found themselves harassed under its strictures. Without fear of legal reprisals, Gardner stepped through the opening.

An adventurous and well-to-do customs agent who had spent most of his life in Borneo, British Malaya, Singapore, and other faraway trading posts of the Empire, Gardner retired to the southern English coast in the late 1930s. He used retirement to further his study of folklore and the tribal rites he had encountered in the Far East. Back home, he was touched by the work of Egyptologist Margaret A. Murray, who postulated the survival of an ancient "witch cult" in England and Western Europe. American folklorist Charles G. Leland had promoted a similar idea at the turn of the century, describing the enduring nature cults as "the old religion." Gardner later claimed he was initiated into one of these covens during World War II, which met secretly in the woods to cast spells against Hitler.

In a move that would reverberate through America, Gardner in 1954 published his slender volume, *Witchcraft Today*. It laid out the surviving beliefs and seasonal rituals of the nature-based cults he was said to discover (though others questioned their existence). Gardner called their members "Wica," an Old English term for "wise or clever folk." Throughout America the faith became known as Wicca. As with the ideas of Noble Drew Ali and his *Circle 7 Koran,* Gardner's new/old theology was borrowed and invented, half dreamed up and half grounded in a mélange of folklore and traditional practices. It was, above all, a new religion that met the needs of the times. Wicca was nature-based, sexually free, and female-affirming. By the late '60s, its message of do-it-yourself spirituality spoke to hundreds of thousands of young people. Wicca, or neo-paganism, became one of America's fastest-growing spiritual movements in the late twentieth and early twenty-first centuries, even gaining recognition as an official religion within the U.S. Armed Forces. Wicca also became a surprisingly popular spiritual choice among teenage girls, for whom its dark imagery and ritual (often a tantalizing taboo amid the landscape of mainstream Christendom) proved an empowering—and fashionable—statement.

In other developments from abroad, the Maharishi Mahesh Yogi—better known as the Maharishi—journeyed from India to California in 1959 and began teaching his technique of Transcendental Meditation. He gained worldwide fame after hosting the Beatles and other youth icons, including members of the Beach Boys and Donovan, at his India ashram. In the process, many Americans witnessed their first mass-media images of an Eastern guru on network news shows and the cover of *Time* magazine. The Maharishi's ability to attract the Beatles to his headquarters at Rishikesh helped usher in a turning point in youth culture. Some of the band's most memorable songs, including the raga-influenced melodies and lyrics of *The White Album* and *Let It Be,* grew from the visit. (While John Lennon famously split with the Maharishi, band members Paul McCartney, Ringo Starr, and George Harrison maintained lifelong ties to his teachings.) Countless young Americans learned the mantra-based method of Transcendental Meditation, while medical authorities and educators began to seriously study its stress-reducing effects.

From a cultural perspective, perhaps no tradition of the East made deeper inroads than Zen Buddhism. Studied by American scholars in Japan and brought to America in large measure by the brilliant teacher D. T. Suzuki in the 1950s and '60s, Zen became an American religion in its own right. Attracted by its message of nonattachment and "just be" spirituality, the Woodstock generation made Zen one of the most widespread of the nation's new religious movements. Zen attracted hundreds of thousands of adherents or loose hangers-on and wielded broad influence on the religious ideals and language of the youth culture. The concept of "mindfulness" joined the American idiom. Almost a century earlier, Theosophy had helped introduce Buddhism to the West when Colonel Olcott and Madame Blavatsky made formal Buddhist vows in Sri Lanka in 1880, probably the first Westerners ever to do so. But it was in the '60s and '70s that Buddhism found its true footing on American soil.

The 1960s also exposed Americans to Native American shamanism, or a certain version of it. A stocky Latin UCLA graduate student named Carlos Castaneda ignited mass interest in the wisdom of a mysterious (and many said invented) Yaqui Indian medicine man in his 1968 best seller, *The Teachings of Don Juan*. In the following decade, critics and some disappointed readers heaped scorn upon the elusive Castaneda when the logistics and circumstances of his Don Juan books failed to hold up under scrutiny. Even Castaneda's own background as a globe-trotting Brazilian was exposed as invention. He was the Peruvian son of a jeweler. As some readers discovered, however, the books' true value did not appear by dissecting the realness of Don Juan or by heading off to the Southwest in search of magic mushrooms or a Native American teacher. Rather, Castaneda's writings made the most sense to those readers who already had a commitment to a religious or wisdom tradition and understood his books as allegories on that path. The resonances, some found, could be remarkable.

The Revolution Will Be Published

If publishers needed any further encouragement about the potential of the new spiritual literature, in 1969 a New York astrologer and former Miss America contestant named Linda Goodman placed the first astrology book on *The New York Times* best-seller list. The popularity of *Sun Signs* made "What's your sign?" into the nation's favorite (and most parodied) pickup line.

Observers could hardly believe how far astrology had traveled from the temples of the primeval world and how appealing it could seem in the present. "I'm a nonbeliever," wrote Marcia Seligson in a charming assessment of modern astrology in 1969 in *The New York Times*. "But in the last few weeks, since I paid a call on Linda Goodman, I've found it impossible to remain unseduced by astrology." Goodman, she continued,

> has an empathic quality that makes you want to tell her everything that's unsettling you, and let her fix it up. Which I did. And she did. Far be it from me to pooh-pooh a science that tells me not to worry about the problems I'm having with my Sagittarius boyfriend because, as Linda so aptly put it: "You have a deep rich Taurus sense of humor and great sensuality and you cook well and are great fun and attractive to men and keep a lovely home." Obviously she's right about astrology being the universal truth and the mother of all law. And that's that.

Like Seligson, almost every American by the late '60s could identify his or her mythological birth sign (and often that of intimates) and note something about its traits. Most daily newspapers ran sun-sign columns, and even *The Washington Post* eventually gave in, at the behest of its chairman, Katharine Graham. "I got tired of Mrs. Graham telling me we should have an astrology column, so I got one," said executive editor Ben Bradlee. Publishers began noticing that women were the most reliable audience for the new spiritual literature.

A 1967 best seller on Edgar Cayce, *The Sleeping Prophet* by tabloid journalist Jess Stearn, brought a rebound of attention to the medical clairvoyant. Cayce's new vogue was followed by a wide array of "channeled" literature—*channel* was a term Cayce had used—under the names of such other-dimensional entities as Seth, Ramtha, and even the figure of Christ in the hugely popular series of lessons called *A Course in Miracles*. Channeled by Helen Schucman, a Columbia University research psychologist, *A Course in Miracles* turned out to be far more substantive and complex than most casual readers were expecting. Hence, many looked to friendlier metaphysical works, such as the popularized *Course-in-Miracles* psychology of Gerald G. Jampolsky and Marianne Williamson or the explorations of channeling and past lives in the memoirs of actress Shirley MacLaine.

This isn't to say that more-demanding books did not find an audience. American readers discovered the ancient Chinese oracle book *I Ching* in its groundbreaking translation by the German Sinologist Richard Wilhelm. Once a sleepy staple on the backlist of Princeton University Press, it was newly embraced in the late '60s by students and seekers. Likewise, the Chinese philosophy of the Tao Te Ching, one of the world's oldest spiritual works, underwent a new range of serious translations. And new editions of the Sufi mystical verse of Jalaluddin Rumi made the thirteenth-century Persian into one of the most widely read poets in American history.

Occult America

In the mid-'70s, the monthly *New Age Journal* had solidified the name for this new spiritual movement. There was no longer any easily discerned "occult" or "Eastern" or "yogic" subculture; rather, America experienced the rise of a vast metaphysical culture that appeared ever-expanding, ever-accommodating, and perpetually ready to adapt to any foreign or homegrown influence that met the needs of those who yearned for self-discovery or personal fulfillment.

Some of its psycho-spiritual offerings rode the winds of trend, like primal scream therapy, the confrontational psychology of encounter groups, or the *me-first* philosophy of EST. Others were substantive and historically rooted, such as the practice of yoga and the advent of transpersonal, or meaning-based, psychology, which began to bridge the rupture declared by Freud between the psychological and the religious.* Psychology could no longer limit the aims of life to love and work; rather, the questions of purposeful existence had entered the therapist's office—and were apparently there to stay.

A core tenet of the New Age was a belief in the fateful convergence of all religious and therapeutic systems, resulting in an era of boundless human potential. Ivy League–educated researchers at residential learning facilities such as California's Esalen Institute—the first in a wave of growth centers that would dot both American coasts—began studying "supernormal" athletic and mental performance, seeing it as a harbinger of humanity's next "quantum leap" in evolution. Indeed, years before the theory of an "end of history" electrified post–Cold War intellectuals, New Age intellects, such as physicist Fritjof Capra and transpersonal pioneer and Esalen cofounder Michael Murphy, articulated their own visions of an apex in social–ideological–individual development.

There also existed serious esoteric teachers who stood aloof from the New Age, carefully absorbing some of the searchers who had sampled and grown dissatisfied with its plethora of offerings. Spiritual movements that did not lend themselves to popular adaptation—from Islamic Sufism to esoteric Christianity—benefited from the interest aroused by the New Age's reach and took in some of its most thoughtful participants.

Meanwhile, the more traditional religious movements— evangelism in particular—heaped scorn upon the New Age, even while lifting some of its most popular therapeutic premises. Late-twentieth- and early-twenty-first-century megachurches and media ministries rapidly took to counseling congregants, readers, and television audiences on everything from the spiritual laws of debt relief and weight loss to the mental secrets of success.

---

* Freud could also reveal a greater openness to the metaphysical than is commonly assumed. In his 1922 paper "Dreams and Telepathy," he noted: ". . . psychoanalysis may do something to advance the study of telepathy, in so far as, by the help of its interpretations, many of the puzzling characteristics of telepathic phenomena may be rendered more intelligible to us; or other, still doubtful phenomena be for the first time definitely ascertained to be of a telepathic nature."

Even tough-skinned skeptics who dismissed the New Age as flim-flam turned to "woo-woo" methods, often unknowingly. When faced with chronic illness, addiction, or stress, rationalists from every reach of life used alternative approaches in medicine and relaxation—ranging from meditation (Edgar Cayce), to hypno-therapy (Mesmer), to positive thinking (Ernest Holmes, et al.), to practices in yoga, herbs, and acupuncture that had entered America through the channel created by arcane subcultures.

The United States Army itself adopted a slogan—"Be All You Can Be"—that some believed echoed the ethos of the human-potential movement. *The New York Times* cited a report that in the early 1980s a group of officers at the Army War College in Carlisle, Pennsylvania, headed up a study aimed at creating a "New Age Army," whose recruits would receive training in potential-building techniques, such as meditation, extrasensory perception, and self-hypnosis. The program was abandoned, but one researcher claimed that the Army's ever-popular slogan grew directly from it.

For all of its inroads into mainstream life, New Age became a term (and sometimes an epithet) that for many serious people connoted nothing more than a softheaded jumble of spiritual–therapeutic remedies or bromides. But the New Age did, in fact, have a core set of beliefs and a definable point of view. Most people, thought schools, or movements identified as New Age from the 1970s through the early twenty-first century shared these traits:

1. Belief in the therapeutic value of spiritual or religious ideas.
2. Belief in a mind–body connection in health.
3. Belief that human consciousness is evolving to higher stages.
4. Belief that thoughts, in some greater or lesser measure, determine reality.
5. Belief that spiritual understanding is available without allegiance to a specific religion or doctrine.

Most twenty-first-century Americans, whatever their background, would probably agree with a majority of those statements. To a very great degree, occult movements and personalities had introduced those ideas, in some of their most popular variants, into American life. Whether the occult changed America, or the other way around, certainly this much is clear: The encounter between America and occultism resulted in a vast reworking of arcane practices and beliefs from the Old World and the creation of a new spiritual culture. This new culture extolled religious egalitarianism and responded, perhaps more than any other movement in history, to the inner needs and search of the individual. At work and at church, on television and in bookstores, there was no avoiding it: Occult America had prevailed.

These notes are intended to supplement attributions that appear in individual chapters. When a source is already cited within a chapter, it is not generally repeated here.

Introduction: *What Is the Occult?*
(And What Is It Doing in America?)

Sources on the Kelpius and Ephrata communes include *The Diarium of Magister Johannes Kelpius,* with annotations by Julius Friedrich Sachse (Publications of the Pennsylvania German Society; v. 25, 1917), *The German Pietists of Provincial Pennsylvania* by Sachse (privately printed, 1895), *Wisdom's Children* by Arthur Versluis (State University of New York Press, 1999), *The American Soul* by Jacob Needleman (Tarcher/Penguin, 2002), and *The Woman in the Wilderness* by Jonathan D. Scott (Middleton Books, 2005), a rigorously researched historical novel.

Éliphas Lévi is quoted from his 1855 *Transcendental Magic,* as translated by Arthur Edward Waite in 1896. Aleister Crowley is quoted from *The Book of the Law* (Weiser, 1926, 1938, 2004).

The works of Frances A. Yates form an extraordinary guide to the intellectual history of Renaissance and Elizabethan occultism, particularly *The Rosicrucian Enlightenment* (Routledge & Kegan Paul, 1972), *The Occult Philosophy in the Elizabethan Age* (Routledge & Kegan Paul, 1979), and *Giordano Bruno and the Hermetic Tradition* (The University of Chicago Press, 1964), from which the epigraph from the Hermetic dialogue *Asclepius* is translated.

Articles on Zolar include "Dean of Astrologers" by John Updike, *The New Yorker,* 10/31/59; "In the Stars," *Time* magazine, 8/24/62; "Publishing Enters the Age of Aquarius" by Marcia Seligson, *The New York Times,* 9/28/69; "Tells Fortunes, Makes a Fortune" by George C. Harlan, *San Mateo Times,* 2/3/60; and "Zodiac Provides Signs of the Times" by Richard Blystone, Associated Press, 3/1/70.

Chapter One: *The Psychic Highway*

General sources on Ann Lee and the Shakers include *The Shaker Experience in America* by Stephen J. Stein (Yale University Press, 1994), *Spirit Possession and Popular Religion* by Clarke Garrett (The Johns Hopkins University Press, 1987), *The People Called Shakers* by Edward Deming Andrews (Dover, 1963), *Mother Ann Lee* by Nardi Reeder Campion (University Press of New England, 1976, 1990), and *Ann the Word* by Richard Francis (Arcade, 2000). The legend of Mother Ann Lee and the averted shipwreck appears in *A Summary View of the Millennial Church, or United Society of Believers, (Commonly Called the Shakers)* by Calvin Green and Seth Y. Wells (Packard & Van Benthuysen, 1823). The stories of Mother Ann's maternal and marital woes, the mob violence against her, and the winter travelers reaching the Shaker colony at Niskayuna (now called Watervliet) appear in *Shakerism* by Anna White and Leila S. Taylor (Press of Fred J. Heer, 1905) and in *Testimonies of the Life, Character, Revelations, and Doctrines of Mother Ann Lee, and the Elders with Her* by Rufus Bishop and Seth Y. Wells (privately printed 1816 and reissued 1888). The story of Mother Ann Lee's "psychometric portrait" appears in *The New York Folklore Quarterly*, autumn 1960. The events of the "Dark Day" are reported in *Historic Storms of New England* by Sidney Perley (The Salem Press, 1891). Henry Steel Olcott's *People from the Other World* (American Publishing Company, 1875) is a useful window on how the Shakers considered their order a forerunner of Spiritualism.

Carl Carmer's phrase is from *Listen For a Lonesome Drum: A York State Chronicle* (Farrar & Rinehart, 1936, 1950). The history of Millerism draws on accounts by historian Whitney R. Cross in his indispensable *The Burned-over District* (Cornell University Press, 1950), Francis D. Nichol in his sympathetic but responsible *The Midnight Cry* (Review and Herald Publishing Association, 1944), and *The Memoirs of William Miller* by Sylvester Bliss (J. V. Himes, 1853).

The most reliable sources I have found on the life of Jemima Wilkinson include *History and Directory of Yates County* by Stafford C. Cleveland (1873), "Jemima Wilkinson" by Robert P. St. John, *The Quarterly Journal of the New York State Historical Association* (April 1930), and *Pioneer Prophetess* by Herbert A. Wisbey, Jr. (Cornell University Press, 1964). Also helpful on the movements of the Burned-Over District are *The Crucible of Ferment* by Emerson Klees (Cameo Press, 2001) and the online book *Saints, Sinners, and Reformers* by John H. Martin (www.crookedlakereview.com, 2005).

Invaluable research into the occult and folkloric beliefs that ran in the family of Joseph Smith appears in *Early Mormonism and the Magic*

World View by D. Michael Quinn (Signature Books, 1998). The folklore of the Central New York region and Mormonism is considered in Whitney R. Cross's *The Burned-over District* (Cornell University Press, 1950) and "Mormonism in the 'Burned-Over District,' " by Cross, *New York History,* July 1944. Governor DeWitt Clinton's remarks appear in his *Discourse Delivered before the New-York Historical Society* (James Eastburn, 1812). Dan Vogel's *Indian Origins and the Book for Mormon* (Signature Books, 1986) provided the initial Clinton reference. An analysis of Mormonism and Freemasonry appears in *The Refiner's Fire* by John L. Brooke (Cambridge University Press, 1994), *No Man Knows My History* by Fawn Brodie (Knopf, 1945), and *Mormonism and Masonry* by E. Cecil McGavin (Stevens & Wallis, Inc., 1947). A useful study of Mormonism's esoteric influences appears in Lance S. Owen's "Joseph Smith: America's Hermetic Prophet," *Gnosis* magazine, spring 1995. Other articles include: "What Is It about Mormonism?" by Noah Feldman, *The New York Times,* 1/6/08, and "As Mormon Church Grows, So Does Dissent from Feminists and Scholars" by Dirk Johnson, *The New York Times,* 10/2/93. Helpful passages on Smith are also found in Harold Bloom's *The American Religion* (Simon & Schuster, 1993) and *Omens of the Millennium* (Riverhead, 1996).

Andrew Jackson Davis is quoted from *The Magic Staff* (J. S. Brown & Co., 1857), *The Principles of Nature* (S. S. Lyon and Wm. Fishbough, 1847), and *The Harmonial Philosophy* (Advanced Thought Publishing Company, 1917). His accounts of being Mesmerized appeared in *The Great Harmonia,* Vol. II (Crown, 1851) and *The Magic Staff.*

The Marquis de Lafayette's letter to Washington is from *Abnormal Hypnotic Phenomena, Vol. 4: The United States of America* by Allan Angoff, edited by Eric Dingwall (J. & A. Churchill, 1968). Washington's reply to Mesmer appears in *Franklin in France,* Volume II, by Edward Everett Hale (Roberts Brothers, 1888). The marquis's visit with the Shakers is described in *Spirit Possession and Popular Religion* by Clarke Garrett (The Johns Hopkins University Press, 1987) and *The Shakers and the World's People* by Flo Morse (University Press of New England, 1987). The role of Mesmerism in Poyen's aversion to slavery is noted in "Charles Poyen Brings Mesmerism to America" by Eric T. Carlson, *Journal of the History of Medicine and Allied Sciences* (April 1960), and "How Southern New England Became Magnetic North" by Sheila O'Brien Quinn, *History of Psychology* (August 2007). Poyen's relationship to the mayor of Lowell is noted in *The Heyday of Spiritualism* by Slater Brown (Hawthorn Books, 1970).

The credulity that greeted Poe's fictional accounts of Mesmerism is noted by historian Michael Gomes in his pamphlet "Colonel Olcott and the Healing Arts" (Theosophical Publishing House, 2007). John B.

Buescher's *The Other Side of Salvation* (Skinner House, 2004) notes Poe reading in a trancelike state. Frank Podmore is quoted from *Mesmerism and Christian Science* (George W. Jacobs and Co., 1909).

Chapter Two: *Mystic Americans*

Olcott left a vast record of his affairs, most usefully his six-volume *Old Diary Leaves* (G. P. Putnam's Sons/Theosophical Publishing Company, issued 1895–1935). His encounter with Andrew Jackson Davis is recounted in a prefatory note to an article by Anna Kingsford in *The Theosophist* magazine in May 1890. Biographies of Olcott are *Yankee Beacon of Buddhist Light* by Howard Murphet (Theosophical Publishing House, 1972, 1988) and *The White Buddhist* by Stephen R. Prothero (Indiana University Press, 1996). Olcott's Civil War career is noted in *The Web of Conspiracy* by Theodore Roscoe (Prentice-Hall, 1959). Edison's psychical experiments are described in *Old Diary Leaves, Vol. I* and "Edison Working on How to Communicate with the Next World" by B. C. Forbes, *The American Magazine* (October 1920). Abner Doubleday's translation of Éliphas Lévi's *Dogma and Ritual of High Magic* (or *Transcendental Magic*) appeared in serial form for several years beginning in 1912 in the occult journal *The Word*. Olcott's travels in the East are noted in *Buddhism* by Edward Conze (Bruno Cassirer, 1951) and *The Buddhist Bible* edited by Donald S. Lopez, Jr. (Beacon, 2002).

Bronson Alcott is quoted on Hermes in Arthur Christy's rare and important 1932 study, *The Orient in American Transcendentalism* (Columbia University Press; reprinted by Octagon Books, 1963). Alvin Boyd Kuhn's *Theosophy* (Henry Holt, 1930) helpfully tracks the arc of metaphysical subjects in Emerson's journals. K. Paul Johnson is quoted from his significant study *The Masters Revealed* (State University of New York Press, 1994).

In the vast literature on Spiritualism, a variety of ages are attributed to the Fox sisters, and historical records are inconclusive. The ages used here—Kate, 11, and Margaret, 14—are from John Patrick Deveney's article in the *Dictionary of Gnosis & Western Esotericism* (Brill, 2006). Survey numbers on Spiritualism are from Whitney R. Cross's *The Burned-over District* (Cornell University Press, 1950). E. W. Capron is quoted from *Modern Spiritualism* (Partridge and Brittan, 1855). The quotation from the *Religio-Philosophical Journal* is from August 26, 1865. Quotes from *The Carrier Dove* are taken from *The Psychic World of California* by David St. Clair (Doubleday, 1972). For summaries of the differing statistics of practicing Spiritualists, see *The Other Side of Salvation* by John B. Buescher (Skinner House, 2004),

The Dawning of the Theosophical Movement by Michael Gomes (Quest, 1987), and *The History of the Supernatural, Vol. II,* by William Howitt (Longman, 1853). Also helpful is *Radical Spirits* by Ann Braude (Indiana University Press, 1989, 2001).

Lincoln is quoted on his son's death from *Behind the Scenes: or, Thirty Years a Slave, and Four Years in the White House* by Elizabeth Keckley (G. W. Carleton & Co., 1868). Mary Todd Lincoln is quoted from *Abraham Lincoln: The War Years* by Carl Sandburg (Harcourt, 1939). Mary Todd's struggles with her son Robert appear in *Mary Todd Lincoln* by Jean H. Baker (Norton, 1987).

Mary Fenn Love is quoted from *Radical Spirits* by Ann Braude (Indiana University Press, 1989, 2001), an invaluable resource on women's rights and Spiritualism. Frederick Douglass is quoted from Barbara Goldsmith's *Other Powers* (Knopf, 1998), a monumental study of Victoria Woodhull. Also helpful is Mary Gabriel's *Notorious Victoria* (Algonquin Books, 1998). For a Spiritualist view of Woodhull, see the pamphlet "Victoria C. Woodhull, A Biographical Sketch" by Theodore Tilton (The Golden Age, 1871).

The Shields episode in the Senate was on April 17, 1854 (the full transcript ran the following day in *The New York Times*). Total signatures on his petition are fuzzy: Shields testified to 15,000, while the document itself reports 13,000. Upon counting them, the industrious historian John B. Buescher found slightly fewer than 12,000 (see www .spirithistory.com/petnote.html).

Anna Blackwell is quoted from *The History of Spiritualism, Volume II,* by Arthur Conan Doyle (1926). Historical information on Caodaism can be found in Ralph B. Smith's two-part study, "An Introduction to Caodaism," *Bulletin of the School of Oriental and African Studies of the University of London,* Vol. XXXIII (1970). Other sources include "Cultural Intrusions and Religious Syncretism: The Case of Caodaism in Vietnam" by Graeme Lang, *Working Papers Series* No. 65, Southeast Asia Research Centre (July 2004); and "Vietnam's Cao Dai Sect Flourishing Amid Hollywood Endorsement," Agence France-Presse, 6/3/01.

Chapter Three: *Don't Try This at Home*

The story of Ouija and the three teens is based on an episode reported in the "True Mystic Experiences" column of *Fate* magazine (July 2006). Special thanks are due to historians/curators Robert Murch and Eugene Orlando for their insights into Ouija and their intellectual doggedness in tracking down its history. Murch has tirelessly traced relations among Ouija's investors. Orlando and historian John B.

Buescher provided references to the "lost link" article from the *New York Daily Tribune*. Fuld is quoted from "William Fuld Made $1,000,000 on Ouija but Has No Faith in It," Baltimore *Sun*, 7/4/20. Thomas Mann is quoted from *The Perfect Medium* by Clément Chéroux (Metropolitan Museum of Art, 2005). The recollections about Truman Capote and about Merrill and Jackson's sexual relations are from Alison Lurie's *Familiar Spirits: A Memoir of James Merrill and David Jackson* (Viking, 2001). Merrill is quoted from *James Merrill* by Judith Moffett (Columbia University Press, 1984) and "The Channeled Myths of James Merrill" by John Chambers, *The Anomalist* (summer 1997).

Chapter Four: *The Science of Right Thinking*

The recollections of Florence Wattles appear in a letter that publisher Elizabeth Towne included in a reprint edition of Wallace D. Wattles's *The Science of Being Great* (1911), which Towne retitled *How to Be a Genius*. Thanks to Tony Mase for help tracking down the source. Emerson's 1841 quote is from "Spiritual Laws." John B. Anderson is quoted from *New Thought, Its Lights and Shadows* (Sherman, French & Company, 1911). Elbert Hubbard is quoted from Stefan Kanfer's "Love and Glory in East Aurory," *City Journal* (spring 2007). The career of Ralph Waldo Trine is explored in *The Positive Thinkers* by Donald Meyer (Pantheon, 1965, 1980, 1988) and *History and Philosophy of Metaphysical Movements in America* by J. Stillson Judah (The Westminster Press, 1967). Articles on Wattles include the following from the *Fort Wayne Sentinel*: "Leaves the Methodists," 6/27/00; "News Paragraphs," 6/13/08; "Totals on District Vote," 11/15/08; "Trouble at Elwood," 7/12/09; and "Indiana Socialist Dies," 2/8/11. Also, "Hoosier Writer Is Dead," *Indianapolis Star*, 2/9/11. Florence Wattles appears in "Says Even Dead Voted in Recent Elwood Election," 1/29/11, *Indianapolis Star;* and "Woman Socialist Speaks to Kendallville Audience," 7/12/11, *Fort Wayne Journal-Gazette*.

Quimby's initial encounter with Mesmerism is variously attributed to his attendance at lectures by Poyen and Collyer; lecture dates of 1836 and 1838 are cited, as are different Maine locales. *The Quimby Manuscripts*, edited by Horatio Dresser (Crowell, 1921), places Quimby at a Belfast, Maine, lecture in 1838 but names no lecturer. The same author cites Collyer as the speaker in his *History of the New Thought Movement* (Crowell, 1919). Poyen had probably left America by that time, as noted by Eric T. Carlson in the *Journal of the History of Medicine and Allied Science* (April 1960). Poyen had appeared in Bangor, Maine, earlier, and the likelihood is that both influences—

Poyen's 1836 demonstration and Collyer's 1838 lecture—aroused Quimby's interest. Further details on Collyer's career appear in *Abnormal Hypnotic Phenomena, Vol. 4: The United States of America,* by Allan Angoff, edited by Eric Dingwall (J. & A. Churchill, 1968). Quotes by Quimby are taken from *The Quimby Manuscripts.* Warren Felt Evans's and Mary Baker Eddy's relations with Quimby are variously described in: *History and Philosophy of Metaphysical Movements in America* by J. Stillson Judah (The Westminster Press, 1967), *Each Mind a Kingdom* by Beryl Satter (University of California Press, 1999), *Mary Baker Eddy: The Years of Trial* by Robert Peel (Holt, Rinehart & Winston, 1971), and *A Republic of Mind and Spirit* by Catherine L. Albanese (Yale University Press, 2007). Eddy's eulogy of Quimby appears in *The True History of Mental Science* by Julius A. Dresser (Alfred Mudge & Son, 1887). Her comment about the "illiterate" Quimby is from the June 1887 *Christian Science Journal.* Eddy's relationship with Emma Curtis Hopkins is described in Satter (1999).

Sources on Ernest Holmes include *Open at the Top* by Neal Vahle (Open View Press, 1993) and *Ernest Holmes: His Life and Times* by Fenwicke L. Holmes (Dodd, Mead, 1970). Norman Vincent Peale discusses Holmes in "The Pathway to Positive Thinking" by Elaine St. Johns, *Science of Mind* magazine (June 1987).

Helpful overviews of many of the figures in this chapter appear in *Spirits in Rebellion* by Charles S. Braden (Southern Methodist University Press, 1963, 1987), *The American Myth of Success* by Richard Weiss (University of Illinois Press, 1969, 1988), and *History and Philosophy of Metaphysical Movements in America* by J. Stillson Judah (The Westminster Press, 1967).

Chapter Five: *The Mail-Order Prophet*

The preeminent works on Frank B. Robinson are *These Also Believe* by Charles S. Braden (Macmillan, 1949), *They Have Found a Faith* by Marcus Bach (Bobbs–Merrill, 1946), and the pamphlet "Psychiana: The Psychological Religion" by Keith P. Petersen (Latah County Historical Society, 1991). Also helpful is Bach's *Strange Sects and Curious Cults* (Dodd, Mead, 1961). For Robinson's conversion experience, I have relied chiefly on the works of Bach and *The Strange Autobiography of Frank B. Robinson* (Psychiana, 1941). I have benefited from a wide range of Psychiana papers, correspondence, and meeting transcripts, including those of the Holmes–Robinson speaking appearances, archived at the University of Idaho Library Special Collections. Key news articles include: " 'Money-Back' Religion," UPI, 3/30/36; "Moscow, Idaho, Once Home to a Booming Religion Known as Psychiana" by Rich

Roesler, [Spokane] *Spokesman-Review*, 9/3/96; "Money-Back Religion," *Time* magazine, 1/17/38; "Death of Psychiana," *Newsweek*, 3/24/52; "Mail-Order Messiah" by Fred Colvig, *Sunday Oregonian*, 12/26/37; "A Visit to the Man Who Talked with God" by Herman Edwards, *Sunday Oregonian*, 12/24/39; and "Idaho Publisher Offers Finns Plan to Beat Reds," UPI, 12/5/39. On the career of Arthur Bell, see *California Cult* by H. T. Dohrman (Beacon Press, 1958) and "Mankind United," 9/20/37, and "Profit's Prophet," 5/21/45, both from *Time* magazine. The recollections of Alfred Robinson are from Bach's *Report to Protestants* (The Parthenon Press, 1948). The columnist who attended the Holmes–Robinson talks was Sidney P. Dones writing in the 9/25/41 *Neighborhood News*. The closing quote is from Braden (1963, 1987). Thanks to John Black (www.johnblack.com/psychiana) and to the Northwoods Spiritual Resource Center (www.angelfire.com/wi2/ULCds/) for compiling a wide range of Psychiana resources online.

Chapter Six: Go Tell Pharaoh

Quotations of Frederick Douglass are from *Autobiographies* (Library of America, 1994), which encompasses *Narrative of the Life of Frederick Douglass, an American Slave* (1845), *My Bondage and My Freedom* (1855), and *Life and Times of Frederick Douglass* (1893).

The invaluable historical resource on hoodoo is a five-volume oral history, *Hoodoo-Conjuration-Witchcraft-Rootwork,* by Episcopal priest and folklorist Harry Middleton Hyatt, who began assembling his material in the late 1930s and early 1940s. He privately published his volumes, based on interviews with more than 1,600 devotees of hoodoo, between 1970 and 1978, and he died before a projected sixth volume, an index, was completed. Where Hyatt's volumes can be found (there exist fewer than 600 complete sets), they are the most remarkable records of African-influenced magic in America. Hyatt's finest written interpreter and a hoodoo master scholar in her own right is Catherine Yronwode, whose resources include an extensive Web site (www.luckymojo.com), her online and print books (*Hoodoo in Theory and Practice* and *Hoodoo Herb and Root Magic*), and her indispensable *Hoodoo Rootwork Correspondence Course*. Carolyn Morrow Long's *Spiritual Merchants* (The University of Tennessee Press, 2001) is a masterly record of the hoodoo supply dealers of the twentieth century, as well as a history of African-influenced magic. Important texts on religious and folk beliefs among African slaves and their descendants are *Slave Religion* by Albert J. Raboteau (Oxford University Press, 1978, 2004)—from which I drew the Georgia Writers' Project quote—and *Black Magic* by Yvonne P. Chireau (University of California Press, 2003). Also helpful are: *Voodoo*

& Hoodoo by Jim Haskins (Scarborough House, 1978, 1990) and *Folk Beliefs of the Southern Negro* by Newbell Niles Puckett (H. Milford, 1926).

Jim Magus's delightful history, *Magical Heroes* (Magus Enterprises, 1995), has been a very helpful source on the career of Black Herman, particularly for the dialogue of Herman's stage act. Other quotes are from Herman's memoirs. Articles on Black Herman from the *Chicago Defender* include: "Harlem Healer Given Setback by Woman Cop," 6/18/27; " 'Black' Herman Given Penitentiary Sentence," 10/22/27; "Black Herman," 10/18/30; and "Black Herman, Noted Magician, Dies," 4/21/34. Articles from the *New York Amsterdam News* include: " 'Black Herman,' Magician, Held for Trial in Special Sessions as 'Quack,' " 9/7/27, and " 'Black Herman' Given Sentence in Penitentiary," 10/19/27. Black Herman's death certificate (April 17, 1934) lists the cause of death as chronic myocarditis, a viral inflammation of the heart, which led to cardiac failure.

The pioneering work of UCLA historian Robert A. Hill has highlighted the connections between Marcus Garvey and New Thought. Hill has meticulously assembled and annotated *The Marcus Garvey and Universal Negro Improvement Association Papers* for the University of California Press. Volumes I (1983) and VII (1990), in particular, explore Garvey and New Thought. Hill's volume with Barbara Bair, *Marcus Garvey Life and Lessons* (University of California Press, 1987), is similarly valuable. I am grateful for Hill's work and advice. For biographical background on Garvey, I have benefited from the documentary *Marcus Garvey: Look for Me in the Whirlwind* (American Experience, 2001) and *Black Moses* by E. David Cronon (University of Wisconsin Press, 1955, 1969).

Sources on L. W. de Laurence include: "William Lauron DeLaurence and Jamaican Folk Religion" by W. F. Elkins, *Folklore*, vol. 97:ii (1986); "Academic Freedom: Manley's Heritage," *The Sunday Gleaner* (Kingston), 2/18/73; and Carolyn Morrow Long's *Spiritual Merchants* (The University of Tennessee Press, 2001).

On the career of Noble Drew Ali, two sources merit special mention: "Shoot-Out at the Circle 7 Koran" by Peter Lamborn Wilson, *Gnosis* magazine (summer 1989), and "Mystery of the Moorish Science Temple" by Susan Nance, *Religion and American Culture* (2002). Wilson's work, including his *Sacred Drift* (City Lights, 1993), has been groundbreaking, and Nance has written with unprecedented thoroughness. Also helpful are: "Black Gods of the Inner City" by Prince-A-Cuba, *Gnosis* magazine (fall 1992); "Who Was Noble Drew Ali?" by Isa al-Mahdi (Ansaaru Allah Publications, 1988); "Man of Myth and Fact," *The New York Times*, 6/29/64; *The Black Muslims in America* by C. Eric Lincoln (Beacon, 1961); *Islam in the African-American Experience* by Richard Brent Turner (Indiana University Press, 1997, 2003); *African American Islam* by Aminah Beverly McCloud (Routledge, 1995); *Black Pilgrimage to Islam* by Robert Dannin (Oxford University Press, 2002); and Robert Hill, *The Marcus Garvey and Universal Negro Improvement Association Papers, Vol. VII* (University of California Press, 1990).

In addition to the efforts of historian Christopher Paul Moore, the career of Robert T. Browne has been elucidated by Robert Fikes, Jr., in his article and postscript, "The Triumph of Robert T. Browne," in the January–April 1998 issue of *The Negro Educational Review*. Arthur A. Schomburg is quoted from *Arthur Alfonso Schomburg: Black Bibliophile and Collector* by Elinor Des Verney Sinnette (Wayne State University Press, 1989). I am grateful to Thelma Calvo for information on Browne's Hermetic Society.

Chapter Seven: *The Return of the "Secret Teachings"*

Details of Manly P. Hall's early life appear in *A History of the Occult Tarot, 1870–1970,* by Ronald Decker and Michael Dummett (Duckworth, 2002). Hall offered his own reflections in "Recollections of M.P.H." from the Winter 1959 edition of the *PRS Journal,* "Manly P. Hall and the Secret Teachings of All Ages" in the December 1978 *PRS Contributors' Bulletin,* "Reflections of M.P.H." in the Winter 1986 *PRS Journal,* and in a talk transcribed in the Autumn 1955 edition of the PRS magazine *Horizon.* Additional details were provided by Obadiah Harris, president of PRS, and Hall's longtime friend Colonel Clarke Johnston. Hall's sermon on crime is from "Buddha Quoted on Crime," *Los Angeles Times,* 11/1/23. For the conversion of Hall's *Secret Teachings* into a new edition, see "Bringing the Secret Teachings into the 21st Century" by Mitch Horowitz, at www.LapisMagazine.org. Articles about the interests of Marie Bauer Hall appeared in the Richmond (Virginia) *Times-Dispatch:* "New Age Christian Mystic Sure Group Will Unearth Bacon Chest," 8/30/92; "Pair Seeking Vault Fined for Trespassing," 9/25/92; and "Mystics Seek New Dig; Say Church Site Holds Secret Keys to Peace," 3/19/03. For Hall's participation in *Black Friday,* see *The Lima News* (Ohio), 6/27/40. Bob Pool of the *Los Angeles Times* provided useful accounts of PRS's legal issues in "Search for Peace Leads to Court Brawl Estate," 5/3/93, and "A Materialistic Fate for a Philosophical Legacy," 12/23/94. Other *Los Angeles Times* articles include: "Research Center Pursues Ideas Most Won't Consider" by Alan Citron, 10/31/82; " 'Last Western Mystic' Thrives in Los Feliz" by Santiago O'Donnell, 7/6/89; and Hall's obituary by Louis Sahagun, 9/3/90. The most meticulously detailed account of Hall's death, as well as much other material elucidating Hall's life, appears in Louis Sahagun's well-researched biography, *Master of the Mysteries* (Process Media, 2008). Also useful on the controversies around Hall's death is Stephan A. Hoeller's 2003 interview in *Paranoia* magazine, conducted by Robert Guffey. The quote about the unduly influential Fritz appeared in Cliff Johnson's 1/10/95 letter in the *Los Angeles Times*. Irving Howe is quoted from *The Portable Kipling* (Penguin, 1982). Hall's encounter with Bragdon appeared in "America's Timeless Philosopher" by Basanta Koomar Roy from *Wynn's Astrology Magazine*, as reprinted in the Nov.–Dec. 1941 edition of *Horizon*. For an example of recent scholarship verifying the esoteric accounts of Delphi, see "For Delphic Oracle, Fumes and Vision" by William J. Broad, *The New York Times*, 3/19/02.

Chapter Eight: *New Deal of the Ages*

Accounts of Truman Capote's appearance on *The Tonight Show* and the reaction to it appeared in *Time* magazine: "The Assassination According to Capote," 5/10/68; "Ray's Odd Odyssey," 6/21/68; and "Cult of the Occult," 7/19/68. No taping of the live appearance has been found to exist. *The New York Times* reported Sirhan's reading material in "Suspect Requests Theosophic Works and Newspapers," 6/7/68. *The Fresno Bee* reported the John Birch controversy in "Fresnan Backs Author of Book Sirhan Reads in Jail," 6/28/68. I am indebted to Michael Gomes's *Theosophy in the Nineteenth Century: An Annotated Bibliography* (Garland, 1994) for first directing me to the incident.

Details on the life and career of Henry A. Wallace are from *American Dreamer* by John C. Culver and John Hyde (Norton, 2001), *Henry A. Wallace: His Search for a New World Order* by Graham J. White and John R. Maze (University of North Carolina Press, 1995), *Tournament of Shadows: The Great Game and the Race for Empire in Central Asia* by Karl Ernest Meyer and Shareen Blair Brysac (Basic Books, 2006), and "Who Was Henry A. Wallace?" by Arthur Schlesinger, Jr., *Los Angeles Times*, 3/12/00. Jim Farley's criticisms of Wallace and Roosevelt's responses are from *Jim Farley's Story* (Whittlesey House, 1948). Useful information on the Liberal Catholic Church appears in *These Also Believe* by Charles S. Braden (Macmillan, 1949). Wallace's interest in the Great Seal is explored in *The Eagle and the Shield: A History of the Great Seal of the United States* by Richard S. Patterson and

Richardson Dougall (University Press of the Pacific, 1976). Roosevelt's handwriting on the designs of the dollar bill can be seen in the pamphlet "The Great Seal of the United States," published by the U.S. State Department in 2003. The quotes from Henry M. Morgenthau, Jr., are from "The Morgenthau Diaries," part V, in *Collier's* magazine of 10/25/47. In the same article, Morgenthau quotes Roosevelt asking, "What's the matter with Wallace?" Westbrook Pegler's writing on Wallace includes syndicated columns of 5/18/47, 8/27/47, 3/11/48, and 7/26/48.

Sources on William Dudley Pelley include *William Dudley Pelley* by Scott Beekman (Syracuse University Press, 2005), *The Old Christian Right* by Leo P. Ribuffo (Temple University Press, 1983), "The Great Anti-Cult Scare 1935–1945" by Philip Jenkins (a paper presented at the 1999 conference of the Center for Studies of New Religions), and "New Age Nazi" by Jon Elliston, *Mountain Xpress* (North Carolina), 1/28/04. Useful biographical information and images are found in the William Dudley Pelley Collection at the University of North Carolina at Asheville. Pelley's extended version of "Seven Minutes in Eternity" appeared in 1932 from his Galahad Press. Quotations from Pelley's memoirs are from a copy of his hand-typed manuscript, *The Door to Revelation: An Intimate Biography*, produced between April 1934 and April 1935, in the holdings of the Humanities Center of the New York Public Library. The Humanities Center also holds bound editions of Pelley's magazine, *Liberation*. The federal government's case against Pelley is summarized in 132 F.2d 170 *United States v. Pelley*, 7th Circuit Court of Appeals, 12/17/42.

Sources on the nationalist conceptions of Aryanism include *The Aryan Myth* by Leon Poliakov (Basic Books, 1974), *Arktos: The Polar Myth in Science, Symbolism, and Nazi Survival* by Joscelyn Godwin (Phanes Press, 1993), and probably the finest study on Nazism and the occult, Nicholas Goodrick-Clarke's *The Occult Roots of Nazism* (New York University Press, 1992). An excellent analysis of Theosophy and fascism appears in Robert S. Ellwood, Jr.'s notes to "The American Theosophical Synthesis," from *The Occult in America*, edited by Howard Kerr and Charles L. Crow (University of Illinois Press, 1986). A clear-minded look at the Third Reich and religion appears in David Sutton's "How the Nazis Stole Christmas," *Fortean Times*, No. 218. Hitler's remarks about Alfred Rosenberg are from *Inside the Third Reich* by Albert Speer (Simon & Schuster, 1970). The career of Karl Ernst Krafft is considered in *Astrology: A Recent History Including the Untold Story of Its Role in World War II* by Ellic Howe (Walker and Company, 1967) and to a lesser degree in *Astrology: An Historical Examination* by P. I. H. Naylor (Robert Maxwell, 1967). Sources on Karl

Germer include *Sexuality, Magic, and Perversion* by Francis King (Citadel, 1972) and Bill Heidrick's essay, "Ordo Templi Orientis, A Brief Historical Review," at www.hermetic.com.

Accounts of Gandhi's experiences with Theosophy appear in his *Autobiography: The Story of My Experiments with Truth* (Public Affairs Press, 1948), *Gandhi in London* by James D. Hunt (Nataraj Books, 1993), and *The Life of Mahatma Gandhi* by Louis Fischer (Harper & Brothers, 1950). Gandhi's relations with Annie Besant are explored in *Annie Besant: A Biography* by Anne Taylor (Oxford, 1992) and *Gandhi: A Life* by Yogesh Chadha (John Wiley & Sons, 1997). Gandhi is quoted from those sources and from his *Collected Works,* Vols. 36, 41, and 44. A. O. Hume's encounter with "advanced initiates" is considered in Edward C. Moulton's introduction to *Allan Octavian Hume: 'Father of the Indian National Congress' 1829–1912* by Sir William Wedderburn (Oxford University Press, 1913, 2002).

Chapter Nine: *The Masters Among Us*

Spalding's engagements in Helena, Montana, are reported in the *Helena Daily Independent:* "Free Lenten Talks Given by Miss Chew," 3/1/31, and "Church Notes," 5/16/37 and 5/23/37. Ruth E. Chew's career is noted in "Shine, Shimmer & Scintillate," *Time* magazine, 7/16/56. Paul Brunton is quoted from *Notebooks of Paul Brunton, Category 16: The Sensitives,* "Chapter 13: The Occult" (www.wisdomsgoldenrod.org). A. W. Chadwick is quoted from *A Sadhu's Reminiscences of Ramana Maharshi* (Sri Ramana Ashram, 1961). Chadwick misstates Spalding's name as "Bierce Spaulding." Stella Spalding's divorce from her husband appears in the legal notices of the *Los Angeles Times,* 7/21/37. Articles about Spalding's tussles with the law include the following from the *Los Angeles Times:* "Mine-Fraud Charged," 9/8/28; "Occultist Bound Over in New York," 12/11/29; "Daughter Allowance Asked from Author," 7/12/31; and "Lawyer-Beating Charge Dropped," 12/23/34. Also, "Bay Area Lecturer Arrested for Failure to Provide," 8/7/35, *The Fresno Bee.* The murder of Douglas DeVorss is reported in "Rich Publisher Slain at Desk," 9/25/53, *San Mateo Times,* and "Publisher Murdered; Suspect Held," 9/25/53, *Los Angeles Times.* Also helpful is John Chambers's "The Strange and Brilliant Life of Baird T. Spalding," *Atlantis Rising,* No. 46. The sole record I have been able to locate of David Bruton's death is a notice for a memorial service, which identifies his passing on March 11, 1955, and announces a service on March 27, 1955, at the Calicinto Retreat near San Jacinto, California. I am grateful to historian John B. Buescher for directing me to the census information on Spalding and to the current president and publisher of DeVorss & Company, Gary Peattie, for discussions about Spalding and Douglas DeVorss.

Swami Vivekananda is quoted from Stephan F. Walker's delightful essay, "Vivekananda and American Occultism," from Kerr and Crow (1986).

Sources on I AM include *These Also Believe* by Charles S. Braden (Macmillan, 1949); "The Great Anti-Cult Scare 1935–1945" by Philip Jenkins (1999); "The 'I AM' Sect Today: An Unobituary" by David Stupple, *Journal of Popular Culture*, Spring 1975; "Mighty I AM," *Time* magazine, 2/28/38; and *Psychic Dictatorship in America* by Gerald B. Bryan (Truth Research Publications, 1940). The last is a controversial work by a former student of I AM who later sought to expose the organization; its basic premises and facts are affirmed by historian Braden, who knew the author and considers the book in *These Also Believe*. Frank B. Robinson's comments on I AM appeared in Westbrook Pegler's syndicated column of 12/5/39. Guy Ballard's initial encounter with Saint Germain is described in *Unveiled Mysteries*, written under his pseudonym Godfré Ray King (Saint Germain Foundation, 1934, 1939, 1982). For Justice Robert H. Jackson's landmark dissent, see *United States v. Ballard*, 322 U.S. 78 (1944). Key issues in the I AM case are summarized in *Ballard v. United States*, 138 F. 2d 540 (9th Cir., 1943) and *Ballard v. United States*, 329 U.S. 187 (1946).

Chapter Ten: *Secrets for Sale*

The timeline and events of Case's life are drawn from federal census data, B.O.T.A. publications, and *A History of the Occult Tarot, 1870–1970*, by Ronald Decker and Michael Dummett (Duckworth, 2002). Though some of our dates and references diverge, Lee Moffitt's Paul Foster Case timeline (www.kcbventures.com/pfc/documents/timeline .pdf) has been a helpful resource. The story of Case encountering the "stranger" is told by Ann Davies in *Adytum News-Notes* (July–September 1963). Case is quoted on Tarot meditation from his 1927 pamphlet, "A Brief Analysis of the Tarot." The Case–Mathers–Geise correspondence appears in Mary K. Greer's *Women of the Golden Dawn* (Park Street Press, 1996), one of the finest works on the occult milieu of the late nineteenth and early twentieth centuries. The International Brotherhood of Magicians meeting at which Case performed with Davies is reported in *The Linking Ring* magazine, Vol. 26 (1946). *The Linking Ring* noted Case's cards-up-the-sleeve routine in Vol. 25 (1945). I am grateful to historian Jim Steinmeyer for providing references and material on Case's stage career.

On the career of Benjamin Williams/Elbert Benjamine, I have greatly benefited from Christopher Gibson's "The Religion of the Stars," *Gnosis* magazine, Winter 1996, and from Decker and Dummett (2002), who trace the sources of Benjamine's Tarot. I have also found assistance in correspondence with historian K. Paul Johnson. For the "hidden hand" theory, see: *The Theosophical Enlightenment* by Joscelyn Godwin (State University of New York Press, 1994); Godwin's four-part series in *Theosophical History* (April, July, October 1990, and January 1991); and Christopher Bamford's introduction to *The Transcendental Universe* by C. G. Harrison (Lindisfarne Press, 1993). The career of the H.B. of L. is covered in *The Hermetic Brotherhood of Luxor* by Joscelyn Godwin, Christian Chanel, John Patrick Deveney (Weiser, 1995) and *Paschal Beverly Randolph* by John Patrick Deveney (State University of New York Press, 1997). Paul Christian's theories on the Egyptian origins of Tarot appear in his *The History and Practice of Magic* (Forge Press, 1870, 1952).

Jeane Dixon's career is explored in Marcia Seligson's "Dixonmania," *The New York Times Book Review,* 10/19/69. Evangeline Adams is considered in Karen Christino's biography, *Foreseeing the Future* (Reed Publications, 2000). An overview of Ronald Reagan and astrology appeared in "All the President's Astrologers," *People* magazine, 5/23/88. Also helpful is "Nancy Reagan's Astrologer," *Time* magazine, 5/16/88. Sydney Omarr is quoted from "In the Stars," *Time* magazine 8/24/62; *Omarr: Astrology and the Man* by Norma Lee Browning (Doubleday, 1977); *Answer in the Sky . . . Almost* by Sydney Omarr (Hampton Roads, 1995); "Blind Seer Is Still Stargazing" by Louis Sahagun, *Los Angeles Times,* 12/13/02; "Sydney Omarr, 76; Astrologer to Stars Wrote World's Best-Read Horoscopes," by Sahagun, *Los Angeles Times,* 1/2/03; and "The Signs Are Right for Astrology," by Tom Buckley, *The New York Times,* 12/15/68. Damon Runyon wrote about Professor A. F. Seward in his syndicated column, "As I See It," of 1/9/37. Seward's "land cruiser" was the subject of articles in *The Lima News* (Ohio) of 1/21/30 and 7/25/55.

Historical material on modern numerology appears in *Numerology, or What Hath Pythagoras Wrought* by Underwood Dudley (Mathematical Association of America, 1997). The terms *numerology* and *scientology* first appeared in Stephen Pearl Andrews's 1871 *The Primary Synopsis of Universology and Alwato.* He expanded on his use of numerology the following year in *The Basic Outline of Universology.* Julia Seton's 1929 *Western Symbology* is the work that helped popularize the occult use of the term and linked it to the Balliett system.

A useful history of newspaper astrology appears in Penelope

McMillan's "Horoscopes: Fans Bask in Sun Signs," *Los Angeles Times,* 6/5/85, and in Geoffrey Dean and Arthur Mather's "Sun Sign Columns," *Astrological Journal* (May–June 1996).

Chapter Eleven: *"The Greatest Mystic Who Ever Lived in America"*

The Cayce literature is vast and of widely varying quality. Three works merit special mention: *Edgar Cayce: An American Prophet* by Sidney D. Kirkpatrick (Riverhead, 2000), *Edgar Cayce In Context* by K. Paul Johnson (State University of New York Press, 1998), and *Edgar Cayce's Bookshelf* by David Bell (California Institute of Integral Studies, unpublished dissertation, 1998). Also helpful are: *The Lost Memoirs of Edgar Cayce,* compiled and edited by A. Robert Smith (A.R.E. Press, 1997), *Hugh Lynn Cayce: About My Father's Business* by Smith (Donning Company, 1988), *A Seer Out of Season* by Harmon Hartzell Bro, Ph.D. (New American Library, 1989), and *The Charisma of the Seer* by Bro (University of Chicago Divinity School, unpublished dissertation, 1955). David Kahn is quoted from his memoir, *My Life with Edgar Cayce* (Doubleday, 1970).

The organization Cayce founded, the Association for Research and Enlightenment (A.R.E.), is now an active New Age center in Virginia Beach, encompassing a school of massage in the old hospital building and a reconstituted Atlantic University. A.R.E. maintains an electronic archive of readings and follow-up files that document Cayce's diagnoses and treatments (though only occasionally from the perspective of medical doctors). The organization categorizes the readings by hyphenated numbers, the first representing the subject and the second representing the sequence. Cayce's reading for the ex–Silver Shirt official is 2449–1. The subject of 2449–1 is also quoted from *Psychic Dictatorship in America* by Gerald B. Bryan (Truth Research Publications, 1940). The June 18, 1923, reading is 3744–1. Cayce's reversal is from June 16, 1939, 3976–24. The so-called Hitler Reading of November 4, 1933, is 378–17. It is further analyzed in Rabbi Yonassan Gershom's *From Ashes to Healing* (A.R.E. Press, 1996). Martin Ebon is quoted from *Prophecy in Our Time* (New American Library, 1968). The extended quote from the October 18, 1923, reading for Arthur Lammers (5717–2) is from a revised but faithful adaptation of the original by Thomas Sugrue in his Cayce biography, *There Is a River* (Holt, Rinehart and Winston, 1942). Quotes from Lammers are also taken from Sugrue, who did not observe the events recorded but was an intimate of the Cayce circle. J. Gordon Melton made a comprehensive study of Cayce's past-life readings in "Edgar Cayce and Reincarnation," *Journal of Cayce Studies* (February 1999). *The Elder Brother* by Gregory

Tillett (Routledge & Kegan Paul, 1982) is a helpful source on Charles Webster Leadbeater, who is also written about in *Krishnamurti: The Years of Awakening* by Mary Lutyens (Shambhala, 1975) and *Star in the East: Krishnamurti and the Invention of a Messiah* by Roland Vernon (Palgrave, 2000). William Sloane is quoted from "Publishing Prophets for Profit" by Nora Ephron, *The New York Times,* 8/11/68. Margueritte Harmon Bro's articles are "Explain It As You Will," *The Christian Century,* 6/2/43, and "Miracle Man of Virginia Beach," *Coronet,* September 1943. *Life* magazine's coverage of the Bridey Murphy phenomenon is from 3/19/56. Cayce's statements on patience and visualization are from reading 705–2. His correspondence with his cousin appears in the supplementary material to reading 1089–2, dated 12/26/35; 1/5/36; and 1/9/36. I am grateful to K. Paul Johnson's excellent *Edgar Cayce in Context* for initially directing me to that material.

Epilogue: *Aquarius Rising*

Sources on Ray Palmer and Richard Shaver include Bruce Lanier Wright's outstanding article, *Fear Down Below,* initially posted in 2000 on www.softcom.net (and presently off-line). Also helpful is Walter Kafton-Minkel's chapter on Palmer from *Subterranean Worlds* (Loompanics, 1989) and Jerome Clark's "UFO Report" column from *Fate* magazine (August 1991). Palmer is quoted from *Mystic* magazine, November 1953 and April 1956. Clark wrote a singularly excellent history of *Fate* in *Fortean Times* No. 237. Jacob Needleman is quoted from *The New Religions* (Doubleday, 1970). Sources on the career of Eden Gray include *A History of the Occult Tarot, 1870–1970,* by Ronald Decker and Michael Dummett (Duckworth, 2002); Gray's obituary from the *Chicago Tribune,* 1/25/99; Mary K. Greer's "Tarot Blog" of 3/27/08; federal census data; and Gray's books, *A Complete Guide to the Tarot* (Crown, 1970) and *Mastering the Tarot* (Crown, 1971). She is quoted from the latter. Sources on the career of Gerald Gardner include *Triumph of the Moon* by Ronald Hutton (Oxford University Press, 2001), *Drawing Down the Moon* by Margot Adler (Penguin/Arkana, 1997), *An ABC of Witchcraft* by Doreen Valiente (Phoenix Publishing, 1973), *Gerald Gardner: Witch* by J. L. Bracelin (Octagon Press, 1960), and an annotated edition of Gardner's 1954 *Witchcraft Today* (Citadel Press, 2004). Useful details on the artistic influences the Beatles found on their trip to Rishikesh appear in *With the Beatles* by Lewis Lapham (Melville House, 2005). On the growth of Zen, I have benefited from Needleman (1970). For the holes in Castaneda's background story, see "Don Juan and the Sorcerer's Apprentice," *Time* magazine, 3/5/73. Seligson's account of Linda Goodman is from *The New York Times,*

9/28/69. Ben Bradlee is quoted from Penelope McMillan, *Los Angeles Times*, 6/5/85. On *A Course in Miracles*, I have benefited from D. Patrick Miller's pamphlet, "A Different Kind of Miracle" (Fearless Books, 2005). Jeffrey J. Kripal's outstanding *Esalen* (University of Chicago Press, 2007) explores the history of this influential growth center in a manner that exceeds my scope here. Material on the U.S. Army is from "Spiritual Concepts Drawing a Different Breed of Adherent" by Robert Lindsey, *The New York Times*, 9/29/86.

An author stands on the shoulders of his editors, and I have been blessed with four at different stages of this project. They are: Paul Barrett, a great friend and ally, who gave generously of his time and intellect in working through the manuscript with me; Laurie Fox, a wonderful literary agent and a deeply thoughtful friend, whose guiding hand greatly strengthened the book; Allison Orr, my wife and eternal rock, whose insights guided me through the work's inception and its earliest stages; and Philip Rappaport, senior editor at Bantam, whose incisive eye, thoughtful comments, and personal support across the whole arc of the project have made it a privilege to work with him. Thanks also to my colleague Gabrielle Moss, editor at Tarcher/Penguin, for the benefit of her great intellect and dedicated efforts as I completed this work. I am also grateful for the copyediting efforts of Kathy Lord and Loren Noveck at Bantam.

My special gratitude is due Lisa Barnes, publicity manager at Random House, who promoted the book with terrific commitment, intelligence, and doggedness—her written materials and perfect framing of the book's themes were an author's dream. I can't thank her enough. Random House senior editor Jill Schwartzman shepherded the book into its present paperback and electronic editions with grace, enthusiasm, and care—she's an editor who makes a writer feel right at home.

My gratitude goes to the biannual journal *Esopus*, which published earlier portions of the chapter on Ouija; to *Science of Mind* magazine, and especially its editor Amanda Pisani, who ran an earlier version of the chapter on Frank B. Robinson; and to the magazines *New Dawn, Sub Rosa, Atlantis Rising,* and *Lapis,* in whose pages I worked through parts of the chapter on Manly P. Hall.

While writing this book, I have greatly benefited from discussions with Joel Fotinos, Michael Gomes, Obadiah Harris, K. Paul Johnson, Jay Kinney, Robert Murch, Jacob Needleman, Richard Smoley, Jim Steinmeyer, Mark Thurston, Kevin Todeschi, and Ptolemy Tompkins.

And a thank-you in more than words can say to my sons, Caleb and Tobias, who put up with a father's occasional absences as this book was being completed, and to their mother, Allison, the sun in our skies.

Index

Mitch Horowitz is a widely known writer and speaker on the history and impact of alternative spirituality. For more than twenty years, he has been an editor at New York publishing companies and is currently editor-in-chief at Tarcher/Penguin, one of the leading publishers of spiritual and metaphysical literature. Horowitz has written for *The Washington Post, U.S. News and World Report, Parabola,* Boing Boing, *Esopus, Fortean Times, Venture Inward, New Dawn, Atlantis Rising, Sub Rosa, Science of Mind,* and the Religion News Service. He has discussed occult and paranormal topics on *CBS Sunday Morning, Dateline NBC, All Things Considered,* The History Channel, *The Montel Williams Show, Coast to Coast AM,* and other national media. *Occult America* is his first book. Horowitz lives in New York City with his wife, Allison Orr, a network news producer, and their two sons, Caleb and Tobias. His website is www.MitchHorowitz.com.